Cisco Network Security

ISBN 0-13-091518-1

90000

9 790130 915183

PRENTICE HALL PTR CISCO TECHNOLOGY SERIES

◆ *Cisco Certification: Bridges, Routers and Switches for CCIEs, Second Edition*
Andrew Bruce Caslow and Valeriy Pavlichenko

◆ *CCNA 2.0 Certification: Routing Basics for Cisco Certified Network Associates Exam 640-507*
Robert N. Myhre

◆ *CCNP 2.0: Routing — Exam 640-503*
Robert N. Myhre

◆ *Cisco Network Security*
James Pike

JAMES PIKE

Cisco Network Security

PH PTR Prentice Hall, Upper Saddle River, NJ 07458
http://www.phptr.com

Library of Congress Cataloging-in-Publication Data

Pike, James.
   Cisco network security / James Pike.
     p. cm.
   Includes index.
   ISBN 0-13-091518-1
   1. Computer networks--Security measures. I. Title.

   TK5105.59 .P59 2001
   005.8--dc21   2001036430

Editorial/Production Supervision: *Patti Guerrieri*
Acquisitions Editor: *Mary Franz*
Marketing Manager: *Dan DePasquale*
Manufacturing Manager: *Maura Zaldivar*
Cover Design Director: *Jerry Votta*
Cover Design: *Design Source*
Interior Design Director: *Gail Cocker-Bogusz*
Series Design: *Patti Guerrieri*
Composition: *PreTeX, Inc.*

© 2002 Prentice Hall PTR
Prentice-Hall, Inc.
Upper Saddle River, NJ 07458

Prentice Hall books are widely used by corporations and government agencies for training, marketing, and resale.

The publisher offers discounts on this book when ordered in bulk quantities.
For more information, contact: Corporate Sales Department, Phone: 800-382-3419;
Fax: 201-236-7141; E-mail: corpsales@prenhall.com; or write: Prentice Hall PTR,
Corp. Sales Dept., One Lake Street, Upper Saddle River, NJ 07458.

Printed in the United States of America

10 9 8 7 6 5 4 3 2

ISBN 0-13-091518-1

Pearson Education LTD.
Pearson Education Australia PTY, Limited
Pearson Education Singapore, Pte. Ltd.
Pearson Education North Asia Ltd.
Pearson Education Canada, Ltd.
Pearson Educación de Mexico, S.A. de C.V.
Pearson Education—Japan
Pearson Education Malaysia, Pte. Ltd.

To Candy, Justin, Jory, Jarrod, Jason, and Sam

Contents

Chapter 12 Cisco's Other Security Products   283

Preface

*T*he phenomenal acceptance and growth of the Internet and internetworking technologies, in general, has brought with it the requirement to look at information security in a new light. While network security has been an issue since the advent of computer networking and remote communications, today's environment calls for a fresh approach.

In prior years, the "network" was a relative closed, controllable environment. Access was limited, and access points were readily identifiable. The Internet defies both of these premises, in that it is essentially an "open" environment. Access is virtually and, intentionally, unlimited, and the access points are vast and unpredictable. Organizations seeking to take advantage of the benefits of this open, interconnected system also inherit the risks and liabilities that come with this complex environment. To defend against hostile or malicious action, an organization must understand the nature of the threats and the range of tools available for defense.

While many knowledgeable information systems professionals are aware that there are risks and threats, the nature of these, and the available defensive tools and technologies, are often a great mystery. Like many maturing technologies, the information may be available, but scattered in many places, and requires familiarity with an entirely new vocabulary. Likewise, the information is not always in a readily useable form, often too abstract and theoretical for those who need to apply the defensive remedies, or too oversimplified to ensure confidence in the thoroughness and completeness in the application of the tools.

This leads to a situation where the technical professional has too much or too little information, yet is still expected to exercise professional judgment in the selection and application of "appropriate" solutions.

This book attempts to bridge the gap between the theory and practice of network security. We have tried to provide enough detail on the theories and protocols for reasonable comprehension, so that the networking professional can make informed choices, and coupled that with the "how-to." Although the focus is on the Cisco product offerings, the principles apply to many other environments, as well. Although the user interface and configuration details may vary, the functionality is often similar across comparable products.

The most difficult task is often choosing among many options and choices. Hopefully, the discussion of some of the design theory and protocol details will make these choices a little more clearly understood.

Although this work might be directed toward the technical professional, we believe that students, educators, auditors, management personnel, and others interested in network security will probably find much of the material helpful, as well.

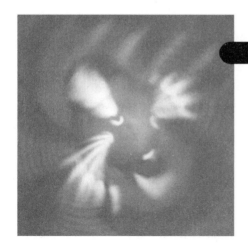

Understanding Security Risk and Threats

*T*oday, businesses, organizations, and individuals expect the convenience of the ready availability of information that has been made possible by interconnected computers, or computer internetworks like the Internet. Along with the advantages of these internetworks come certain disadvantages and additional risks.

These additional risks include increased exposure of your system to intruders and others whose purpose is malicious or hostile, and whose presence is unwanted. The popular press has developed the habit of labeling these interlopers as simply "hackers." This term has also been used by many computer enthusiasts to describe themselves. They prefer the term "cracker" to describe those with malicious intent. To avoid confusion and conflict, we will avoid both terms. Instead, we will use the term "intruder" to describe these unwanted visitors.

The risk is possible exposure to various forms of threats. The subtle distinction between risks and threats is that all risk does not result in direct threats. With that in mind, a prudent system administrator should be prepared nonetheless. The assumption that we can completely eliminate risk, and thereby avoid threats, is not realistic. Instead, we should plan to *manage* risk (and correspondingly, threats) to an *acceptable* level. The difficulty is 1) understanding the nature and degree of risk and 2) determining and defining what constitutes an acceptable level. No system is 100 percent safe, and the higher degree of safety that may be desired carries an associated cost. This cost includes tangible monetary cost, as well as the less tangible administrative time and attention, and reduced ease-of-use by system users. Each organization must assess their own specific situation and determine what they are willing to sacrifice (financial and ease-of-use) to obtain a greater degree of security, and, hence, lower risk.

Many falsely assume that security is a just another technology product that you can buy and apply. While there are a wide variety of network security products available, security is not solely a technology issue. There is also a human element that must be addressed by appropriate employee awareness of the issues, user education, and a clear statement of acceptable organizational policies, procedures, and practices by management.

One of the first steps is to examine the reasons that various security issues exist. The reasons fall primarily in one of the following categories.

Technology Weaknesses

There are several aspects of the technology itself that may contribute to the weakness of the overall system. These weaknesses usually appear in one of the following forms.

Protocol

Most computer and networking technologies suffer from some inherent security deficiencies. The TCP/IP protocol suite is one glaring example. The family of protocols known collectively as the TCP/IP suite had simple connectivity as its basic design emphasis, with no provision for security. For nearly 20 years, capabilities and functions were added to improve its flexibility and usability, but only in the last few years has any serious attempt been made to provide for secure communication. IPSec (IP Security) is a recent collection of sub protocols that attempts to retrofit secure communications into the IP protocol suite, and will be discussed further in a later chapter.

One common TCP/IP application is Sendmail; a program that sends, receives, and forwards most electronic mail processed on UNIX and Linux computers. Sendmail's widespread use on the Internet makes it a prime target of attackers. Several flaws have been found over the years. The first advisory issued by CERT/CC in 1988 made reference to an exploitable weakness in Sendmail. In one of the most common exploits, the attacker sends a crafted mail message to the machine running Sendmail. Sendmail then reads the message as instructions requiring the victim machine to send its password file to the attacker's machine (or to another victim) where the passwords can be cracked.

Several of the other applications that make up the TCP/IP suite make no provision for even simple login/password authentication (e.g., TFTP) and are subject to abuse. Even those that do provide login/password commonly send the login name and password as clear text, which can be easily intercepted. The Simple Network Management Protocol (SNMP) is widely used by network administrators to monitor and administer all types of network-connected devices ranging from routers to printers to computers. SNMP uses an unencrypted password or "community string" as its only authentication mechanism. The default community string used by the vast majority of SNMP devices is "public," although a few "clever" network equipment vendors change the string to "private." Attackers can use this vulnerability in SNMP to reconfigure or shut down devices remotely. Eavesdropping on SNMP traffic can reveal a great deal about the structure of your network, as well as the systems and devices attached to it. Intruders use such information to pick targets and plan attacks.

The Berkeley Internet Name Domain (BIND) package is the most widely used implementation of Domain Name Service (DNS), the mechanism used to locate systems by name without having to know the specific IP address. This factor makes it a favorite target for intruders. According to a recent survey, about 50 percent of all DNS servers connected to the Internet are running vulnerable versions of BIND. In a typical example of a BIND attack, intruders erased the system logs and installed tools to obtain administrative access. They then compiled and installed IRC utilities and network scanning tools, which they used to scan more than a dozen class-B networks in search of additional systems running vulnerable versions of BIND. In a matter of minutes, they had used the compromised system to attack hundreds of remote systems abroad, resulting in many additional successful compromises. This illustrates the chaos that can result from a single vulnerability in the software for ubiquitous Internet services such as DNS. These examples are representative of the TCP/IP protocol suite, applications, and utilities it provides.

Operating Systems

All of the operating systems in common use today suffer from a variety of security problems. Many of these are well known and documented, but aren't included in the training curriculum comprising the common body of knowledge that is required to administer these operating systems. Each of the common operating systems has a long list of vulnerabilities. Many of the various Windows® 95, 98, NT®, and 2000 vulnerabilities are avoidable by keeping the operating system updated to the most current level. Service packs and individual patches are available from Microsoft® to eliminate most of these vulnerabilities; however, the burden rests on the system administrator to keep up with a constant stream of newly discovered weaknesses.

A representative example is NetBIOS. This service allows file sharing over networks. When improperly configured, it can expose critical system files or give full file system access to any hostile party connected to the network. Many computer owners and administrators use these services to make their file systems readable and writeable in an effort to improve the convenience of data access. In one reported incident, administrators of a government computer site used for software development for mission planning made their files world readable so people at a different government facility could get easy access. Within two days, other people had discovered the open file shares and stolen the mission-planning software.

When file sharing is enabled on Windows machines they become vulnerable to both information theft and certain types of quick-moving viruses. A recent virus called the 911 Worm uses file shares on Windows 95 and 98 systems to propagate and causes the victim's computer to dial 911 on its modem. Macintosh® computers are also vulnerable to file sharing exploits. The same NetBIOS mechanisms that permit Windows File Sharing may also be used to enumerate sensitive system information from NT systems. User and Group information (usernames, last logon dates, password policy, RAS information), system information, and certain Registry keys may be accessed via a "null session" connection to the NetBIOS Session Service. This information is typically used to mount a password guessing or brute force password attack against the NT target.

A catalog of many of these (and others) can be found in a listing known as NTBugtraq, which can be found at *http://archives.neohapsis.com/*. Another excellent source of information on various system vulnerabilities is maintained by the Sans Institute and can be found at *http://www.sans.org*. The Sans Institute also publishes a listing of the Top 10 Security Exploits. Both of these organizations allow you to subscribe to a mailing list that provides weekly alerts and bulletins via email.

A number of other organizations serve as valuable sources of information network security and related topics. Among the best known are the Computer Emergency Response Team (CERT) operated by Carnegie–Mellon University (*http://www.cert.org*) and the Center for Education and Research in Information Assurance and Security (CERIAS) at Purdue University (*http://www.cerias.purdue.edu*).

Networking Equipment

Various types of internetworking equipment suffer from lack of password protection or other forms of authentication. The routing protocols currently in common use are mixed. Neither RIP nor IGRP provide any meaningful form of authenticating of router table exchanges among routers. Routers running these routing protocols "trust" any incoming routing information to be legitimate. Although both Open Shortest Path First (OSPF) and Cisco®'s Enhanced IGRP (EIGRP) provide for authentication and encryption for routing updates, organizations rarely take the extra steps to configure these options.

Structured wiring systems can be a problem. In the past, it has been common practice to wire network outlets to each work location, including empty offices. If Ethernet networks are built upon coaxial cable, or 10BaseT hubs, anyone who "plugs into" the network at any open outlet can view all of the traffic on the network with simple packet decoding software like EtherPeek™, TCPdump, Sniffer™, and others. Some of the leading vendors provide "port lockout" protection. This is usually accomplished by disabling the port at the hub, or by configuring the hub port to accept a connection only from a network interface card with a specific MAC address. Once a legitimate user is assigned the data outlet, or a device matching the preconfigured MAC address is attached to the port, the hub port becomes active. Ethernet switches aren't as susceptible to eavesdropping as hubs or multiport repeaters, but they, too, often provide similar port lockout protection.

Even routers with password protection are vulnerable. On Cisco routers, one can perform "password recovery" simply by attaching a terminal device to the console port and power cycling the router. Similarly, booting from a floppy disk rather than the hard disk can sometimes compromise network operating systems. For these reasons and others, network equipment should be kept in a secured area, with physical access limited to those with proper authority.

Firewall "Holes"

Nearly all firewall devices are configured to allow some traffic to originate outside the organization. If the rules are not carefully defined, unwanted traffic can infiltrate the network through these intentional "holes." For example, many organizations allow Internet Control Message Protocol (ICMP) packets through the firewall, so that they receive various diagnostic messages, and can utilize handy applications such as the Ping utility. Unfortunately, ICMP can also be used as a preferred carrier for malicious packets. Also, Web server hosts outside the firewall are often configured for read/write access to database servers inside the firewall. If the outer Web server is compromised, direct access to the inner database server is readily available. These servers and services should also be configured with great care. Mail servers and DNS servers are also usually outside of the firewall, and are also susceptible to compromise. As a result, access through the firewall for these devices should be considered carefully.

IMAP and POP are popular remote access mail protocols, allowing users to access their email accounts from internal and external networks. The "open access" nature of these services makes them especially vulnerable to exploitation because openings are frequently left in firewalls to allow for external email access. Attackers who exploit flaws in IMAP or POP often gain instant root-level control.

Configuration Weaknesses

Badly configured devices can also be a problem. Among the problems in this category are unsecured user accounts, or those with simplistic or easily guessed passwords (e.g., admin, cisco, pass, etc.). Pets' names, a spouse's name, favorite hobbies, and other similar sources are not good choices for passwords, but are commonly chosen because they are easy to remember.

Services like Java®, JavaScript®, and ActiveX® can allow intrusion or attacks via hostile applets. The attraction of these software tools is that they allow applications or "applets" to be downloaded from the server to execute on the client. While these provide local execution of sophisticated functions, they can also be used to provide a direct path for hostile application. Users can be lured into activating these downloaded applets with enticing "click here for a free offer" messages. Badly configured access lists and routing protocols can also open up large security holes.

Most current Web servers support Common Gateway Interface (CGI) programs to provide interactivity in Web pages and to support functions such as data collection and verification. All too often, these Web servers come with sample CGI programs installed by default. Further, many CGI developers fail to consider ways in which their programs may be misused or subverted to execute malicious commands. Vulnerable CGI programs present a particularly attractive target to intruders because they are relatively easy to locate, and they operate with the privileges and power of the Web server software itself. Intruders are known to have exploited vulnerable CGI programs to vandalize Web pages, steal credit card information, and set up back doors to enable future intrusions, even if the CGI programs are secured.

In one reported intrusion, Attorney General Janet Reno's picture was replaced with that of Adolph Hitler at the Department of Justice Web site. An in-depth assessment later determined that a CGI hole was the most likely avenue of compromise. As a general rule, sample programs should always be removed from production systems.

All too often, those responsible for configuring routers or hosts may actually enable *additional* security breaches, unaware of the security implications of various features and services. Some systems come with "demo" or "guest" accounts with no passwords, or with common default passwords. Service workers often leave maintenance accounts with no passwords, and some database management systems install administration accounts with default passwords. In addition, careless system administrators often select system passwords that are easily "guessable" ("pass," "admin," "wizard" are common favorites) or just use a blank as the password. Default passwords provide easy access for attackers. Many intruders try default passwords, then attempt to guess passwords before resorting to more sophisticated methods. Compromised user accounts get the attacker's access through the firewall and inside the target machine. Once inside, most attackers can use a variety of widely available exploits to gain root or administrator access.

Policy Weaknesses

The weaknesses due to organizational policy are numerous.

- Lack of written security policy — all too often there is no written security in place. In the absence of a written policy, there is no way to provide consistency or enforcement. Each administrator or user is left on his or her own to determine what is allowed or appropriate, a sure recipe for problems.

- Politics — internal, organizational politics provide many opportunities for problems. One group may set a policy, only to have another ignore or override it. Consistency is not possible, and accountability nonexistent.

- Lack of continuity — high turnover or frequent replacement of personnel commonly leads to an erratic approach to policy. The new administrators rarely verify that existing policies are in place or adequate. There are often no authoritative sources of "acceptable" policy.

- Passwords — poorly chosen, easily guessed, or default passwords are all too often the norm. Passwords written on Post-it® notes stuck on the computer monitor are not uncommon in some organizations. Most current network-aware operating systems provide for minimum length and aging out of passwords, although these safeguards are not always implemented. These features can require passwords to be of some minimum length (often eight or more characters) and require password replacement on a regular basis. The longer a password has been used, the greater the likelihood it can or will find its way into the wrong hands.

- Lax administration — inadequate monitoring and auditing allow intrusions to continue undetected for a period of time beyond the initial intrusion, wasting the organization's resources, and exposing the organization to possible legal liabilities. Logging of relevant activities is important, with "alerts" and periodic review of the logged data equally important.

- Software and/or hardware changes — unauthorized and undocumented changes to the network equipment and/or topology, along with unauthorized user applications, can also increase exposure to additional risk. All too often, the users or administrators of these applications don't have an awareness of the security issues. Direct dialup access from desktops is another source of problems as this allows a "backdoor" opening for additional network intrusions, bypassing established security checkpoints.

- Lack of disaster recovery or incident response — the lack of an incident response or contingency plan insures that in the event of an attack or intrusion, panic, chaos, or confusion will rule. This will obviously not solve the problem, and may even make it worse. Legal recourse, including insurance claims or prosecution, is not likely to be successful since records are often incomplete or unavailable.

Sources of Security Threats

We should now look at the sources and types of threats that may exist. Although most discussions of network security assume that the threats originate from outside the organization, statistically, the greatest number of threats actually comes from within the organization. For this reason, it is considered inadequate to merely secure the outer perimeter of the organization. Instead, a multilayered security arrangement provides more thorough, and realistic, protection. A further discussion of a "layered" defensive strategy will be discussed in a later chapter

What are the sources of the threats? The common impression of the typical intruder profile is that of simple network vandals. In reality, there are numerous types. The source of the various intruder types may consist of any combination of the following.

Thrill Seekers and Adventurers

The prototypical hacker; technically skilled, this hacker's motive can include self-amusement, sport, vandalism, or the admiration of his peers. To this group, network intrusions are recreational intellectual activities. Although any organization can be a random target, if your organization has high visibility, you may attract unwanted attention from these network vandals. In the intruder "underground," additional prestige is gained for attacking "worthy" targets. Obvious examples are organizations like the IRS, FBI, CIA, military sites, political and religious organizations, and others who attract significant negative attention. The successful intruder is rewarded a certain level of esteem among his peers.

This profile is the one many people associate with the term "hacker," due in part to its use as a title and/or story line in several popular films. To further confuse the image, the Hollywood hackers are often brilliant, technically talented, but misunderstood, nonconformist good guys who ultimately save the day. For every movie portrayal of an antagonist "evil" hacker, there is a counterpart in the form of protagonist "good" hacker who triumphs. These are the same ones who can break into any computer in minutes, guess passwords within a few attempts, decode any encryption with simple programs they write in minutes, and gain total knowledge of, and control over, all systems they compromise. Probably more than one impressionable teenager has decided to become a hacker after seeing these films.

Notwithstanding the above, few organizations willingly choose to serve as their playground. Like "graffiti artists," little social benefit can be attributed to their acts of simple vandalism, despite their romantic depictions.

Competitors

Knowledge of product plans, marketing strategies, and the like can provide advantage to your competitors. The nature of your organization, the value to be gained, and the "culture" of your competitors will dictate the likelihood of this form of intrusion. Based upon these factors, one can surmise that a charitable organization or medical institution is less likely to suffer attacks of this nature than an aerospace company or semiconductor manufacturer.

Thieves

Motivation is typically to take something of value or gain unauthorized access to assets. Customer lists, with or without credit card numbers, are vivid examples. Unauthorized usage of assets, resources, or services also qualifies. Loss may be realized even if data is only copied, not removed or destroyed. Data may be "taken" and the "loss" may go unnoticed. As noted above, intrusions may be sophisticated since there is tangible gain from the intrusion.

Clearly, this category can also include industrial espionage, theft of trade secrets, and other intellectual property. Companies engaged in military and/or other advanced technologies are particularly tempting targets of international competitors or foreign governments, both friends and foes alike. Intrusions of this latter type may be well financed and more technically sophisticated, since significant value may be gained from the intrusion, and government sponsorship is not beyond the realm of the possible.

Enemies or Spies

Although similar to the above category of thieves, the objective may be to gain information, provide misinformation, or engage in simple harassment, rather than theft, per se. Government-sponsored information warfare, espionage, or cyber-terrorism is an obvious source of this type of intrusion. However, spies are not always enemies, and there have been reported cases where friendly governments or allies have spied upon one another.

Similarly, religious organizations may also become targets of "enemies" whose motivation may include zealotry, idealism, spite, revenge, or other similar motives. Likewise, political parties or similar organizations may be concerned with activities initiated by "enemies" or "spies." Other examples include timber companies, tobacco companies, furriers, and others who may have their own particular sort of enemies or spies in the form of political or environmental activists.

Hostile Employees

This group consists of those who exploit their employer's trust for personal gain. This type is most difficult to identify and defend against because their hostility may be well hidden. Their activities might not be closely monitored since they may appear to be trustworthy. The statistics on "attacks" by these intruders can never be accurate, since their activities are often not discovered. Even when discovered, organizations are sometimes reluctant to discuss or confirm these types of attacks, unless they have substantial evidence, due to the risk of slander or other legal complications arising from such accusations. There are no security "products" that can eliminate this threat; however, proper access controls, coupled with audit controls, policy and policy enforcement, backup procedures, and other administrative safeguards can reduce the risk or minimize the damage.

Hostile Former Employer

This category covers those who seek revenge or profit, and use "insider knowledge" to avoid or defeat existing security mechanisms. Privileged user accounts that remain active after termination allow ready access to these intruders. There are occasional reports of sabotage or "time bombs" that are difficult to detect and avoid. Like the above category, thoughtful administrative and security policies, in conjunction with appropriate termination policies, can minimize exposure to these intrusions.

Other Employee Sources

This group includes examples such as employees that are pursuing intentional or unintentional activities that may put the organization, or its reputation, at risk. Downloading of illegal software or sexually offensive software files are common examples. Use of organizational assets for personal benefit is a simple form of theft, although each organization must define what level of personal use is acceptable. In many cases, personal email, checking online sports scores or stock prices, online shopping, and other activities may be allowed to some extent. Of particular interest are those cases where an organization was held liable for allowing an activity to occur, even in cases where the activity was not sanctioned by the organization. Sexual harassment, discrimination, and other suits have been brought, where the company was held liable, because they didn't take "appropriate, reasonable" steps to prevent the event from happening.

Depending upon your organizational type, some of the examples noted here may pose a greater threat than others. Each organization must determine which pose the greatest real threat, determine their likelihood, calculate how much risk is allowable, and budget the funds for equipment and staff to reduce the risk to an affordable, acceptable level. Expenditures on security are a form of insurance, and should be budgeted accordingly. More funding *should* result in less risk, but *zero risk* (like unlimited funding) is not possible in practice.

Threats to Network Security

There are a variety of basic threat types. While their source and purpose will vary by circumstances, most fall into one of several basic categories. In many cases, the intrusive activity may include several of these threat types simultaneously.

Electronic Eavesdropping

As the term implies, eavesdropping consists of secretly observing the flow of traffic, or "listening" to the traffic traveling between parties. This traffic flow may include such things as login and password information, plus the general body of data that may be exchanged between parties, some of which is intended to be private and confidential. This intrusion may also include interception and modification of the traffic, or insertion of false information. Eavesdropping can occur anywhere along the path between two parties, including both private and public portions of the path. In the case of Internet traffic, there are a multitude of points where traffic can be observed, with neither party being aware that their "conversation" is being monitored or recorded. In addition, existing wiretap laws don't adequately cover this new internetwork mode of communication.

A local area network (LAN) environment may be particularly vulnerable to eavesdropping, since LAN technologies, such as Ethernet, are shared-media environments. As such, all stations on an Ethernet segment are capable of "listening" to all traffic. Under normal circumstances, the network interface card's (NIC) driver software accepts Ethernet frames only if they are addressed to the station itself, or sent to the hardware broadcast or multicast address (i.e., the MAC address) that applies to the station's NIC. However, it is relatively easy to modify the driver software, instructing it to operate in *promiscuous mode*, that is, to collect all frames on the segment. This is undetectable since the station in promiscuous mode merely copies the frame, leaving no trace, and passes it up to software designed to analyze all network traffic. Networks built from coaxial cable or 10BaseT hubs are particularly vulnerable, although switch-based networks minimize the ability to eavesdrop, since, with an Ethernet switch, each segment and its single station device are isolated from other segments. The only place that all traffic can be observed is from *within* the switch, making eavesdropping more difficult, if not impossible.

This type of intrusion is sometimes known as "sniffing," the term being borrowed from Network Associates' Sniffer®, one of the earliest and best-recognized network analysis tools. The Sniffer, and other similar protocol analysis tools, are intended to read, decode, and analyze all of the traffic on a network segment for the purpose of diagnostics and troubleshooting of network problems. Like any powerful tool, it can also be misused for other purposes. For instance, an intruder could user packet-sniffing software to capture and record login packets on the network, and then use the captured login information to gain access to protected resources. Packet sniffing could also be used to collect confidential data or messages as they travel the network for later analysis. Since the path that traffic follows (both LAN and WAN) may often be unprotected, or outside the control of either sender or receiver, the only real protection against eavesdropping is encryption.

Denial of Service

The denial-of-service attack is one of the most common and easiest to accomplish. There are dozens of well-known techniques to cause denial-of-service (DoS). The basic goal of a denial-of-service attack is to overwhelm the target with activities or services requests that causes the victim to be unable to provide services to other legitimate users. The basic design of the TCP/IP protocol suite provides dozens of characteristics and features that can be misused to create this situation. Many individual forms of denial-of-service attacks are well documented and are preventable, with proper application of sound security practices, coupled with defensive features that are incorporated into current networking products. These attacks have often been given colorful names like TCP SYN Flooding, Smurf attacks, land.c attacks, WinNuke attacks, Teardrop.c, Ping of Death, and others.

The newer, more sophisticated forms are more dangerous, particularly those that are commonly described as Distributed Denial of Service (DDoS). These DDoS attacks have a common thread. They marshal the resources of a large number of machines by covertly planting "agent" software on unsuspecting machines, under the control of some "master" controller source. The controller can direct the "zombie" machines to launch a coordinated, simultaneous attack on a target victim, greatly amplifying the effect. Although avoidable, these DDoS attacks have proven to be highly effective, and are thought to be the source of the February 2000 service outages experienced by Yahoo!®, eBay®, Amazon.com®, and several others. Their broad-based attack, and use of traffic that looks like regular traffic, but in arriving in extraordinary volumes, makes them particularly difficult to detect and defend against.

Unauthorized Access

This category covers various forms of access to, or use of, resources without permission. It covers unauthorized use of disk drive capacity; CPU time; access to applications, files, or services; and other organizational computing assets. The financial cost to the organization may range from negligible to significant, depending upon the circumstances. There are sometimes other costs associated with this activity, including damage to the organization's reputation or public image, public embarrassment, or possibly legal liability if the unauthorized access provides a basis to conduct an illegal activity (e.g., storage of illegal software, child pornography, etc.). This type of activity can often be prevented or minimized with appropriate access controls.

Session Replay

This threat typically consists in recording all or a portion of a transaction or "session" between two parties. The session is later replayed, imitating an additional transaction. An example might be a payment authorization session that is later replayed, effectively resulting in additional payments to appear to be authorized. This technique is often difficult to employ, since it requires access to the data stream representing the original transaction or session, as well as the ability to inject the replayed session into a new data stream. The logistics and technical skill level required to effectively accomplish this type of attack make it less common that some other attacks. Session replay is difficult, but not impossible to accomplish. There are several forms of protection available, including certain tools like the IPSec protocol suite, which provide specific antireplay protection. These tools often use some form of sequencing of packet numbers beyond those that are inherent in TCP segments.

Session Hijacking

Although one of the most difficult to accomplish, this threat is accomplished by taking over one end of an exchange between two parties. Its power is that, if successful, the hijacker assumes the role of one participant after the authentication phase has successfully completed. It effectively bypasses even strong authentication controls by intercepting the session after authentication checks have verified the identity of one or both of the parties. It requires the intruder to carefully imitate the actions of one party, requiring "spoofing" or falsifying the original IP source address, matching the pattern of sequence and acknowledgement numbers (for TCP-based sessions), and simultaneously eliminating the participation of the displaced party. This may be possible by sending a connection-reset message (TCP RST) to the displaced party and/or launching a denial-of-service attack, effectively prohibiting the displaced party from continuing the exchange. This attack requires significant technical skill and careful logistics to accomplish, and is therefore less common than other attacks.

Impersonation

As the term suggests, impersonation consists of one posing as another, presumably, to gain access to resources authorized to the party who is being impersonated. Other potential motivations include authoring documents that appear to have come from another party, or other acts of fraud. This approach can take on several forms. The imposter could use the logon credentials of another to gain access to files, programs, documents, or other resources. Forging of email, electronic documents, or various forms of authorization are other possible goals. Falsifying or "spoofing" of IP addresses can mask the identity of the true origin, and appear to come from another device. One goal might be simply "covering one's tracks" in situations like denial of service, or other situations where the true identity might be traceable. Another goal might be so that packets appear to originate from a different location, such as situations where the source address is used to determine some approval criteria (e.g., packet filter or access lists).

Malicious Destruction

This threat covers intentional destruction of files or programs. Once access has been gained, resources are damaged, destroyed, or deleted. Sometimes the damage or destruction results from the inadvertent acts of an authorized user. The preventive defense is different for the two, while the remedy may be the same. In the case of malicious destruction, preventive measures include limiting access through proper access controls such as authentication. In the case of unintentional destruction, user education and training can minimize the occurrences. The remedy is essentially the same for both cases. Network security policy or administrative policy should provide for backup and recovery procedures for all crucial files, programs, or services.

Repudiation

This risk is not an attack in the commonly understood manner but, instead, describes the ability of one party to generate traffic; create, modify, or delete data; or conduct various activities and later deny that he or she actually *did* perform the action. The claim could potentially be made that the action was actually performed by some other party using falsified credentials, captured login information, or other forms of unauthorized access or impersonation. Although tight access controls can minimize the potential, the only sure method is to utilize IPSec or some other mechanism that provides specific antirepudiation measures. IPSec will be covered in greater detail in subsequent chapters.

Viruses, Trojan Horses, and Worms

This category is one of the most common, widespread, and visible forms of attack. While each is slightly different, they share a common characteristic. Each involves covertly downloading a program to a host, where the malicious program executes, producing the intended result. This can be accomplished by secretly downloading the program or the currently more popular forms, where an unsuspecting user is lured into voluntarily downloading the program and/or executing the malicious program. These methods often involve hiding the malicious program inside of another program or file to hide or disguise its presence and intention. The action of the malicious program could be to copy, delete, modify, or transfer files; collect confidential information; generate messages; or simply replicate and multiply copies of itself, which are then unwittingly propagated by the unsuspecting user. In many cases, its only purpose is to propagate itself, creating a nuisance. Although no real damage may be caused, the necessity of removal and cleaning up the mess is sufficiently costly and time-consuming to constitute indirect "damage."

Rerouting

While this form of attack is less often observed, rerouting is nonetheless potentially damaging. If the redirection of traffic permits eavesdropping or modification of the data in transit, the goal can be accomplished, often unnoticed by the sender and receiver. This redirection of traffic may facilitate a "man-in-the-middle" attack, which will be discussed further in our discussion of encryption and authentication mechanisms in IPSec. In most instances, routing information remains within the organizational boundaries, and is not accessible to intruders outside the organization. Even in the event of an intrusion that results in injection of false routing information, little damage is likely done since interior routing protocols rarely affect the path taken by traffic exiting to the outside world. Further, this problem can be minimized, if not eliminated, by simply using EIGRP or OSPF. Both provide for authentication of routing information exchanged between routers.

What Are We To Do?

Now that we have outlined the nature and sources of the threats, we must decide how to approach these potential problems. We need to plan a defensive strategy. As part of this strategy planning we need to determine the answers to a few basic questions.

What Needs Protection?

While the answer might seem obvious, this step is not a trivial task. In fact, this step may be the most difficult. It will require us to thoroughly define all the items that may need protection, assess the risks to which they may be exposed, and determine the *appropriate* level of protection. In short, we need a comprehensive organizational security policy. The information systems and network security professionals will not be able to accomplish this task alone. It will require guidance and involvement from the management with policy and budgeting authority over the applicable areas, as well as input from the organization's legal counsel.

There may be organizational policies already in place that can be expanded to incorporate the network security issues, or that must be consulted to assure conformance with existing policy that may be applicable. In most cases, there will be a formal, written, human resources or employee policy that defines the organization's expectations regarding employee conduct, conflict of interest, confidentiality of organizational information, et al.

The itemization of objects that require security protection will include equipment, programs or applications, data files of various types, services provided, and many other similar items. These types of items may be relatively easy to inventory or quantify. The more intangible items will include things like organizational reputation, customer confidence and goodwill, stockholder confidence, conformity with applicable laws, loss of use of the equipment, timeliness of data files, downtime, revenue loss, and many other factors that will be different for each organization. These represent the greatest challenge to assess, value, and prioritize, but they also may represent the most significant portion of the cost of network security. Their subjective nature and complexity underscores the difficulty of the task of defining an *appropriate* level of network security.

What Is the Nature of the Risk?

Risk assessment is the formal term that encompasses the tasks that must be performed. It essentially requires that we identify the "assets," determine their "value," either monetary or ranked by relative importance, and evaluate the risk involved. The steps must be taken so that we can determine what level of risk an organization is *willing to tolerate*. The concept of risk *management* consists of weighing the possible loss of value or use against the cost of protecting the asset. If the item is replaceable, the replacement cost serves as a useful guideline to determine what level of protection is cost justifiable.

If an asset has a value of $10.00 and is easily replaced, it would be foolhardy to expend $100.00 in protection of the asset. Conversely, if an item has a high replacement cost, or is irreplaceable, the decision process gets more complicated. We need to determine how much we are willing to pay for "insurance" (i.e., protection) versus the level of risk that is tolerable. Even "priceless" items are insurable to some degree and at some price. Lloyd's of London specializes in priceless, uninsurable items, but usually for a significant fee. (Ironically, they also offer insurance against intrusions for computer networks.) Traditional insurance takes a similar approach, in that the level of risk determines the cost of insurance, while the cost of that insurance is weighed against the value of the asset. If the insurance cost exceeds the asset's value or replacement cost, insurance is not cost justifiable.

The specific nature of the "loss" may take a variety of forms. One form is loss of confidentiality of the data. Research information is expensive to generate, and if made available to an organization's competitors, benefit is transferred to the party that obtained the information. Coupled with that may be loss to the organization's reputation, or loss of confidence of investors, impacting stock prices. Financial information might help one's competitors, or possibly permit "insider trading," if released at inappropriate times.

Another form of loss is that of privacy. If a medical institution fails to maintain the privacy of a patient's medical records, they may be in violation of federal law that requires protection of patient privacy, and which prohibits unauthorized disclosure. They may also be subject to civil actions, brought by the patient whose records were disclosed.

Each organization must make its own determination of the "value," or replacement cost, including such intangibles as loss of use or loss of reputation or confidence, so that they may budget an appropriate amount for security "insurance."

What Kind of Protection Is Necessary?

The "asset" we describe above may be data such as administrative records, financial data, client or customer data, research results, or data held in confidence for another party (e.g., patient medical records, credit card information, et al.). Each will have its own measure of value. Unlike physical objects, data is "information" and, as such, it has the relatively unique property that it can be "taken" by copying it, or it can be taken in the conventional sense, where the original is no longer available. It can also be modified, changed, or altered, rendering it tainted or unusable for its intended purpose. Likewise, it may have a confidential or private nature that, if revealed, could diminish its value (a secret formula), cause bodily harm (a list of secret agents), cause property damage (list of buildings to be demolished), result in personal embarrassment (X-rated book purchases of a religious leader), or be in violation of a law (patient's medical records).

Protecting the integrity or validity of the data is also necessary. Often, discovering that data has been altered or otherwise compromised is difficult. Even when detected, repair or recovery may be a tedious and painstaking process, and take significant time, effort, and resources to rectify or reinstate. This, too, has a measurable cost.

The "asset" may also be a service where the unavailability of the service has a measurable cost. Loss of sales or income is a relatively tangible measure, but many other intangibles may be associated with the loss of use. Some of the attacks we described previously, like denial of service, have financial costs, but may also have intangible costs, such as loss of reputation or loss of confidence, that are difficult to quantify.

How Much Can You Afford to Spend?

The answer to this question can be determined *only* after the assets to be protected are identified and valued. If the organization hasn't identified the elements that need protection, they will be unable to properly determine their value. If the value cannot be established, there is no basis to determine the *correct* amount to budget for protection. In such an instance, the security budget becomes an arbitrary number.

The amount that an organization can *afford* to spend is not necessarily the same as the amount the company *has available* to spend, nor the amount it *chooses* to spend. In the insurance analogy we referred to earlier, the periodic policy payments must be compared to the amount of protection provided. Likewise, the network security budget must be related to the degree of protection afforded. Any other basis is likely to result in 1) insufficient funding to provide adequate protection, or 2) overspending beyond what is necessary and sufficient — a waste of resources. If the amount is arbitrarily set, it will also be arbitrarily raised or lowered, compounding the problem.

The answers to these questions should be answered fully before one can properly apply the right type and level of protective measures. Likewise, the organization's position should be detailed in some form of an official policy statement. This network security policy will be the benchmark for audits, and the arbitrator regarding questions of policy. If sufficiently detailed, it will serve as the guideline for planning and implementation.

While this book will not go into detail regarding the elements that should be included in the organization's Network Security Policy, there are numerous good sources of information regarding development of such a policy. One good reference example is the Site Security Handbook (RFC 2196), a part of the Internet documentation. As defined in that document:

"A security policy is a formal statement of the rules by which people who are given access to an organization's technology and information assets must abide."

RFC2196 — Site Security Handbook[1]

There are a number of reasons to develop such a policy:

- Provides an overall blueprint for implementing and deploying network security
- Describes organization's expectations regarding acceptable behavior
- Defines responsibilities of users and administrators
- Assists in definition of procedures that may be required
- Assists in identification of appropriate network security technologies
- Provides a basis for audit and verification of existing network security
- Defines the procedures to be followed in the event of network security incident
- Creates the foundation for any subsequent legal action (civil or criminal)

Once defined, the Network Security Policy can be used to define the critical items to be protected, the measures to be taken, and the extent that the organization is willing to go in defense of those critical items, as well as the assignment of responsibility and authority to implement and enforce the policy.

It will serve as a checklist to identify and verify the critical assets, define the threats to which they are exposed, and determine the degree of risk they may experience. This is crucial in selecting the appropriate technologies to employ and/or administrative procedures that may be required.

An additional source of guidance may be found in another Internet document, RFC 2405, User Security Guide.

---

1. Copyright © Internet Society, September 1997. All Rights Reserved.

Summary

In this chapter we introduced various forms of security risks to which networks may be exposed, along with a brief description of the threats posed. Also discussed was risk evaluation and management, since some risk is probably unavoidable. Emphasis was placed on the organization's Network Security Policy as the starting point for any discussion of security safeguards. This document should include a definition of the organization's expectations and policies, and serve as the guideline for implementation and configuration of appropriate network security devices.

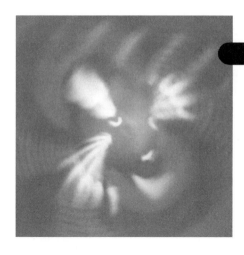

Security
Architecture

In This Chapter

*N*ow that we have addressed the need for a Network Security Policy, we are ready for the next step — designing the Security Architecture. We should first define what things are *not* included in the Security Architecture, The Security is not a product or a group of products, but rather it is a definition as to how you will achieve the objectives as defined in your Network Security Policy. All too many organizations take the position that if they purchase and install the XYZ product, they will be secure. That is simply not the case. Instead, we must align the security goals with appropriate policies, practices, and available technologies to match the protection that is required with what is available. It will consist of defining the goals of the security policy in terms of our objectives, then matching those objectives with the right mix of policy and technology.

The objective of the Security Architecture is to define appropriate levels of protection for data and information technology networks against various types of threats. Organizations face a significant challenge, because taking fullest advantage of the technology requires providing access to organizational networks and the resources they contain to users inside and outside of the organization. This requires that they exert control over the access granted to different users and different resources.

The primary objective is to ensure that system resources are available to legitimate users. Systems resources typically consist of the data, programs, and services over the entire range of systems from individual desktops to shared servers and services.

Organizations may also need to make certain resources available to outside users, such as customers, business partners, or the general public. It is often critical that these outside users have access to the data and services. Specific examples might be online shopping and banking applications. Timely, reliable access for these users is a primary element of the service offering, and, as such, service outages can be highly detrimental. The risks associated with this "public" access include additional exposure to attacks. In particular, denial-of-service attacks are of great significance, since their objective is to render the data or service unusable or unavailable.

The conventional wisdom is that network security can't be an "add-on;" rather, it must be integrated seamlessly as part of the network's infrastructure. Effective network and Internet security is built-in, not bought. It involves more than simply having the latest antivirus software and a firewall, although some organizations appear to believe otherwise. Further, it must become a part of the organization's standard operational policies and procedures. Network security may be less effective and is clumsy if one attempts to add it to the infrastructure after the fact. It must be planned from the start, as an integral part of the network's design.

Engaging in commerce on the Internet is fraught with hazards, and must be approached with that in mind. Part of the problem is that it is a "public" network, with no central management, authority, or control. Individual organizations, from Internet Service Providers (ISPs) to users, make their own independent decisions, with little or no consensus on policy matters. A fitting illustration is the February 2000 denial-of-service attacks on several major Web sites.

Reports indicated that the attacks were some form of Distributed Denial of Service (DDoS). In this type of attack, unwitting hosts were compromised with a "zombie" program planted by the intruders, which was not detected by the users and administrators of the affected machines. These "zombie" programs operate under the control of a "master" program that can direct them to generate a large volume of traffic at a chosen target victim. The resulting flood of traffic came from a large number of hosts, with no discernible pattern or connection to one another, and with false or "spoofed" IP source addresses. The argument was made that the situation could have been avoided by proper controls from the administrators of the recruited "zombie" hosts. The counterargument was also made that the ISPs could have minimized the damage by monitoring traffic originating from their clients, disallowing traffic from devices with improper IP source addresses. This incident further emphasizes the point that there is little common consensus regarding the assignment of responsibility.

The security infrastructure provides the means to implement a centrally managed policy that is enforceable at every point that data is manipulated. It should facilitate the addition of new devices, applications, and users, and extend the safeguards to those additions. As such, there is no out-of-the-box solution to remedy potential problems.

Ideally, various hardware and software components used to enforce organizational security policy should be aware of one another, and work well together in a coordinated fashion. In practice, this is not often the case, and organizations tend to add security in piecemeal fashion, with each element providing its own self-contained functions, oblivious to other security components. Network professionals who are deploying Internet-oriented applications face a baffling combination of firewalls, screening routers, virus or other content-based protection, encryption devices, virtual private network (VPN) devices and software, monitoring and logging tools, access control mechanisms, intrusion detection systems, network management systems, configuration aids, and a variety of other hardware and software tools. The expectation is that these will work together in a coordinated fashion, as a "system," but this is rarely the case.

The vast majority of network security tools, both hardware and software, are "point products." In most cases, the vendors of these tools have only a single product, or very narrow product offering, making integration of these tools into a cohesive system difficult, if not impossible. Vendors such as Cisco have the advantage, in that they have a broad array of complementary products that can be coordinated and synchronized to maximize each other's strengths.

The above factors contribute to the fact that network security is a complex, multidimensional undertaking. It affects not only the origin point of the data, but also the numerous points throughout the network that data passes through.

Goals of the Security Policy

As a starting point, let's consider some of the universal goals of network security. To some degree we expect our security architecture to provide some or all of the following assurances.

- Confidentiality and privacy of data
- Availability of the data
- Integrity of the data

- Identity — Authentication and authorization
- Nonrepudiation

Let's explore each of these to better understand exactly what we mean by each of these terms.

Confidentiality and Privacy of Data

Preventing others from observing what we are doing is the primary aspect of confidentiality. Internal business practices, employee data, financial and accounting data, trade secrets, marketing plans, et al., are obvious examples of things that need to be kept confidential by an organization. Sometimes the activities we are engaged in are also required to remain private.

Merger discussions, launching a new product, recruiting new employees, criminal investigations, and many other activities fall into this category, as well. The confidentiality extends to many forms of the data; printed, stored on disks or in file cabinets, as well as when the data may be transmitted across a network. Different policies and technologies may provide this functionality. In the case of technology solutions, we will see that virtual private networks (VPNs) and/or digital encryption technologies are the primary tools to provide confidentiality and privacy. VPNs can provide some degree of privacy in that data in transit is not easily intercepted for examination. However, to achieve a more complete guarantee of confidentiality, some form of encryption will probably be necessary. Each of these will be explored in later chapters.

Availability of the Data

The data or services are of no use to us, if they are unavailable. The availability may be impacted by a number of circumstances. Data may be accidentally damaged or destroyed, therefore requiring that backup copies should be generated and secured. It may be damaged, taken, or removed by an intruder. Even with appropriate backup procedures, the data will be unavailable during the period of time that it takes to restore the backup copy, possibly resulting in lost productivity or revenues. One of the forms of intrusions we discussed in a previous chapter was denial-of-service (DoS). The specific goal of a DoS attack may be to render the information or services unavailable for some period of time. To help ensure the availability of data we can utilize multiple technologies in combination. One of the first things we can do is limit access to authorized parties. We also need to prevent or defend against denial-of-service attacks. Since there are many DoS attack techniques, both known and those that may appear in the future, we will need to employ multiple technologies. Access lists on routers can block certain types of traffic altogether, eliminating some known type of attacks. ICMP is a commonly used "carrier" for a number of attacks. By blocking all or some ICMP traffic we can eliminate some. Firewalls have a better ability to analyze traffic flows, or packet exchange sequences, and can eliminate others. Vulnerability scanners can identify hidden weaknesses that should be addressed, while intrusion detection systems (IDSs) provide the highest level of traffic analysis and pattern recognition. Further, an IDS can optionally be configured to trigger dynamic access lists on routers, to block a specific activity. Denial-of-service is one of the most common attacks, one of the easiest to create or launch, and one of the most difficult to defend against, and therefore may warrant special attention.

Integrity of the Data

Likewise, the data has diminished value or is useless if it is not valid and accurate. If the data is intentionally or unintentionally altered, modified, or corrupted, we suffer a loss of the usefulness, accuracy, or reliability of the data. This may be one of the most difficult to prevent, detect, or correct, since many times the alteration is not noticeable. The goal of an intrusion may be specifically to falsely modify the data covertly.

If the data is accidentally altered in transmission across a network, there are several common mechanisms that will detect, and possibly correct, the error. Ethernet has a frame check sequence (FCS or CRC), TCP has an acknowledgement and retransmission capability, and applications sometimes have their own mechanisms to detect or correct transmission errors.

However, if the alteration was intentional, the intruder will make every effort to defeat these simple mechanisms, that is, recalculating the FCS, modifying the TCP header fields, and so forth. Various other technological methods can be employed to detect or prevent these forms of intentional alteration. Data integrity is an issue when stored on hosts and during transmission.

Identity Authentication and Authorization

Sometimes referred to as "identity" technologies, these techniques are typically applied to limit access to only designated individuals. The *authentication* verifies their identity, commonly using some form of password protection, whereupon, they are afforded *authorized* access to the data. There are various means to verify the identity of those who need access to the data, in order to restrict access to those without authorization.

The identity technologies typically consist of either a password or a combination of username and password. While the distinction between the two may seem insignificant, the latter, consisting of username in conjunction with a user-specific password allows for more granularity. When we configure Cisco switches and routers, we typically use password-only, and it is applied to a specific *port*. We lose the ability to remove any individual user's authorization. All users that possess *the* password can gain access. To exclude a previously authorized user, we must change the password for all the other users.

Alternatively, with the combination of user name and a password that is specific to that particular user, we maintain the ability to withhold access, simply by removing the appropriate user name and password configured for that individual.

Cisco implements several optional identity features beyond that which is commonly implemented. The most common method of access control on Cisco routers, Catalyst switches, and PIX firewalls is to apply a port-level password. There are two primary levels of access granted: basic user and privileged user. While the individual commands for each class vary by product line, they share a common theme. The basic level allows for limited administrative access, essentially "look-but-don't-touch," with limits on what can even be viewed. Privileged user access effectively provides "superuser" access, with unlimited rights. (Note: There is also a little known third category of user between basic and privileged, which will be discussed in a later section.)

While this is sufficient for many environments, Cisco also offers an alternative that utilizes a combination of user name and user-specific password. This latter method provides better "granularity" and is advantageous in situations such as when access rights need to be withdrawn for a specific user. In instances where all administrative users share a common port-level password, access rights can only be removed by changing the password for all the other users. If access control is based upon a user name and password combination, we need only to remove references for the individual user name and password, while all others retain their existing rights.

In addition, Cisco provides an option for a common database of user names, their associated passwords, and authorizations via the Cisco Secure Access Control Server (ACS). The ACS supports both the RADIUS (Remote Authentication Dial In User Service) and TACACS+ (Terminal Access Controller Access Control System) protocols, and implements what is commonly referred to as "AAA," an acronym for authentication, authorization, and accounting. This feature is available on the range of Cisco's routers, Catalyst switches, and PIX firewalls. Scalability and central administration is made possible via the Cisco Secure ACS. The Cisco Secure ACS also operates in conjunction with a number of token card servers. The ACS server provides a mechanism to authenticate and authorize users for varying degrees of access rights. The Cisco Secure ACS will be discussed in more detail in a later section.

Nonrepudiation

This unfamiliar-sounding term refers to the ability to prove that an action took place. The mechanisms that afford this protection verify that the party or parties to an event actually did participate in the action. One or the other is not able to deny that they participated, by claiming that someone fraudulently impersonated them. Nonrepudiation usually involves some variation of encryption, coupled with additional functionality (for Cisco implementation details, see section on IPSec). Conventionally, parties to a negotiation or contract *sign* documents to indicate their participation and acceptance. The only recourse is to claim that the signature was a forgery, not signed by the contesting party. Nonrepudiation in a data security context likewise uses *digital signatures,* with additional forms of "proof." While not all data communications require this capability, it may be required for some. Nonrepudiation will be covered in a later section on IPSec.

The characteristics described in the preceding section can be obtained through the appropriate use of various technologies. We will not attempt to describe the policies and procedures that may also be used to provide or enhance these functions, but will instead focus on the nature of the technolonts, which may be both physical and procedural.

The network diagram in Figure 2-1 represents a "typical" organization.

As can be seen in the drawing, the connection from the Internet first passes through a perimeter or "screening" router, which is directly connected to the "outside" Ethernet interface on the PIX firewall. The "inside" interface is connected to the protected "internal" network, consisting of various hosts. For the sake of simplicity, the drawing omits the additional detail of the organization's internal network that typically includes various servers or other host computers, client workstations, Ethernet switches, and a variety of other information assets. The third interface on the PIX firewall is connected to a publicly accessible, semi protected network commonly referred to as the demilitarized zone or DMZ. This DMZ is typically the location for Web servers, DNS servers, mail servers, or other devices that must be accessible to the outside world.

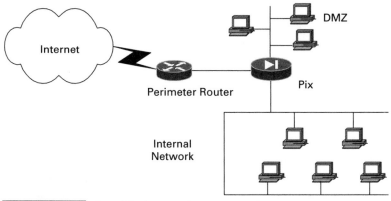

FIGURE 2-1   Simplified network security architecture.

Although this diagram is highly simplified, it illustrates the major connection points. These connection points, and the devices that facilitate them, give us a number of strategic "choke" points to control access to the data, as well as an opportunity to monitor data transmission. One method of identifying the relevant issues is to divide the "network" into logical zones. As indicated in the diagram, the relevant zones are:

- Internet access (public) consisting of the area outside the firewall, including the perimeter router, connection to the ISP(s), and any hosts/servers located in the DMZ (e.g., Web servers, mail hosts, DNS servers, etc.).

- The organization's internal network infrastructure, typically consisting of local area network (LAN) technologies and other infrastructure devices, such as Catalyst switches and route switch modules (RSMs), clients, servers, "campus" routers, plus associated cabling, patch panels, et al. It is further assumed that the geographic boundaries are limited and under the control of the organization.

- Other logical zones that may be relevant, such as remote locations or offices (commonly referred to as Intranets).

- External "partner" organizations (commonly referred to as Extranets).

- Any special cases like dialup access directly into the internal network from remote users. These could be Intranets, Extranets, or logical extensions to the internal "campus" network.

Each of these logical zones will likely have their own particular requirements, and should therefore be treated individually. Some or all of these may be present, and the mix will vary from one organization to another.

While network security applies to both network devices as well as hosts, we will focus our discussion on network security for the data as it travels through the network infrastructure and equipment, and leave it to others to address the specific host-related issues. There are certain external tools, features, and techniques that can reduce the threats to individual hosts, but the ultimate place to protect the host and its data is at the host itself.

Before we examine the tools and approaches, we should also discuss several interrelated issues. The first issue is with regard to the source of the threats. While the common perception is that the greatest threats come from outside the organization's network, this point is debatable. Most surveys and studies indicate that, on a percentage basis, the majority of threats actually come from *within* an organization. The percentages vary by study, but all arrive at a similar conclusion. The nature of the intrusions may vary, due to the nature of "inside" access and "inside" information. If this is the case, the challenge may seem daunting — how to protect the network from both inside and outside attacks.

The answer may lie in a popular adage: "Protect what you can and monitor the rest." This approach is also consistent with the conventional wisdom that recommends a "layered" approach, using multiple technologies, at multiple levels, and at multiple control points.

Physical Security

Any serious discussion of network security architectures should begin by first emphasizing the necessity for physical security. Most organizations limit physical access to hosts and servers, yet are not as diligent when it comes to networking devices, such as routers, switches, and the like. Even such simple elements as cabling and wiring closets require consideration.

Cabling

The cabling plant is a good place to start. Depending upon the type of cabling your organization has chosen to implement, you may be vulnerable to different types of intrusions. In the days when coaxial cabling and 10BaseT hubs were more common, it was often possible to simply choose an unused office wall outlet and plug into the network. Any number of readily available software packages would allow an intruder to eavesdrop on *all* the traffic on a particular network segment, including clear text Telnet logons to routers or other equipment, ftp logons, SNMP community strings (passwords), email (SMTP), and various other types of traffic. These passive taps on the network were essentially undetectable. Ethernet switches have made this less common, since each port is effectively its own segment, limiting the ability to see the entire network. A notable exception is the "span" or "mirror" port on some Catalyst switches, which effectively provides a view into *all* ports, comparable to the older mechanism described above.

Switches

Enhancements such as port lockout on Catalyst switches provide an additional hurdle, but can sometimes be defeated. A document available on the SANS Institute Web site details how this can be done (*http://www.sans.org/ infosecFAQ/firewall/port_security.htm*). Many people would contend that switches are not vulnerable to various forms of attack, but this is contradicted by the facts, as well as security bulletins from Cisco.

In December 1997 they reported that Catalyst 5xxx and 29xx switches were vulnerable to the attack. For further details see Cisco's interim field notice, *TCP Loopback DoS Attack* at *http://www.cisco.com/warp/public/770/ catalyst*.

In the Field Notice it is also pointed out that there are several issues with switches. It has been claimed that switches are not susceptible to DoS attacks, since they operate at the Ethernet frame level, and are thereby immune to attacks directed at the IP stack. However, that claim is not always correct because in many cases a Catalyst switch does in fact "run IP." The Catalyst switch has a management entity that has an IP address, and can be managed via a Telnet connection. By virtue of the fact that switches may be exploited, and tend to be at the core of many networks may make them opportune targets. In an example, Cisco reported that the attack might cause the supervisor module to reload. If attack is repeated, a denial of service can be achieved.

While this clearly is not intended to be an indictment of Cisco, and other switch vendors may have similar problems, it is a reminder that good security doesn't happen in a vacuum. Network security professionals must constantly be on their guard.

Routers

Routers have always been, and will continue to be, tempting targets, by virtue of the fact that they are key elements of any network infrastructure. The common first step used by serious intruders is to perform surveillance, with address scans and port mapping to gather information about the layout of the network. Access to the routing table can add a significant amount of detail to these reconnaissance efforts. Beyond that the routers sit in strategic positions in their respective networks, making them attractive targets for a variety of intrusions, especially rerouting and eavesdropping. These factors further indicate that the network equipment should be kept in a room with access restricted to only authorized individuals.

The Cisco training curriculum even documents how to perform "password recovery" for their router, switch, and PIX firewall products. The technique requires that one simply be able to reboot (power cycle) the router and send the "break" character to the console port.

In addition to their role as traffic cop, routers also share some "host" functionality, requiring similar physical safeguards. A more complete discussion of the router's role is contained in a subsequent section. Its inclusion here was intended to emphasize the common overall need for physical access controls for networking devices, whether switch, router, host, or other.

As is apparent from the previous sections, it is not only host computers and servers that should be kept in a secure climate-controlled environment. Instead, we should also treat the network infrastructure, consisting of cabling plant, hubs, switches, and routers, in a comparable fashion. Since each type of network equipment is vulnerable to various forms of compromise, we can minimize or eliminate those that are based upon having physical access to the equipment.

An additional consideration is for various forms and types of redundancy. This may be implemented using redundant servers, mirrored disk drives, or other techniques to achieve redundancy. Larger sites may implement load balancing across multiple servers for performance reasons, and thereby indirectly enjoy some degree of redundancy. The Domain Name Service (DNS) provides a comparable mechanism to achieve redundancy by defining a primary server, secondary (backup) server, and possible tertiary servers in the form of "caching" servers. Since the data in DNS is relatively static and stable, appropriate use of these mechanisms, in conjunction with proper backup and recovery procedures (to tape or otherwise), should provide an adequate means to achieve reliability.

The final element in this limited discussion of physical security is backup and recovery procedures. This topic has been covered exhaustively in other forums, so its wide scope will not be duplicated here. The point to be made here is that while thorough, well-planned backup and recovery procedures may not prevent or minimize the *threats*, such procedures can make a significant contribution to minimizing the *damage* those threats could cause. Prompt complete recovery procedures should be carefully considered when planning for disaster recovery or incident response.

Basic Network Security

It would be appropriate at this point to review the range of security tools that are currently available. We will not cover those that are host-specific, those that are part of the host or server operating system feature sets, nor those that are based upon administrative policies and procedures. Instead, we will focus on those that are protocol-based or network-based. Since our focus is on Cisco-based network security, we will identify the applicable Cisco products or supported features that provide the various forms of security protection.

Passwords

In the previous section we discussed various ways that passwords could be used to control administrative access to Cisco switches, routers, and PIX firewalls. In addition to these, there are a variety of methods to implement password protection that are used or supported by Cisco products.

Authentication methods using passwords is one form of "identity technologies." In general, identity technologies rely upon one or more of the following:

- Something you know
- Something you have
- Something you are

The underlying assumption behind using passwords is that a secret password is something you know. The ability to identify or authenticate an individual relies upon the secrecy of the password. If the password is kept secret, known only by one person, it serves as proof that the person that knows and can produce the password upon request is the correct person. Since passwords are assumed to be unique to, and known only by the rightful owner, mechanisms that implement password protection require the user's name, in order to associate it with the correct password. As a result, most logon procedures consist of the familiar username and password combination.

The deficiency of this approach is that it may be possible for others to learn or guess the password, and subsequently impersonate the genuine party. One mechanism to strengthen the proof provided by password protection methods is to make the password difficult to guess. For that reason, common words like cisco, admin, pass, et al., are bad choices for passwords. Likewise, words that can be associated with an individual, such as a spouse's name, hobbies, or pets' names are comparably bad choices.

One of the attacks on password-protected systems is to apply "the brute force method," or attempt to guess every combination of letters or numbers that a password may contain. These brute force methods look for shortcuts to avoid the necessity to try every possible combination. Since passwords are often common language terms, brute force methods will often employ a "dictionary attack" with the hope that by choosing words from a dictionary they may get a match without having to try every possible combination. For these reasons, some password protection methods require passwords to be a minimum length (e.g., six or eight characters), and require that they consist of some combination of numbers and letters. Using longer passwords results in exponentially more combinations that must be attempted. This defeats the ability to use shortcuts or "good guesses," and forces more combinations to be tried. Even so, a motivated party with sufficient computing power can still "calculate" all the possible combinations. This factor can be overcome if only a few attempts are permitted (three is common) and the password file is secured. Nonetheless, password files are often targets of intruders because calculating all combinations is feasible. There are a number of readily available programs that do brute force password cracking that can be found on many "hacker" Web sites.

A variation of the common password protection method is to require that the password be changed on a periodic basic. By using this "password aging," we limit the time that a password is valid. The result is that, even though a password may be learned or discovered, it is only useful for a limited time period.

A further improvement is the one-time password (OTP), the ultimate case of password aging. With this method, a password is used only once and then discarded. Even if the password is learned or discovered, it is not useful after it has been used for the first time, since subsequent attempts require a new password.

Since the use of a one-time password (OTP) would create an administrative nightmare, if we had to manually change the password after each use, a method to dynamically update the password database is necessary. S/Key, developed by AT&T®, is one such method. With S/Key, a client requests an S/Key server to generate a list of passwords for use by that client. The server generates the list, makes it available to the client (via floppy disk or printout), and keeps a copy for itself. The client uses the passwords in the sequence they are listed. As each password is used, it is "crossed off the list" by both the client and the server. Once the list of passwords is exhausted, the client must request another batch of passwords from the S/Key server, making the process less than fully transparent to the user. Note that the user receives a list that might also be compromised. A better method would provide a "perpetual" list of one-time passwords, which is not subject to compromise. Token-based systems provide such a method.

Token-based systems using token cards (or alternatively token software — "soft tokens") are an improvement that addresses the shortcomings of basic OTP methods. In addition, they provide an additional authentication factor — something you have — in the form of the token card itself. For this reason, they are sometimes referred to as two-factor authentication systems. The token card is typically an electronic device, about the size of a credit card-sized calculator. Often, the token card is activated when the user enters a PIN number (something you know), with the OTP displayed on an LCD screen. The token card runs an algorithm that continually generates new passwords, with each one valid for a short period of time (a minute or a few minutes). The token card server runs a similar algorithm that is generating the same OTP passwords. This method is applicable to time-based methods, but synchronization between the token card and the token server may be achieved one of two ways:

- Time-based, in which the server algorithm generates a similar sequence of passwords. User supplied PIN number activates the token card. If the card-generated OTP the user enters matches the password generated on the server (within the previous minute or so), the user is authenticated.

- Challenge-response, in which the token server sends a random string of digits then sends the string to the client. The client enters the random string, which the token card uses along with a secret encryption key, to generate a response (the OTP). The response is sent to the server, which has also encrypted the random string with its own copy of the secret key. The server evaluates the client's response. If it matches the server's encrypted result, the user is authenticated.

With either method, additional equipment is required: both the token card (or soft tokens) and the token server. Cisco supports authentication from the following token-card servers:

- CRYPTOCard RB-1 from CRYPTOCard Corporation
- SecurID® and ACE Server from RSA Security (formerly Security Dynamics)
- SafeWord™ from Secure Computing® (using DES Gold Card token card and SofToken)
- Axent Technologies® token server

While the token-based systems provide a superior authentication method, they require the user to always carry the token card. If they leave it at home, they are unable to access the system. The end result is that we have a higher degree of protection (i.e., more reliable authentication), but at the cost of the token cards and server, as well as less ease-of-use on the part of the user.

An even better form of authentication is afforded by the use of biometrics. These methods rely upon the other characteristic — something you are — and typically use some unique physical characteristic, such as fingerprints, retinal scans, voice recognition, et al. Currently, their cost puts them out of reach for many organizations, although this situation is likely to improve over time.

A special case of authentication was developed specifically for dialup environments as part of the Point-to-Point Protocol (PPP). PPP was developed to be a standardized, serial-line (wide-area network) protocol. Since one of the intended environments was dialup access from device to device (e.g., router to router), provision was made so that these devices could authenticate one another. The underlying issue was that if two network devices needed to authenticate one another over a dialup line, who or what would enter the user name and password on behalf of the devices? The answer was that the device could provide this information on its own behalf by extending the functionality of the PPP protocol. Additional, optional sub-protocols were added to PPP to accommodate this functionality, specifically the Password Authentication Protocol (PAP) and the Challenge Handshake Authentication Protocol (CHAP). While a complete discussion of PPP, PAP, and CHAP is beyond the scope of this material, an overview is provided.

PAP

PAP provides a simple user name and password method for one device to authenticate to another. It assumes a one-way, master/slave relationship with the calling party (client-side) providing login information (i.e., username and password). The called party (server-side) assumes the role of authenticator verifying the username and password against the database of usernames and passwords stored at the server-side of the connection. The PAP option is exercised after the physical establishment of the link (via the Link Control Protocol, or LCP) and before the Network Control Protocol (NCP) negotiates the connection's protocol parameters. Once the connection is made, PAP (repeatedly) sends the username password until authentication is acknowledged, or the connection is terminated. If the PAP authentication is unsuccessful, LCP "tears down" the connection.

CHAP

CHAP is more sophisticated and complex, and differs from PAP in several distinctive ways. First, it can be bi-directional, in that each end of a connection can require authentication of the other end. Additionally, CHAP can request a re-authentication at any time during the connection. It also utilizes a "three-way handshake" for negotiation. The "initiator" of a CHAP negotiation provides its user name and indicates that it wants to use CHAP. The "responder" issues a challenge consisting of an incrementally changing identifier and a variable changing value. The initiator uses these values in a calculation along with its password. This calculation results in a MD5, keyed hash (discussed in later chapters) that is sent to the challenger/responder. The challenger looks up the password in his username and password database. He also performs the same calculation with the same numbers and the password for that user from his database. If the result of his hash matches that of the initiator, authentication is granted.

Although more complicated, CHAP also provides additional functionality. The "password" is never sent over the network in "clear text," eliminating the possibility of eavesdropping. Further, protection against replay of the original CHAP handshake is provided by the variable changing values (loosely equivalent to a time stamp).

The negative aspect is that the challenger must maintain its copy of the password in clear text, so that the keyed-hash can be generated and compared for each authentication. This is problematic in environments (like the Windows NT SAM hive) where irreversible, encrypted password files are used. Microsoft has developed it own variation of CHAP, known as MS-CHAP, to deal with this special requirement.

Cisco supports both PAP and CHAP on Cisco routers and access servers in dialup environments. CHAP is the preferred choice due to its superior functionality. Additionally, Cisco provides support for MS-CHAP in the Cisco Secure Access Control Server (ACS) that may be used in conjunction with Windows NT to provide an authentication database.

Network Security Solutions

As defined by Cisco, their network security solution is comprised of five key elements[1]:

---

1. Source: *http://www.cisco.com/warp/public/cc/so/neso/sqso/index.shtml*

- **Identity** — Identity is the accurate and positive identification of network users, hosts, application, services, and resources. Standard technologies that enable identification include authentication protocols such as RADIUS and TACACS+, Kerberos, and one-time password tools. New technologies, such as digital certificates, smart cards, and directory services, are beginning to play increasingly important roles in identity solutions
- **Perimeter Security** — This element provides the means to control access to critical network applications, data, and services so that only legitimate users and information can pass through the network. Routers and switches with access control lists (ACL) and/or stateful firewalling, as well as dedicated firewall appliances, provide this control. Complementary tools, including virus scanners and content filters, also help control network perimeters.
- **Data Privacy** — When information must be protected from eavesdropping, the ability to provide authenticated confidential communication on demand is crucial. Sometimes, data separation using tunneling technologies, such as generic routing encapsulation (GRE) or Layer 2 Tunneling Protocol (L2TP), provides effective data privacy. Often, however, additional privacy requirements call for the use of digital encryption technologies and protocols such as IPSec. This added protection is especially important when implementing VPNs.
- **Security Monitoring** — To ensure that a network remains secure, it's important to regularly test and monitor the state of security preparation. Network vulnerability scanners can proactively identify areas of weakness, and intrusion detection systems (IDS) can monitor and respond to security events as they occur. Through the use of security monitoring solutions, organizations can obtain unprecedented visibility into both the network data stream and the security posture of the network.
- **Policy Management** — As networks grow in size and complexity, the requirement for centralized policy management tools grows, as well. Sophisticated tools that can analyze, interpret, configure, and monitor the state of security policy, with browser-based user interfaces, enhance the usability and effectiveness of network security solutions.

Let's take a closer look at some of the specific tools that address the five key elements as defined by Cisco in the above.

Perimeter Routers — First Layer of Defense

One of the key devices to secure any network that connects to the Internet, or any other non-private internetwork, is the IP router. It will typically be found anywhere that the LAN connects to the wide-area network (WAN), using dedicated lines, frame-relay, ATM, or other WAN technologies, including those that are purely private to an organization.

Referring to Figure 2-1, one can see that this is the first line of defense, at the point where the private network connects to the public network, typically through an Internet Service Provider (ISP). The network security functionality provided (and referred to in the above section) consists of several items.

- Access control lists (ACLs) — rule sets that are applied to inbound or outbound traffic, at specific interfaces, defining whether individual packets that match a criteria are to be permitted or denied to pass through the router. The criteria are defined by specifying any combination of source address, source port, destination address, destination port, protocol, or TCP connection status (ACK bit set). A mask may be applied to define specific addresses or ranges of addresses, and Boolean operands to define specific ports or a range of ports. Access lists provide for a minimum level of protection.

- Stateful-packet filtering — in the recent past, this optional software add-on was referred to as the "firewall feature set," and has also been called Context-Based Access Control (CBAC). It effectively adds the equivalent of PIX firewall functionality to a router. In its current offering, it has been renamed the Cisco Secure Integrated Software, and now also includes a subset of the intrusion detection system functionality. It is positioned as a lower cost, but lower performing alternative to the PIX firewall (with some added intrusion detection). This product will be covered in greater detail in a later chapter. When used as an alternative to the PIX dedicated firewall appliance, the separate perimeter router and firewall, as shown in Figure 2-1, are collapsed into the perimeter router, with the DMZ typically implemented as an additional interface on the perimeter router.

- Denial of Service protection — specific support to protect hosts from certain types of DoS attacks (SYN flooding). This feature, referred to as TCP Intercept, has been a part of the basic router Internetwork Operating System (IOS) for several years (IOS, version 11.2). A different, but equivalent functionality, is included as part of CBAC in the Cisco Secure Integrated Software.

Firewalls — Perimeter Reinforcement

As illustrated in Figure 2-1, the PIX firewall serves as an inner wall, and a more complete barrier than that provided by a perimeter router with ACLs alone. Several variations on Figure 2-1 are possible. These variations will be further explored in later chapters.

When we use the term "firewall" in a Cisco context we are talking about the PIX (or PIX-like functionality). In general, the addition of a true firewall provides an additional layer of protection beyond what can be provided with stateless access lists. As shown in the figure, the DMZ can be isolated from the more protected internal network. Since the DMZ must allow for some degree of public access to Web servers, mail servers, and DNS servers, we need to isolate it from the internal network. If an intrusion on one of these DMZ-based hosts results in compromise of that host, the intruder would still need to get through the firewall to access the internal network. In contrast to the perimeter router, which must be at least slightly permissive, the PIX begins with the premise that *no* traffic originating on the outside will be permitted. The common impression is that a firewall (as shown in the configuration of Figure 2-1) will be adequate. While that may not be completely true, it does provide a solid foundation to apply additional protective measures. A thorough discussion of firewalls and the PIX, in particular, will be found in later chapters.

Virtual Private Networks

Although not illustrated in the figure, a VPN could extend from the perimeter router or the PIX firewall to one or more external sites. A VPN allows a public network like the Internet to be treated like a private network. VPN technologies provide the convenience and cost savings of the public network, while providing the characteristics of a private network. VPNs have generated significant interest since organizations can often eliminate private networks at a significant cost savings. Of particular interest are dialup users. In the conventional scenario, an organization would need to provide their own incoming phone lines, modem pools, access servers, and security methods, along with the overhead for installation, maintenance, and management. They would also have to deal with upgrades and expansion to accommodate additional users. This clearly entails significant time, effort, and expense. With VPN technologies, the organization can off-load much of this burden to an ISP. Instead of dialing into the organization's private dialup network, the user can now take advantage of simple Internet dialup connections. The user traffic is then carried to the "home" network in a VPN "tunnel," which maintains most of the characteristics of a private network. The traffic enters the organization via the Internet, eliminating dialup lines, modems, et al. Several methods for creating VPNs are available, using PPP derivatives (at Layer 2), or IPSec (at Layer 3). Cisco provides VPN support for IP traffic using PPTP, L2TP, and IPSec. Support for non-IP protocols such as Novell® IPX or AppleTalk® is provided through Generic Routing Encapsulation (GRE).

Data Privacy and Integrity

The task of providing confidentiality, privacy, data integrity, and authentication of data origin and non-repudiation requires digital encryption and related technologies, such as digital signatures, keyed-hash algorithms, et al. The industry standard method to provide these features is IPSec. Cisco provides full support for the current standard for IPSec, and also includes additional support for Certificate Authorities, a prestandard feature that has not yet been included in the IPSec standard. IPSec provides for confidentiality, authenticity, data integrity, and non-repudiation of data flows over public and private networks.

Cisco also continues to support their older, pre-IPSec encryption method, Cisco Encryption Technologies (CET). CET does not provide all of the features and functionality that are provided by IPSec, but may be used to provide backward compatibility. It may also be used in Cisco router-to-router environments, if the full functionality of IPSec is not required. Because CET is less sophisticated than IPSec, it is also more mature and easier to configure. Encryption technologies and IPSec, in particular, will be covered more thoroughly in later chapters.

Vulnerability Assessment

Vulnerability scanners operate by running a series of test (including passive intrusion techniques) to discover vulnerabilities to possible threats and intrusions. The specific Cisco product that provides this functionality is the Cisco Secure Scanner (formerly Net Sonar).

Intrusion Detection

Intrusion detection systems provide 24/7 surveillance of traffic flows, in search of traffic patterns that are characteristic of known intrusion methods. *Sensors* are placed at strategic points in the network. These sensors analyze traffic flows and report any anomalies to a *Director*, a management, database, and reporting platform. The Cisco Secure Intrusion Detection System (IDS [formerly Net Ranger]) provides this functionality. A subset of the IDS is also included in the Cisco Secure Integrated Software for router platforms.

Access Controls and Identity

Access controls for dialup users provide a means to authenticate users when they attempt to connect to the network. Using authentication protocols such as RADIUS and TACACS+, a network access server (NAS) can relay logon information to a centralized database for authentication and authorization on a per-user basis. The database may be local to the RADIUS or TACACS+ server, or the server may be configured as a proxy front-end to an existing Microsoft NT Domain, Novell NDS, or token card server. This same functionality may be used to extend authentication, authorization and accounting (AAA) to non-dialup environments, such as router and firewall logons. It can also be used as an additional layer of AAA protection for traffic traversing the firewall. This functionality is provided in the Cisco Secure ACS.

Security Policy Management and Enforcement

As the size and complexity of networks increase, the security measures increase in complexity, as well. To provide consistency checks and security policy enforcement, a supervisory platform will prove to be essential. Cisco provides such a policy-based platform in the Cisco Security Manager. Although initial support is limited to the PIX firewall, future extensions are planned to cover the entire range of Cisco security products. Also currently available is the PIX Firewall Manager that provides a convenient, GUI-based interface for managing one or many PIX firewalls. The PIX Firewall Manager functionality will eventually be fully integrated into the Cisco Security Manager.

Summary

We started this chapter by describing a Security Architecture, why we need one, and what it might include. We defined the goals we hoped to achieve, namely, confidentiality and privacy of data and transactions, availability of data and services, integrity of data, and non-repudiation. We then outlined where the architecture would be applied, to both the physical protection of the network infrastructure, and the logical areas we may need to protect. The logical areas were loosely defined as outside the network perimeter, inside the internal network, in the semipublic area (i.e., DMZ), and noted considerations for special cases, such as dialup, Intranets, and Extranets. We discussed the functionality of various technologies we could employ to satisfy our goals, how each one might be employed to reach the goals, and identified specific Cisco products, features, and technologies that provide that functionality.

In the next section we will begin to explore, in more detail, some of the key Cisco products, the functionality they provide, along with the information to configure and implement the relevant features.

First Line of Defense — The Perimeter Router

In This Chapter

- Passwords
- Disable EXEC-Mode
- Establish a Line-Specific Password
- Establish User-Specific Passwords
- Limit Access Using Access Lists as Filters
- Other Issues
- Router Services and Protocols
- Traffic Management
- Router-Based Attack Protection
- Routing Protocols
- Summary

*T*he perimeter or border router is defined as the router that connects an organization's network to the rest of the public world, including the Internet. Since it is the first device on an organization's network that incoming traffic passes through, the perimeter router plays a critical role in providing protection for the organization's internal network.

While there are a number of different basic designs using perimeter routers, with and without firewalls, we will not attempt to discuss each one individually in this chapter. We will be covering various "firewall" strategies in the next chapter. Instead, we will focus here on the common threads that each of those strategies share.

In Figure 3-1, we show the perimeter router as used in a "classic" firewall design. In this scenario, the semiprotected, semiprivate, DMZ area, where publicly accessible Web servers, mail servers, and DNS name servers are located, is between the perimeter router and the PIX or other firewall. In this case, the perimeter router will be solely responsible for protecting the servers in the DMZ. The functionality provided by the perimeter router in these cases is crucial. The primary tools we have at our disposal

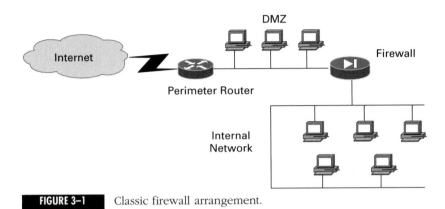

FIGURE 3-1   Classic firewall arrangement.

are access control lists (ACLs) configured on the router. There are several other network security features that Cisco includes as an integral part of the Internetwork Operating System (IOS), as well as additional, optional software that is available.

The ACLs on a Cisco router are essentially "packet filters." They can be defined as basic *standard* access lists, or more advanced *extended* access lists. The fundamental difference between a standard and extended access list is the scope and degree of detail we can define. Extended access lists are a superset of standard access lists and allow us to define additional criteria to examine.

An alternative, preferred design is to move the DMZ "behind" the firewall. This allows the additional functionality of the firewall to be employed to provide a higher degree of access control. Cisco support for this design on the PIX has existed for several years and consists of permitting an additional "third" interface" to be installed on the PIX, beyond the two that are assumed by the classic design. Recent PIX operating system versions have expanded support for as many as six interfaces, depending upon interface type and PIX platform. Figure 3-2 illustrates the current preferred design.

In the following discussion, we will assume that the second scenario applies. We will discuss additional considerations that may be necessary for the case of the classic design at the end of this section, and more fully in the chapter on the IOS Firewall

One additional note: While it may be possible to employ a router with access lists alone, as the sole line of defense, this approach has significant limitations and is not recommended. If budget or other considerations preclude a firewall, the next best alternative would be to implement what has been referred to as the "firewall feature set," an optional, additional IOS software product that provides a Cisco router with most of the functionality of the PIX.

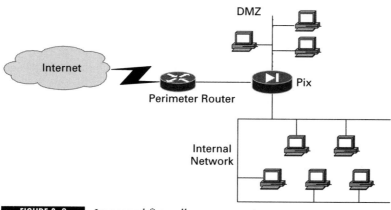

FIGURE 3–2   Improved firewall arrangement.

This feature set has been known by several names: the firewall feature set, CBAC, and the current name the Cisco Secure IOS Firewall. This product will be discussed in a separate chapter. This chapter focuses primarily on securing the router, with a limited treatment of the issues regarding protecting other network devices.

Given the above, in this chapter we will present various configuration methods and settings to "harden" the perimeter router. Many of these configuration choices or options have the effect of protecting the router, in addition to implementing the router features that complement the functionality of the firewall. Other recommendations represent the best current practices. This is particularly important since several of the recommendations we will present are to disable features that are enabled by default. These configuration options may also be applicable to the organization's other routers, as well, but are particularly important considerations for perimeter or border routers. Some represent configuration assumptions that were valid in the past, but no longer serve their original purpose. Others may be appropriate for some routers, but result in additional, unnecessary vulnerabilities if implemented on the perimeter router.

Passwords

Cisco routers utilize password protection using several different approaches. Since they are the primary defense against unauthorized access to an organization's routers, they warrant thorough treatment.

Privileged Users

Cisco implements two primary levels of passwords: basic user and privileged user. The basic user level permits some administrative functions, but severely limits those functions. In particular, it prevents a basic administrative user from viewing, modifying, replacing, or otherwise altering the existing configuration. Basic users are permitted to view various conditions and statistics, but the approach might be best described as "look-but-don't-touch." On the other hand, privileged users are treated as "superuser" and permitted unlimited software access.

Privileged user access is controlled by the "enable" password. This password gets its name from the Cisco IOS command **enable** used to enter this mode. Cisco recommends that an enable password should always be set. There are two forms of the enable password. The appropriate global configuration commands are:

```
Router(config)#enable password sometextstring
```

or

```
Router(config)#enable secret sometextstring
```

The differences are both historical and functional. The first command was introduced in Cisco IOS version 10.0 and is written to the configuration text file as clear text. The second command was introduced several years later in IOS version 11.0. The reference to "secret" is based upon the fact that the password is written to the configuration text file in an irreversible, MD5-based cryptographic form. Cisco also provides an additional global configuration command (i.e., **service password-encryption**) that will encrypt any clear text passwords found in the configuration file. However, this second form of encryption uses a weak encryption algorithm, which any competent amateur cryptographer could easily reverse. There are, in fact, numerous sites on the Internet where one can download the "crack" program to decrypt passwords encrypted with this mechanism. A WWW search on the phrase "Cisco crack" discovered multiple sites:

- http://www.kazmier.com/computer/ — The site's home page refers to itself as the 26th Floor, and has an online Java applet to decode passwords. A second applet is described as a tool to verify access list address references.
- http://www.cotse.com/route.htm — Cult of the Swimming Elephant offers an executable program, explanation of the algorithm Cisco uses, and a Palm Pilot™ version of the password-cracking program. Also included are several other Cisco related documents that describe various vulnerabilities.

- http://www.l0pht.com/~kingpin/pilot.html#ST1 — L0pht Heavy Industries provides a downloadable, zipped program. This is also a primary site for password cracking tools, which seems to be one of L0pht's specialties.

As a result, Cisco recommends you should always use the **enable secret** *textstring* form of the command. If you use the "setup mode" on a Cisco router, you will be required to provide a password for both types, and each password must be different. This double password was once considered a safe precaution, but is rarely necessary today. When the newer, preferred form of the command was first introduced, Cisco recommended that the older form *also* be used as a *backup* password. Their reasoning was that if the configuration was used under a version of the IOS that predated the newer command form, the **enable secret** *textstring* command would not be recognized, and, therefore, the router would start up with no privileged password set. Simply typing the **enable** command would permit privileged user access with no password checking. Conversely, if the IOS version did recognize the **enable secret** format, the **enable password** format would be useable. In either case (and depending upon the IOS version), the result is the only one **enable** password could be used.

The MD5 hash algorithm has had considerable review by the cryptographic community and is believed to be irreversible; however, even irreversible encryption is vulnerable to *dictionary attacks*, a brute-force method that hashes every word in its dictionary looking for a match. These vulnerabilities will be covered in the discussion of encryption contained in a later chapter.

Basic Users

Even nonprivileged access should be controlled for several reasons. First, if anyone can log into the router, there is still a significant level of information available which should remain private. Second, anyone who can log into a router can also open an outgoing Telnet session, and possibly use it a launching pad for attacks on other network equipment. If the attack was traced back to your equipment and IP address, the results could range from embarrassment to legal liability, depending upon the circumstances.

It is considered good practice to include basic user passwords on all ports, including console 0, auxiliary 0, and any other asynchronous ports that may be applicable. (Cisco supports low-speed asynchronous ports or *lines* on some router models that can also serve a dual purpose as access servers.) Cisco describes terminal-oriented access as "tty," a historical reference to "teletype," one of the original terminal types manufactured by the Teletype® Corporation. Remote access via Telnet, rlogin or other similar methods is described as "vty," or virtual Teletype. These remote access mechanisms have the effect of making a remote terminal appear to be locally attached, hence *virtually* locally attached. Virtual ttys are not ports in the physical sense, but configuration statements in the Cisco IOS use a "line" analogy.

The underlying difference between locally attached terminals and remote access via virtual terminals is simple. With a locally attached terminal, raw ASCII characters are sent directly to the port. With remote access, the same ASCII characters are processed by the Telnet client application, encapsulated in a TCP segment, which is encapsulated in an IP packet, which is encapsulated in some data link layer frame, such as Ethernet. These are delivered to the router or other host device through one of its interfaces. The host function reverses the encapsulation process, first at the data link layer then IP layer, and then the TCP layer. The TCP segment header indicates the appropriate TCP port number (e.g., port 23), with the final unwrapping of the character performed by the Telnet host process. Responses from the host to the client reverse this process. (The relevance of this description will become more apparent when we discuss access lists. Access lists will allow us to control Telnet traffic at either the interface level or at the Telnet process level.)

We can control basic user access for line console 0, line aux 0, line vty 0 through 4, and any other low-speed asynchronous lines, using several methods. Special attention should be given to any of the line types that may provide dialup access via modem or ISDN, since devices connected to these are treated as locally attached terminals.

Disable EXEC-Mode

Disable the command line interface (CLI) altogether. Cisco also refers to the command line interface as EXEC-mode access. This method may be applicable for low speed asynchronous lines, when the router is used as an access server. It may be applicable to Telnet access (via line vty 0 to 4) or auxiliary 0, but would be inappropriate for console 0. Without some CLI or EXEC-mode access, you could not manage or reconfigure the router. The configuration statements would look something like this:

```
Router(config#)line aux 0
Router(config-line#)no exec
```

Establish a Line-Specific Password

This would permit anyone with knowledge of the password to gain "login" access to the basic user level (i.e., EXEC-mode). This is probably the most common approach, and is the approach taught in Cisco's basic router configuration course. The configuration statements would look something like this:

```
Router(config#)line vty 0 4
Router(config-line#)login
Router(config-line#)password somepassword
```

A common mistake when configuring passwords for various line formats is to forget to include one or the other of the commands. If one configures the **login** command, but no **password** is set, anything entered (including a carriage return) is considered an acceptable password. Conversely, if one configures the **password** but doesn't include **login**, no login is required, and access is automatically granted. The exception to these rules is Telnet access. If no password is configured, all Telnet access is blocked by default.

Establish User-Specific Passwords

The command syntax to accomplish user-specific passwords is a simple modification of the above, with the username and password configured in global configuration mode, not associated with the specific line. This command effectively creates a "local" database of usernames and passwords.

```
Router(config)#username yourname password somepassword
Router(config)#line vty 0 4
Router(config-line)#login local
```

This method is often described in the context of AAA. The benefit is that we may establish passwords on a per-user basis, rather than a per-port basis. To provide scalability, an extension this concept of AAA is to have the username and password database stored on a centrally located database, rather than replicated on each router or other device.

An example of such a database is the Cisco Secure ACS that will be outlined in a later chapter. A full discussion of AAA is beyond the scope of this material. For a more complete description, refer to the Cisco IOS documentation.

Limit Access Using Access Lists as Filters

There are two approaches to access control filtering. Since access lists are IP addresses-based, they are often used in conjunction with one of the other approaches described above, rather than an alternative. We will describe these in our discussion of access lists later in this chapter.

Other Issues

In the specific case of console 0, there are additional considerations. *The password recovery procedures* documented by Cisco operate by sending the BREAK signal on the console port during the boot cycle. If a reboot can be forced via power cycling the router, or otherwise causing a reboot, these password recovery procedures can result in total control of the router by any malicious party who has access to the console 0 port. Whether by a directly connected terminal, modem-connection, or reverse Telnet on a terminal server, intruders have the ability to breach any security measures you may configure. As a result, such access should be considered as part of your physical security preparations.

There is also a little-known category between basic and privileged modes. These are sometimes described as privilege level modes. With privilege levels, Cisco provides a method to elevate and add to the access rights of a basic user, without allowing fully privileged user access. You can specify 16 levels, from level 0 through level 15. Level 0 is a special case that can be used to specify an even more limited subset of commands than those afforded by basic user. Level 1 is normal, basic user EXEC-mode privilege, and level 15 is the conventional fully privileged user. The remaining levels from 2 through 14 can be established by defining a "dictionary" of privileged user commands that are applicable to that specific level.

The steps to define a privilege level are:

1. Define the privilege level
2. Define the commands that apply to the level
3. Set the password for the level

The example below illustrates the steps to create a privilege level 5 on the console port 0, to permit "configure" commands, and set the secret enable to "xyzzy" for level 5 users. For additional information on privilege levels see Cisco IOS documentation.

```
Router(config)#privilege exec level 5 configure
Router(config)#line console 0
Router(config-line)#enable secret level 5 xyzzy
```

A final note on use of passwords relates to the "login banner." These are the on-screen informational messages that greet users when they attempt to login. It is recommended that these not use phrases that could be interpreted as invitations. There are reported cases in which an intruder was apprehended, and during the ensuing prosecution, the intruder made the claim that they were not intruding, but had, in fact, been invited or "welcomed" to the breached site. Illogical as this may seem, it has been used as a successful defense. As a consequence, it is recommended that any such login banners advise that access is for authorized users only.

On a similar note, monitoring of authorized user activities may be required. Some organizations have elected to monitor various activities, such as the Web sites users frequent, files that are uploaded or downloaded, email, or other similar practices.

If such monitoring is part of an organization's policies and procedures, it may be legally necessary to warn users that they may be subject to monitoring. This issue pits the rights of the organization to protect their assets against the individual user's right to privacy. To further complicate the matter, this is an immature part of the law. Since technology progresses at a faster pace than the applicable law, this is uncharted territory from a legal perspective. The existing laws typically address posted mail, telephones, and other telecommunications (like telegraph), but don't begin to address the myriad of legal issues introduced by Internet technology. Since the law varies from jurisdiction to jurisdiction, you should consult your own legal counsel to determine what may be necessary and appropriate in your individual circumstances.

Router Services and Protocols

In addition to establishing passwords, there are a variety of other things that can be done to "harden" the router against attacks. As indicated previously, there are certain features on a Cisco router that are commonly enabled by default, which could make the router more vulnerable to attack. While the basic recommendation is that these features be disabled, there are some circumstances where this may not be possible or desirable. We will provide basic background information regarding their potential for abuse, so that network security professionals can measure the feature's value against the potential risks.

Simple Network Management Protocol

The Simple Network Management Protocol (SNMP) was introduced as a simple data retrieval mechanism to facilitate management of network objects. SNMP doesn't *do* network management, but merely provides a method for a network management application (i.e., a *manager*, such as CiscoWorks, HP OpenView, SunNet Manager, et al.) to gather information from individual client devices (i.e., the *agent* function imbedded in the device). The relevant information for any given device type or class is described in a Management Information Base (MIB) for that device type. Originally designed to manage routers, the original MIB (replaced by MIB II) covers things such as TCP segments in and out of a device, UDP datagrams in and out, IP packets in and out, ICMP packets in and out, etc. It also provides for device identification in the form of text string fields for contact name, location, etc. The original SNMP protocol has been expanded to include MIBs for a wide variety of device types in addition to routers.

The SNMP protocol itself consists of a small set of verbs or operands (GET, GET NEXT, SET, TRAP, etc.) that are used by a Manager station primarily to poll individual device Agents on a periodic basis. The exceptions are the SET and TRAP operands. As its name implies, the SET command is used to set or reset some value contained in the MIB. This is a value *sent by the Manager to the Agent*. The other exception is the TRAP operand. This allows the Agent to initiate transfer of information to the Manager, without waiting to be polled. The TRAP operand is commonly used as an alert for some special event that warrants immediate attention. The Manager station processes, counts, or manipulates the gathered information into various charts, graphs, icons, change to the color of an icon, etc., for human interpretation.

Cisco supports the SNMP Agent function in the IOS of the router. SNMP is not enabled by default, but if it is necessary to enable SNMP support, special care should be taken. The Cisco IOS includes a feature referred to as Setup Mode. This is a simplified user interface for very basic router configurations. It consists of a simple question and answer dialog. At the end of the dialog, Setup builds a configuration file with the correct command syntax, allowing a novice administrator to configure a Cisco router without knowing the precise command syntax. The dialog asks a question like "do you want to enable SNMP?" An administrator who didn't understand the ramifications is tempted to reply "*Yes,*" even without understanding why. Setup then proceeds to ask what to use for the "community string" for read-only access, and offers the default, "public." The administrator unfamiliar with SNMP is tempted again, this time to accept the default community string of "public." The next question asks what community string to use for read-write access and offers the default "private." Again, the temptation is to accept the default.

To summarize the above: A user has just enabled access via SNMP to the router and set the community string (i.e., password) to *public* and/or *private*, allowing anyone with a simple SNMP MIB browser access to the router! Using the appropriate SNMP commands, one can ask the router for a copy of the routing table (among other things). The routing table can be very instrumental in mapping your network. This mapping of the network is almost always part of an initial surveillance that precedes a serious intrusion.

Even when SNMP is desired, *never* allow the community string (a.k.a. password) to be "public." However, setting the password to something less obvious is only partially effective. The underlying problem rests with the SNMP protocol. SNMP version 1.0 is most commonly used and sends this password in clear text, so even if you take the precaution to establish a better password, the password is susceptible to eavesdropping. A preferred alternative would be to use SNMP version 2.0, which supports a more secure MD5-

based authentication scheme. If SNMP is not necessary, Cisco recommends that it not be enabled on any router.

There are, however, two basic scenarios where SNMP might be necessary or desirable on a perimeter router.

- The SNMP Manager station is internal to the organization's network and thereby inside the perimeter router. For this case, configure SNMP (version 2.0 if possible) and establish unique passwords; *never* accept the defaults *public* and *private*. If read-write (i.e., the SET operand) is not required, configure SNMP for read-only access. SNMP cannot be selectively disabled on any individual interface, therefore you should filter all SNMP traffic on the interface that connects to the Internet or other public network. The SNMP Manager host contains a wealth of information for the would-be intruder and should be protected accordingly.

- The SNMP Manager station is outside the organization's network. This is typical with managed router services offered by a number of third-party outsourcing companies. In this case, SNMP version 2.0 is strongly recommended, and the previous comments are applicable. Even though we can't filter all SNMP traffic on the public-side interface, an inbound extended access list can selectively permit access from the specific source address of the external Manager, and to the specific destination addresses of devices inside your network. Additionally, Cisco configuration options for SNMP can restrict access to a specific Manager device using the **snmp-server community** command with the option that refers to an access list. The thorough "belt and suspenders" approach would be to implement both.

The following basic format is to set the community string *for version 1.0 only*. It should never be used in version 2.0, since it *specifically enables* SNMP version 1.0. The SNMP version 1.0 format is:

```
Router(config)#snmp-server community string RO [listnumber]
```

Using the Cisco documentation convention, *string* is the community string, RO indicates values are read-only, and [*listnumber*] is an optional, standard access list number (1 to 99) that lists the IP addresses of devices that are allowed to use this community string to gain access. Note: RW (for read-write) could be used in place of RO in the above example, but allowing write-access is strongly discouraged, particularly for SNMP version 1.0.

For SNMP version 2.0, Cisco recommends that digest authentication be configured with the **authenticate** and **md5** keywords of the **snmp-server party** configuration command. For details, please refer to the Cisco IOS Configuration Guide for the specific Cisco IOS version.

HTTP

Beginning with IOS version 11.0, Cisco provides the ability for limited http server functionality on routers. This permits remote configuration and monitoring of the router using a common Web browser such as Microsoft Internet Explorer or Netscape Communicator. The authentication mechanism for http access is comparable to other interactive access to the router (e.g., Telnet). It shares the same sort of limitations as Telnet access; the password is sent as clear text. Although it currently doesn't offer any native provision for challenge-based or one-time passwords, use of the **ip http authentication** command in conjunction with a RADIUS or TACACS+ server, such as Cisco Secure ACS, can provide greater functionality. For command details, please refer to the appropriate configuration documentation. The Cisco Secure ACS will be discussed in a later chapter.

In addition, there is a specific access list command (**ip http access-class)** for use with http. This access control is effectively applied to the http process, at the application level, rather than being applied to a specific interface. (Note: There is a comparable command for Telnet access that will be covered later in this chapter.) Http support is disabled by default. The configuration command would resemble the following:

```
Router(config)#ip http server
Router(config)#access-list 10 permit 10.20.30.40
Router(config)#ip http access-class 10
```

Please note that named access lists could also be used. Also note that **ip http access-class** is applied as a global command.

TCP/IP Services

There are a number of TCP, UDP services or IP features that are commonly enabled by default. Beginning with IOS version 12.0, some of these are now disabled by default. The approach we suggest applies to both possible situations. If the feature is enabled, by default or otherwise, the feature will be disabled. If the feature is already disabled, the disabling commands have no effect. As a result, the commands we will discuss *may* be useful as "boilerplate" for any router configurations; however, they *should* be implemented on all perimeter routers.

Disable IP Source Route

The original IP specification provided for several optional features, collectively described as the IP options. They are implemented using the variable length fields that follow the standard 20-byte IP header. Of the IP options, there are three that are specific to source routing: Record Route, Loose Source Route, and Strict Source Route. These should not be confused with Source

Routing Bridging as defined by IBM, but there are fundamental similarities. These options once served a useful purpose for diagnostics and troubleshooting, but no longer are used.

In the original intended function, a station would send an IP packet to a target destination, with the Record Route option set. Each router along the way would add its own IP address to the record. The packet would effectively "learn" the route it followed. The second part is where the problem arises. A sending host could then specify the route the packet should take, either strictly (exactly as described) or loosely (as close to the original as possible).

This functionality has great potential for misuse. More specifically, these options can facilitate IP address masquerading or address spoofing. Since any host can be configured with any IP address, if an attacker attempts to impersonate another device by using a false IP address, the impostor's packets could potentially fool IP access lists that permitted only certain addresses, or other access controls that may be based upon IP source address. Some of Sun™ Microsystems NFS-related applications use the concept of "trusted hosts," and use the host's IP address as a verification mechanism.

Under normal circumstances, this approach will not be successful over any physically or geographically extended range. If an attacker falsifies the IP source address describing the packet origin, the intervening routers will not cooperate in returning any response to the bogus station, for the simple reason that routers will attempt to forward the packet to the legitimate network where that address range is located. If the intruder attempted any activity, especially one that required a reply from the victim host (e.g., all TCP-based applications), the logistic problem of sending the response to the impostor provides a minimal degree of security, because the relaying routers would be unable to return the packet to the impostor's intruder's true location. This all changes if the interposing routers enable support for IP Source Route.

If the intervening routers have enabled support for IP Source Route, they will be provided instructions to return the response packets to wherever the Source Route option indicates, and follow whatever path it describes. Since IP Source Route rarely provides any currently useful function, and its potential for misuse is so great, support should be disabled. The command syntax to disable support is as follows:

```
Router(config)# no ip source-route
```

Disable Non-Essential TCP and UDP Services

The Cisco router IOS provides a number of applications, or more correctly, system services that are common to most TCP/IP implementations. These utilities typically have no specific use on a router, and can also be misused and abused. It is recommended that they be disabled. These utilities are known as the "small services" due to the fact that they utilize low-numbered TCP and/or UDP ports. More specifically, the TCP small services are:

- Echo (TCP port 7) — The Echo server will echo whatever characters are sent on the connection.
- Discard (TCP port 9) — The Discard server will discard any characters sent on the connection.
- Daytime (TCP port 13) — Responds with the system date and time in human-readable format, if available. The time can be set via two different methods. It may be manually set from the command mode, or it can be learned from the Network Time Protocol service.
- Chargen (TCP port 19) — The Chargen server will generate a continuous stream of ASCII characters, until the TCP connection is terminated.
- Time (TCP port 37) — Server returns the time as a 32-bit binary number, which represents the number of seconds since midnight January 1, 1900 (UTC).

The UDP small servers are defined as:

- Echo (UDP port 7) — Server echoes back the data portion of the UDP datagram it is sent.
- Discard (UDP port 9) — Server discards the UDP datagram it is sent.
- Daytime (UDP port 13) — Server responds with the time and date in human-readable format. The time can be set via two different methods: 1) It may be manually set from the command mode, or 2) the Network Time Protocol service is running.
- Chargen (UDP port 19) — Server discards the UDP datagram it is sent, but responds with a string of 72 ASCII characters, and ends with a carriage return and line feed.
- Time (UDP port 37) — Server returns the time as a 32-bit binary number, which represents the number of seconds since midnight January 1, 1900 (UTC).

The UDP services, in particular, are the ones that are most frequently misused by attacks. The "fraggle attack," which uses the UDP Echo service, will be described under the Directed Broadcast topic later in this chapter.

The commands to disable the above TCP and UDP services is:

```
Router(config)#no service tcp-small-servers
Router(config)#no service udp-small-servers
```

Disable the Finger Service

TCP/IP implementations typically include a service known as finger (TCP port 79). The service is typically activated with the command **finger x.x.x.x,** where x.x.x.x is the host IP address or name. The same effect would result if one were to Telnet to port 79. The original purpose was to examine information about users currently logged on to a given host, and to retrieve information such as logon name and email address. This service is typically disabled on hosts since the information that it provides is considered private by most system administrators. On a Cisco router, this service lists users that are currently logged on. Even though it provides little in the way of valuable information to intruders, it should be disabled nonetheless. The command to disable the finger service is:

```
Router(config)#no service finger
```

Disable Proxy ARP

In the late 1980s, one of IP's several redefinitions took place. Prior to this time there were *no subnets*. Most IP networks consisted of a single, flat, bridged network, with a single "gateway" (i.e., router) connecting the organization to the outside world (the ARPAnet or Internet). As these organizations tried to deal with the problems of large bridged networks, they began to deploy routers *inside* the organization to *localize and control broadcasts*. Since IP addressing prior to this time assumed that each organization had a single Class A, B, or C network, individual device addresses referred to a specific host on that *one single* network. The goal was to extend the total usable address space, increasing the total number of network numbers, but still maintain the IP address length of 32 bits. The concept of a subnetwork or subnet was invented. Since the 8-bit or 16-bit or 24-bit prefixes of Class A, B, or C addresses would remain unchanged, any additional subdivisions of that A, B, or C network would be taken from what *had* been referred to as the *host bits*.

Under the new rules, the host bits would be treated as what could be more appropriately described as *locally administrable bits*. With this new interpretation, each organization could use some of these locally administrable bits as extensions to the Class A, B, or C network number, and the balance of the remaining bits for host addresses. The concept of a subnetwork was born.

Each individual, autonomous organization could redefine the locally administrable bits as they saw fit, but such election would be transparent to anyone outside that network. The organization would still be identifiable by their Class A, B, or C prefix, and any subnet definition would be internal and known only inside that organization. Each organization would specify their internal-only subnets, by applying a *subnet mask* to all IP devices, instructing them how to interpret the address: network part and device-specific part, commonly referred to as the subnet number and host ID.

Since routers play a crucial role in determining what networks exist and how to reach them, it was critical that routers be able to properly interpret the subnet numbers. Using the subnet masks that were configured on their interfaces, routers were able to distinguish one subnet place from another subnet place. The problem at the time was that most host operating systems did not understand subnets and subnet masks. To take advantage of this new functionality, all hosts would have to be upgraded simultaneously.

To assist in making this transition more graceful, router vendors implemented a new feature (i.e., work-around) known as Proxy ARP. The way it works is as follows.

When a host station needs to send IP data to another host station, the IP process needs to make a preliminary decision: Is the destination host on the same network or is it elsewhere? At the IP layer, each host compares the destination IP address to its own IP address. If the transmitting host discovers that both hosts share the same network number, the transmitting host concludes that the other host is local, and that they are attached to the same network. Under those circumstances, the transmitting host needs to provide the appropriate Layer 2 hardware destination address (e.g., Ethernet MAC address) in order to transmit it on the local segment.

The IP process on the transmitting host calls upon the Address Resolution Protocol to discover the appropriate MAC address that correlates to the known IP address. ARP sends an ARP request as a broadcast on the appropriate network segment. The ARP Request indicates the IP address for which it needs the MAC address. All IP devices on the local segment receive the broadcast, each examining the IP address in the query. The device that recognizes its own address as the target of the query responds with an ARP reply containing its MAC address. The transmitting station places the IP packet in a MAC frame addressing it to the destination address that was provided in the ARP reply, and caches the IP address and MAC address correlation in an "ARP cache" (i.e., a temporary holding area in RAM memory).

A different procedure applies if the transmitting station concludes that the destination IP address is on another network. Since the destination is not local, the transmitting host will send the IP packet to the default router for forwarding. The IP packet is addressed to the other host, but the MAC-layer frame is addressed to the router. How does the transmitting host know where to send the data for forwarding? In most cases, the default router (or default gateway) is defined as part of the IP address configuration on each host. Like before, if the transmitting host needs the MAC address of the router, it follows the above procedure with an ARP request query for the default gateway's MAC address.

Where does Proxy ARP fit is all of this? We first need to consider a transmitting host that does not understand subnets. At the time that subnets were first introduced, most Internet hosts were running some subnet-unaware variation of UNIX®. These hosts wouldn't be able to distinguish two different subnets of the same major (Class A, B, or C) network from the major network. Consider the scenario in Figure 3-3. Host A has an address of 10.1.0.1/24 while Host B has an address of 10.2.0.1/24 on a different subnet. The two subnets are both connected to Router X.

Under the presubnet rules, Host A would incorrectly conclude that Host B was on the same network segment and would broadcast its ARP request, looking for the MAC address of Host B. Routers (by default) would not for-

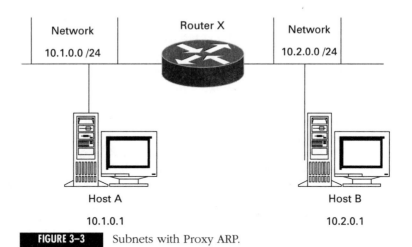

FIGURE 3–3   Subnets with Proxy ARP.

ward the broadcast, since ARP messages are carried directly inside MAC-layer frames and don't have an IP layer. Even if Router X did forward the ARP request onto the subnet 10.2.0.0 that Host B is located on (and forwarded the corresponding ARP reply), the MAC address provided in the reply from Host B would be useless. When Host A tried to send data, no device on network segment 10.1.0.0 would recognize the address, including Router X. (Routers typically only respond to frames sent directly to their own MAC address, or broadcasts intended for all devices.)

Proxy ARP alters this normal behavior of the router. When Router X receives the original ARP request, it will recognize that the IP address that is the target of the query is not his own IP address. Normally this would indicate that Router X should ignore the query, since it is presumably intended for some other device on the segment.

However, with Proxy ARP enabled, Router X will also notice that the target IP address is on a subnet that the router can reach. Router X assumes the transmitting host incorrectly believes that 10.1.0.1 and 10.2.0.2 are both located on network 10.0.0.0/8, and does not recognize that there are two different subnets, 10.1.0.0/24 and 10.2.0.0/24. Router X will attempt to be helpful, and proxy the ARP request on behalf of the target. Router X will send its own APR request to Host B to verify its reachability. If this second APR request initiated by Router X to Host B is successful, Router X will reply to Host A, as proxy for Host B. He does so by responding to the original ARP request with his *own* ARP reply, indicating his own MAC address in the reply.

Host A dutifully sends the packet to the IP address of Host B, but to the MAC-layer address of Router X. Router X behaves in the same fashion that he would in the role of default gateway, and everything works. Host A does not know that Router X interceded, since Host A sent an ARP request and received an appropriate ARP reply. This Proxy ARP feature allowed nonsubnet-aware hosts to function correctly in a subnet environment.

We started this section by describing Proxy ARP as a potential problem. The description above makes it seem to be a handy feature, except for two small points. First, it is unlikely that today, nonsubnet-aware host software is still in current use. Second, and more importantly, it can be used as a surveillance tool for intruders to gather information about your network. Consider the following scenario: Intruders don't know what hosts exist on your organization's network. If the intruder generates ARP requests for hidden hosts, and the router performs Proxy ARP on their behalf, the intruder is able to discover which hosts exist. For this simple reason, Proxy ARP should be disabled and is rarely necessary in today's network. The notable exception is in situations where Network Address Translation (NAT) is performed by the router. In these special cases, it may necessary to enable Proxy ARP for NAT to function properly. The command syntax is:

```
Router(config-if)# no ip proxy-arp
```

Notice that this command is interface-specific, and should be applied to any interface that is accessible from outside an organization's network.

Disable Directed Broadcasts

An IP directed broadcast is a message sent to the broadcast address of a particular network or subnet. The originating station would be located on another network or subnet. The packet travels throughout the network as any other unicast packet. When it reaches the intended network or subnet, the last router recognizes the host portion of the address as a broadcast to all hosts. The last router "expands" the packet into a MAC-layer broadcast, which is received by every host on that segment. There are few legitimate applications that use or require directed broadcasts, and, therefore, support is rarely required. In particular, there are virtually no imaginable circumstances that would warrant allowing incoming directed broadcasts at a perimeter router. In fact, directed broadcasts are the mechanism used in smurf attacks, one of the more infamous denial of service (DoS) attacks.

In a "smurf" attack, the attacker pings (ICMP Echo Request) the directed broadcast address using the source address of some victim where the multiple replies (ICMP Echo Reply) are sent. All the hosts on the network or subnet send an ICMP Echo Reply to the victim, amplifying the effect. If used effectively, the amplifier-effect can potentially overwhelm the victim host, resulting in a denial of the service of the victim host. A close relative of the "smurf" attack is called a "fraggle attack." It is fundamentally the same as the "smurf" attack with UDP Echo packets substituted for the ICMP Echo and Reply used in "smurf."

Notice that there are really two victims here. One is the site that is the target of the directed broadcast, and the other is the victim that receives the multiple replies. Also consider the effect. If an attacker can generate a constant stream of directed broadcast traffic at a network with 100 hosts, the result is effectively an amplification of 100 times the original stream. If an attacker can generate the stream at a fractional T1 rate of 500 kilobits per second, the victim gets hit with 50 megabytes per second. This can have a significant impact on both sites.

It should be noted that it might be necessary to disable this feature on all routers, not just the perimeter router. This is due to the fact that only the last router at the final network or subnet level examines the host portion of the address. All the upstream routers look at the network or subnet prefix only. Hence, the final router is the only router that recognizes the packet as a broadcast, and generates the MAC-layer broadcast. If support has been disabled on an interface, the router merely drops directed broadcast packets. The command syntax to disable is as follows:

```
Router(config-if)# no ip directed-broadcast
```

Also, note that this is an interface-specific command and, therefore, should be applied on all interfaces on all routers that might be affected. This feature is enabled by default on all versions of the Cisco IOS through version 11.3. Beginning with IOS version 12.0 it is disabled by default, on all interfaces.

Disable the Cisco Discovery Protocol

The Cisco Discovery Protocol (CDP) was introduced on Cisco routers several years ago. It provides an advertisement and discovery process whereby Cisco routers and other Cisco devices announce their presence, and discover other neighboring Cisco devices. The nature of CDP is that CDP messages are broadcast on every interface. Any CDP-aware device listening on that segment can discover the model, IOS version, protocols running, and various other status information regarding individual devices. The very nature of the information that is broadcasted gives a potential intruder or attacker the advantage of information that most definitely should be kept private. Cisco has published alerts from time to time, documenting vulnerabilities of various features and various IOS versions. Providing the level of detail that CDP offers is clearly not appropriate. The CDP on the perimeter router can be disabled altogether with the following command:

```
Router(config)#no cdp run
```

If it is desirable to enable CDP for only internal interfaces, but not external interfaces, it may be selectively disabled on individual interfaces with the following interface-specific command:

```
Router(config-if)#no cdp enable
```

Disable ICMP Redirects

The ICMP Redirect message is sent by a router to inform a host that another router is a more direct path to the destination. It is only applicable when a host has a choice of two or more routers (or gateways). Usually the host will choose the default gateway, unaware that another gateway might provide a more direct path. Refer to Figure 3-4.

Host C in the lower part of the figure, needs to send data to Host D, shown in the upper right. The default router for Host C is configured as Gateway A at address 10.1.1.1, even though Gateway B at address 10.1.1.2 would provide a more direct path. When Gateway A receives packets to forward to Host D, it will correctly forward them to Gateway B, but through the same interface on which the packets arrived. Recognizing that Gateway B would be a shorter, more direct path to that particular destination, Gateway A will send an ICMP Redirect message to Host C, advising that a better path can be used for future packets to that destination (i.e., redirecting additional traffic for that particular destination to Gateway B). Upon receipt of the ICMP Redirect, Host C will begin sending traffic for Host D directly to Gateway B for forwarding. That specific destination will be treated as an exception, and Host C will continue to use Gateway A as its default router for other traffic.

Notice that there are two possible default routers to use for any nonlocal traffic. This assumes that ICMP Redirects are only applicable on LAN topologies. Hosts do not send redirects, and routers do not *normally* send redirects to other routers. Further, a host should never receive an ICMP Redirect except from its *local* default router; it *should never* come from a device that is one or more hops away. Since this is another opportunity for misuse of the basic functionality of IP, it is considered good practice to not accept ICMP Redirects at the perimeter router. Cisco recommends that *sending* of ICMP Redirects by the router be disabled. The interface-specific command to accomplish this is:

```
Router(config-if)#no ip redirects
```

Also, note that blocking any incoming ICMP Redirects originated outside an organization's network is also a good practice. ICMP Redirects can be filtered using extended access lists, and should be applied to all inbound traffic. We will illustrate this in a later section on access control lists.

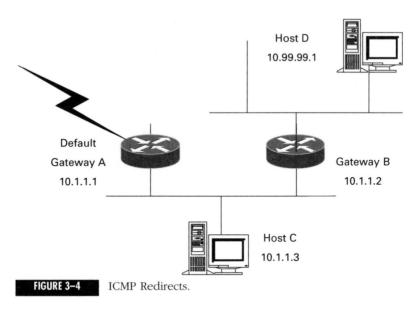

FIGURE 3–4 ICMP Redirects.

Disable the Network Time Protocol

The Network Time Protocol (NTP) provides the ability to synchronize the system clocks within milliseconds for devices that run the protocol. There are quasi-public servers that announce the correct time via multicasting to the Class D address of 224.0.1.1. If it is necessary or desirable to run NTP, Cisco advises that it is necessary to use only a trusted time source, and use proper authentication methods. There are other methods available, including highly accurate network-based devices that could be used within an organization's network. If NTP is not required or desired, it should be disabled on each interface. For a perimeter router, disabling NTP on the outside, public-facing interface should be sufficient. There are two versions of the command, one old, one new. According to the Cisco IOS Command Summary for version 11.3, the appropriate interface-specific command to disable NTP is:

```
Router(config-if)# ntp disable
```

There is also an older form of the command used sometime prior to version 11.3. The previous command is:

```
Router(config-if)# no ntp enable
```

If you are running an IOS version older than 11.3, you may have to experiment with both commands or refer the appropriate IOS Command Reference Summary for the specific version.

Disable ICMP Unreachables Messages

The Internet Control Message Protocol (ICMP) can provide a tremendous amount of information if it is used properly. Similarly, it can be misused in countless ways. It may well be one of the most popular vehicles for all forms of surveillance, intrusions, denial of service, and other forms of attack. It almost warrants a section all of its own, and it is impractical to totally eliminate from an organization's network, since it provides the basis for many useful tools, such as Ping and Traceroute, and also provides a variety of error messages that are indispensable for network diagnostics. On the other hand, it also provides the foundation for the Ping of Death attack, Loki attack, fragmentation attacks, and many others. As an example, consider the Loki program. The Loki "program" uses innocent-looking ICMP Echo Request and Echo Replies (the two components of the Ping utility) as a "courier" to ferry information between the client and server elements used in one form of DoS attack. The message exchanges are hidden in the payload, which normally carries meaningless strings of characters. Its constant presence on the network goes unnoticed, while it transmits covert messages between a "master" program and its "slaves."

The field in an IP packet header that contains the total packet length is a 16-bit field. This allows an IP packet to be up to 64 Kbytes in size, although no LAN or WAN technologies could carry an IP packet of this size. The Ping of Death attack sets this value to its maximum, and some IP implementations are tricked into allocating input buffers to hold these oversize packets. If there is a constant stream of these nonexistent packets, the IP host can exhaust all of its available memory, causing the system to crash.

ICMP defines 16 message types that are collectively known as "destination unreachable." Among the most commonly used are:

- Network Unreachable
- Host Unreachable
- Protocol Unreachable
- Port Unreachable
- Fragmentation need, but do-not-fragment bit was set (used for MTU Discovery)
- Source Route Failed (see previous discussion of IP Source Routing)
- Destination Network Unknown (there is no such network number)
- Destination Network Unknown (there is no host at that address)
- Destination Network Administratively Prohibited (you've been blocked)
- Destination Host Administratively Prohibited (you've been blocked)

Although these clearly provide an organization with information about the status of their network and hosts, this same information is also made available to outsiders. Any serious intruder's toolkit will include tools that will scan and map IP address ranges, port ranges, and the like. By evaluating the response (or lack of response) of these scans, an intruder can learn all sorts of things about an organization's network, including:

- What address ranges exist
- What hosts exist
- What services are running
- What ports provide the services

A motivated individual could document a significant portion of an organization's network simply by scanning. The resulting documentation may be more thorough than an organization's own documentation, because after discovering the hosts and operating system types, these programs can cross-reference those with a catalog of known vulnerabilities. If you have any doubts about the capabilities of these tools, refer to the documentation for the Cisco Secure Scanner. It was designed specifically for the purpose described above. The intent of this class of security products is to allow an organization to scan for vulnerabilities rather than wait for an intruder to do it. The Cisco Secure Scanner will be outlined in a later chapter.

One of the things that can be done to limit the level of detail available to intruders and other outsiders is to reduce the level of helpful, informative detail that ICMP can provide to them. The routers can be instructed not to offer so much helpful information by simply not sending some of the ICMP "network unreachable" messages. Specifically, Cisco allows a router to suppress sending certain of the "unreachable" messages:

- Host Unreachable
- Protocol Unreachable

Cisco has a specific command to suppress these two particular ICMP message types. By applying the following command to the outside interface of the perimeter router, the router will refuse to send these ICMP message types.

```
Router(config-if)# no ip unreachables
```

This command could be used on all interfaces on all routers; however, these two message types are still useful, as long as they remain internal to an organization's network. A better method to suppress these and other ICMP "destination unreachable" message types from more "interior" routers would be to filter them out at the network exit point with access lists.

Traffic Management

The primary task expected of routers is to forward packet traffic. An equally important function is to assist in the management of that traffic. Among the many functions that manage traffic are the filtering of traffic, using ACLs and providing protection from certain types of attacks that the router may be in a strategic position to prevent.

Access Control Lists (ACL)

One of the earliest, and most basic network security features added to router functionality, was packet filters, better known in Cisco parlance as access lists. For IP traffic, there are several types that are applicable. The primary two types are known as standard access lists and extended access lists. There are also several variant ACL types that use the format and syntax of standard and extended to describe a "profile" of the traffic of interest.

When we speak of access lists, we are typically referring to the filters that may be selectively applied to individual interfaces that examine either inbound or outbound traffic. What is sometimes confusing is that the term inbound or outbound is relative to the individual *interface* when we are discussing access lists. In many other cases, we refer to inbound and outbound traffic relative to the organization's internal network, which may not be the same. Consider the illustration in Figure 3-5:

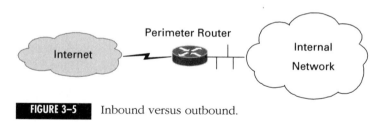

FIGURE 3–5   Inbound versus outbound.

In the Figure 3-5, the Ethernet interface connecting to the internal network would be considered the inside interface of the router, relative to the organization's total network which typically also includes the perimeter router. Similarly, the serial WAN port connecting to the Internet would be considered the outside interface. If we are discussing access lists, the reference point is considered to be the router itself. For example, we could apply an access list on the Ethernet interface, filtering internal users traffic going to the Internet. This *inbound* access list would be applied to *outbound* network traffic. This terminology will be further clarified in a later chapter. At this point, just remember that access lists are described *relative to the interface* where they are applied.

Although we have the option of using standard or extended access lists, it is the extended form that will be more commonly used to control packet traffic flow. The standard access list format allows only the source address of the packet to be examined to determine whether to permit (i.e., pass) or deny (i.e., block) individual packets. The extended form is a full superset of the standard format, allowing evaluation based upon any combination of:

- Source address or address ranges (using *wildcard* bit-masks)
- Source ports (or a range of ports, using Boolean operands)
- Destination address or address ranges (using *wildcard* bit-masks)
- Destination (or a range of ports, using Boolean operands)
- Protocol type or subtype (e.g., IP, TCP, ICMP, IGRP, et al.)
- TCP connection status (TCP header SYN bit-flag, set or unset)

A complete discussion of Cisco access lists is beyond the scope of this material, and it is assumed that the reader has a fundamental knowledge of Cisco access list rules and syntax. For more information, see the IOS Configuration Guide for your specific version. For IOS version 12.1,

http://www.cisco.com/univercd/cc/td/doc/product/software/ios121/121cgcr/secur_c/scprt3/scdacls.htm

Although a more complete discussion of access list statements that may be appropriate will be covered in a later chapter on Context Base Access Lists, there are a few fundamental rules that can be mentioned here. For inbound traffic entering the organization's network at the perimeter router, the following general rules can be applied with an inbound access list, applied to the serial interface shown in Figure 3-5.

- Filter any incoming packets that contain a *source* address from the organization's internal network address space. No origin points on the outside should have any address that applies only within the internal network. Except for VPN "tunneling," or other special circumstances, appearance of this type of address would seem to indicate an attempt to impersonate an internal device to gain unauthorized access.
- Filter any packets with a source address from the reserved ranges specified in RFC 1918, Address Allocation for Private Internets. Specifically:
  - 10.0.0.0 to 10.255.255.255/8
  - 172.16.0.0 to 172.31.255.255/12
  - 192.168.0.0 to 192.168.255.255/16
- Filter incoming bootp, DHCP, TFTP protocols.
- Ping, Traceroute, and other ICMP message types

In addition, it may be appropriate to filter certain outgoing Internet traffic that originates on the internal network.

- Allow only packets that contain a valid source address. This might be thought of as the "good-neighbor-policy," since it reduces the likelihood that your site will be the source of attacks launched against other networks using IP address spoofing. It is also a double check on any "leakage" of private addresses due to misconfigured or misapplied Network Address Translation (NAT) policies.
- Filter any other source addresses that may be restricted by your network security policy. (Note: Cisco firewalls provide more powerful and sophisticated methods to accomplish to same goal.)

Router-Based Attack Protection

Cisco provides a specific feature to protect against certain types of network attacks, specifically those that use a method described as "SYN flooding." SYN flooding takes advantage of the manner by which a basic TCP connection is set up. It gets its name from the fact that a TCP connection request is indicated by the presence of a one-bit "flag" in the TCP header, the SYN, or *synchronizing* bit. In a typical TCP connection setup, an initiator (or client) requests a connection. If the responder (or host) is willing and able to accept the connection request, he responds accordingly to the connection initiator, with a *connection acknowledgement*. Under normal circumstances, the initiator (or client) will *acknowledge* the connection *acceptance* by the responder (host), and the connection setup is completed. This is sometimes described as the "TCP three-way handshake."

Attackers can misuse this simple procedure to their advantage. Specifically, the attacker "floods" a host with connection requests, with no intention of completing the connection. After sending the connection acceptance to the initiator, the responder waits, and waits and waits, for final acceptance from the initiator. In many implementations, the waiting period may be several minutes before the initiator exceeds or reaches a timeout value, and drops the connection request, freeing the resources. Further, the number of "half-open connections" that a responder/host can accept is often far smaller than the total number of fully open connections that the host can support.

This can result in a bottleneck if the half-open connections can't be finalized and converted to fully open connections, aren't cancelled by the initiator, or aren't terminated by timing out on the responder. This bottleneck is just the situation the attacker wants. By sending a continuous flood of connection requests (i.e., TCP segments with the SYN bit set), the attacker can overwhelm the host, resulting in denial of service or possibly system crash.

How can the router prevent this situation? Cisco introduced a feature in IOS version 11.2 named TCP Intercept. They have also incorporated a comparable feature in the IOS Firewall, but it is a CBAC-specific feature and mutually exclusive of TCP Intercept. The PIX Firewall also includes comparable functionality. Each of these produces a similar result, but vary in the implementation details. For purpose of illustration, we will describe TCP Intercept.

TCP Intercept has two modes: intercept and monitor. In *intercept mode*, the router literally intercepts connection requests. The router IOS attempts to establish the connection to the requesting client, by accepting the connection request, on behalf of the host. If the connection is complete, TCP Intercept then establishes a connection with the server on behalf of the client, transparently integrating the two into a single connection between client and host.

In the case of legitimate connection requests, the result is a connection between client and host, coordinated by the router, with the router acting as proxy for each party. In the case of SYN floods, the router uses a shorter, more aggressive timeout period and thresholds, to cancel half-open connections. The configurable thresholds are based upon the total number of half-open connections and/or the arrival rate-per-minute.

In *monitor mode,* the router passively observes the connection exchange directly between initiator and responder. If the connection fails to complete within a configurable time period, the router intercedes and cancels the connection request, by imitating a reset from the initiator. The monitor mode also allows thresholds as described above. For configuration details, refer to the appropriate Cisco IOS Configuration Guide for your version.

While there are still a few other access list considerations that might be appropriate for perimeter routers, we will postpone them until later, since we will revisit the topic again in the IOS Firewall chapter. The primary architecture of the IOS Firewall is built around CBAC, which is fundamentally an enhancement to the same underlying access list concept.

Routing Protocols

Although it may be unlikely that an organization is running an interior routing protocol, such as RIP, RIPv2, IGRP, OSPF, or EIGRP on a perimeter router, it is strongly recommended that the chosen routing protocal supports authentication of routing updates. Of the interior routing protocols only OSPF, EIGRP, and RIPv2 provide this capability, although in practice it is rarely enabled. These protocols can be very sophisticated and, therefore, complex. A more complete discussion is beyond the scope of this book. If perimeter routers must run a routing protocol, one of these three would make a better choice than RIP or IGRP. Further, if either OSPF, EIGRP, or RIPv2 is used, authentication *should* be configured. Refer to the IOS Configuration Guide for the appropriate IOS version, as the features and commands may vary from version to version.

If an exterior protocol is required, Border Gateway Protocol (BGP) is the only practical choice. BGP also offers authentication, and is strongly recommended. As with OSPF and EIGRP, the reader is referred to the appropriate Cisco Configuration Guide.

Audit Trails and Logging

Logging of system related-events is applicable to a variety of different device types, including perimeter routers. The Cisco IOS allows logging to several different destinations: the system console, a remote terminal session, logging buffers on the router, or a syslog server.

The system console (line console 0) is the default destination. Logging to the console terminal may be appropriate for limited cases; however, it should be neither the primary nor only source. The inherent limitation of a terminal device is that there is no mechanism to store the logged data. Once the data scrolls off the screen, it is lost. Worse yet, the generation of console display messages is a fairly CPU-intensive activity. In a crisis situation like a DoS attack, not only would the data scroll off the screen at an unreadable speed and be lost forever, but the display generation could further contribute to the overload of the router. The command syntax (and assumed default) for logging to console 0 is:

```
Router(config)#logging console [level]
```

The optional parameter *level* limits logging to the specified level (i.e., degree of severity) or above, and eliminates log messages below this level. If the *level* option is not specified, messages of all severity levels will be included.

Remote terminal sessions (Telnet; line vty 0 4) have the same limitations as the console terminal, and are further limited by the availability of the network connection from the remote session to the router. It is used to *redirect* console messages to the remote terminal session that is currently active. The command syntax to redirect logging to the specific virtual terminal port where you are connected is:

```
Router(config)#logging monitor [level]
```

Use of the optional parameter *level* is the same as in the previous case above.

Local RAM buffers on the router may be the storage destination for messages that can be later displayed and viewed. The size of these buffers can be configured, but once configured are fixed in size. Once the buffer fills, any new data will replace the oldest data in the buffer (i.e., circular buffers). The command syntax to log to buffers and optionally set their size is:

```
Router(config)#logging buffered [sizeinbytes]
```

Valid buffer sizes range from 4096 to 4,294,967,295 bytes and will depend upon how much free RAM is available. The **show memory** command will display the free RAM available. Without the optional *sizeinbytes* parameter, the default value will be chosen, which varies by router platform. Typical (reasonable) values range from 16,384 or 32,768 for low-end routers to 262,144 for high-end routers with sufficient excess memory.

The **syslog** service (provided with many hosts) is probably the most common and potentially best choice if available. Syslog is a simple logging program available on Unix hosts, with implementations available for other operating systems such as Windows NT. The syslog process writes to a simple text file on disk and can be of virtually unlimited size; however, in practice, periodic (daily or weekly) log files are most common. Log files are for later review and/or analysis and should be sized accordingly. The commands for logging to a syslog server are:

```
Router(config)#logging host-address
Router(config)#logging trap level
```

The *host-address* parameter is the IP address of the syslog server. As before, *level* refers to the degree of severity of the message. The desired level should always be set for syslog logging to prevent the log file from filling up with trivial messages of negligible importance.

On a final note: If NTP service or a network-based real-time clock is available, time-stamping of log message entries is highly desirable to reconstruct event sequence and timing for interpretation or diagnostics. In particular, if the log chronicles a network attack or intrusion, verifiable time stamps will be essential for network forensics, as well as for admissibility of evidence in any civil litigation or criminal prosecution. The command expression for time stamps is:

```
Router(config)#service timestamps log datetime [msec]
```

The optional parameter **msec** includes milliseconds in the date and time stamp. Other optional keywords (not shown) are **localtime,** to time stamp relative to the local time zone, and **show-timezone** to include the time zone name in the time stamp.

Summary

We've seen in this section that there are many precautions we can take on the perimeter router. These precautions include things that protect both the network behind the perimeter router, as well as protect the router. Since much of the heavy-duty network protection will be provided by the firewall (assuming there is one), the primary task may be to protect or harden the router as best we can.

Not every item we discussed will be relevant for every individual situation. Individual circumstances will vary from organization to organization. Likewise, there are a few additional topics we didn't address that may be appropriate for certain types of organizations, such as Internet Service Providers (ISPs) or Web hosting services. The approach was to cover as many of the common issues as practical and attempt to explain why the recommendations might be appropriate.

There is no single point of reference for the range of topics we discussed, although nearly all of the presented information is documented and available from Cisco. There are also various sources that will provide a list of things that an administrator may enable, disable or configure. Since these listings cover the most obvious and most common problems, it may not surprise you to discover that the material overlaps considerably. The difficulty is often in finding all of the pieces amidst the totality of Cisco documentation.

Cisco typically leaves it to the user to discover which are relevant, where to find them, and what they do.

That approach is what prompted the structure used in this book: describe the problem (the *what*), and provide the command syntax (the *how*), along with an explanation for each (the *why*). We thought it important to explain some of the reasons and/or consequences behind the recommendations, rather than simply provide a list of the appropriate commands.

As indicated, Cisco has historically enabled many of these features and services by default. With more recent versions, that has begun to change, and some of the items we covered are now disabled by default. You may have to experiment with the commands to verify the current defaults for the version your organization is using. Even if you take the safe approach and simply apply all of commands we described, no harm will be done. If the feature is already disabled, it will remain disabled.

If we look back on the topics we reviewed, you will see that many of the issues relate to how TCP, IP, ICMP and some of the other protocols operate. Although a more complete explanation of TCP/IP or IP addressing might have been helpful, that is beyond the scope of this book. The goal was to provide at least some explanation of the "how and why" behind the recommendations. If you are new to the network security field, it is strongly recommended that you become fully acquainted with the TCP/IP protocol family. To do otherwise would put you at a serious disadvantage. There are a number of excellent texts covering this topic, such as *Internetworking with TCP/IP, Volume 1: Principles, Protocols & Architecture, 4th Edition*, by Douglas E. Comer (Prentice Hall, 2000).

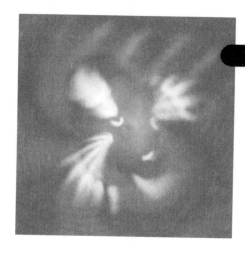

Firewalls

In This Chapter

*T*he Internet is a worldwide collection of networks that are interconnected. It has sometimes been referred to as a "network of networks." The systems are able to communicate by using the TCP/IP protocol suite. Originally intended to provide a simple method for government-sponsored research institutions to exchange information, the Internet today has evolved far beyond its original mission. During the 1980s and early 1990s, the Internet consisted of universities, research centers, and government agencies, with commercial organizations added to the mix in the mid to late 1990s. The internetwork, originally known as the ARPANET, named after its sponsoring agency the U.S. Department of Defense Advanced Research Projects Agency, was merged with the National Science Foundation's NSF-NET, to form what later came to be referred to as "the Internet." The growth rate of new connections, new hosts, and new networks being added to the Internet has been significant for nearly 20 years, but in the last few years, the growth has accelerated. The latest surge in growth coincides with the addition of commercial organizations to the research, academic, and government agencies that constituted the original core of users.

The addition of commercial organizations and the general public has changed the nature of the communication traffic in profound ways. The original intent of the Internet was to facilitate what might be loosely referred to as the free flow of information between peer organizations. This concept is rather foreign in the public world of producers and consumers.

As a result, the underlying architecture, design goals, and evolution of the primary element, the TCP/IP protocol family, is not a good match for the purposes that now dominate Internet usage. When use of the Internet was primarily by academics and researchers, network security was an issue, but not the dominant issue. Security took a back seat to connectivity, reachability, and ease-of-use, and user organizations typically shared common issues, common goals, and common usage patterns.

Many university Web sites were repositories for shareware, freeware, source code, and various other forms of public information. The underlying theme was "here's some good stuff, help yourself." Project Guttenberg was a typical example. The goal of Project Guttenberg was to make many of the classic works of world literature readily available in electronic format. There is an enormous amount of this material currently available that you can download for free. Various government agencies provided information in a variety of formats as a public service. NASA provided pictures from the Hubble telescope on their Web site for public viewing and downloading. The US Treasury's Internal Revenue Service provides nearly virtually every tax form, instruction booklet, and guideline available in PDF format for downloading and printing. If you've ever needed some uncommon tax form at the last minute, you can appreciate the convenience of 24/7/365 availability of the form, without endless hours waiting on hold, or weeks of waiting for the form to be mailed.

What does this all have to do with network security? The simple answer is everything, but the full answer is a little more involved. The intents and purposes of today's Internet users are not so generous, benevolent, or well intentioned as they may have once been. Commercial organizations have discovered Internet commerce or "e-commerce" as a potentially more cost-effective (spelled c-h-e-a-p-e-r), more automated (fewer employees necessary) means to promote their image, products, and services. Technical product companies have long made use of dialup 800 numbers for downloads, patches, spec sheets, and so forth, but today an organization's Web site can significantly reduce the need to provide staff, equipment, and expense for 800 toll-free calls. Promotional information, product literature, first-level technical support, and self-help diagnostics are incredibly less costly to provide from a

Web site than to answer phone calls and mail materials. Email is a nearly free method to promote or sell many things, as evidenced by the volume of email most people receive offering get-rich-quick schemes, secrets to find-out-any-thing-about-anybody, stock advice, and a myriad of other such exciting offers.

For the above reasons and others, security and privacy are far more important issues than they once were. Organizations need to maintain a positive image and ensure the integrity of the material they provide from their Web sites. Alteration and defacement of their Web site would be highly detrimental. Organizations must also maintain the confidentiality of information, such as customer credit card information, that is entrusted to them. If they have an online service offering, they must limit access to authorized users (i.e., paying customers) and therefore have a strong need to authenticate users. One should note that these considerations were not necessarily factored into the TCP/IP protocol suite. As a consequence, many of the features to provide appropriate levels of security are fundamentally lacking, and it is inherently difficult to add these capabilities at a later time. To compound the problem, the underlying TCP/IP protocol and services are essentially in the public domain, and as a result, the protocols and applications are well researched and documented. There are virtually no secrets in their design and/or operation. This openness has been a benefit, and the prime mover behind the virtually universal acceptance of TCP, IP, and their complementary protocols.

On the other hand, this same openness means that those whose purposes are malicious have ready access to the information needed to exploit the inherent weaknesses. This is currently the case. Any number of Web sites will provide documentation, instruction, program tools, and source code to exploit the openness. Even those intruders or attackers with little technical skills have ready access to some very powerful tools. For those who may be more technically skilled, the sky is the limit.

In April 1995, the SATAN software package was introduced. As described by its developers, Dan Farmer and WietseVenema: "SATAN was written because we realized that computer systems are becoming more and more dependent on the network, and at the same becoming more and more vulnerable to attack via that same network." They further said: "SATAN is a tool to help systems administrators. It recognizes several common networking-related security problems, and reports the problems without actually exploiting them". . . "For each type or problem found, SATAN offers a tutorial that explains the problem and what its impact could be. The tutorial also explains what can be done about the problem: correct an error in a configuration file, install a bug fix from the vendor, use other means to restrict access, or simply disable service."

SATAN is the acronym for Security Administrators Tool for Analyzing Networks. Upon its release, SATAN received both criticism and praise by the networking community, as it was the first "shrink-wrapped, intruder toolkit" with a graphical user interface (GUI). The focus on network security was starting to sharpen. It is mentioned here because it was in that same time frame that Internet security started becoming a significant issue, and the early Internet firewalls were being deployed. Prior to the historically significant "Morris worm" in 1988, security wasn't considered such a serious issue. In the early 1990s, research and development of network security tools began in earnest, and the early firewalls were developed and deployed. (For details, see *An Evening with Berford*, William Cheswick in *Proc. Winter USENIX Conference*, San Francisco, CA, January 1992.)

Before we proceed to discuss firewalls, a brief overview of the primary elements of the TCP/IP protocol suite might be appropriate. The source of the popularity of the TCP/IP protocol suite is its ability to be implemented on top of a wide variety of LAN technologies (e.g., Ethernet, Token Ring, FDDI, etc.) as well as wide area technologies, such as X.25, dedicated leased lines (synchronous), low speed dialup (asynchronous), and so forth.

The Protocols of the Internet

The protocol suite has been ported to virtually every computer platform and operating system. Since one of the earliest TCP/IP implementations was developed for Berkeley Unix, many of the common applications and services that were native to that Unix-oriented environment were included as part of the port. When we talk about the TCP/IP protocol family or suite, we are generally talking about a collection of several dozen elements, protocols, or services, which are commonly found as a set. As it is defined, TCP/IP suite consists of both mandatory and optional features. In practice, there are some elements that are virtually universal. The relationships between some of the major elements, protocols, or services, and their approximate relationship to the Open Systems Interconnect (OSI) reference model are shown below in Figure 4-1.

IP — The Internet Protocol

The IP layer receives *packets* or *datagrams* that are delivered by the Data Link layer, such as Ethernet, PPP, Frame Relay, and so forth. Upon receipt of a packet at a destination device, the IP layer passes the data payload "up" to TCP, UDP, or some other higher layer protocol. The appropriate upper-layer protocol is identified using a descriptive field in the IP header. IP is considered unreliable since it takes no steps to verify the packets are error-free, nor in the proper sequence. If the original IP packet had been "fragmented" by

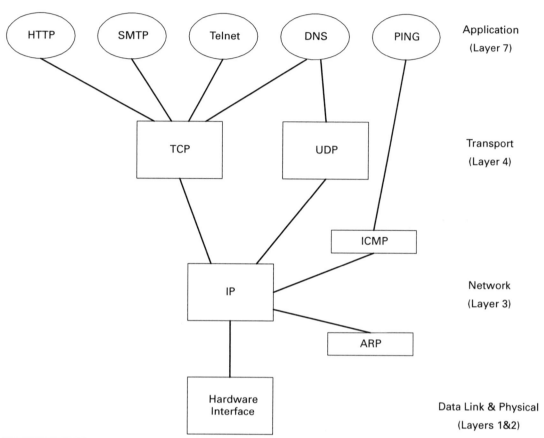

FIGURE 4–1   TCP/IP organization and architecture.

some intermediate relaying device (i.e., router) the destination IP device will accumulate all the fragments, reassemble them, and attempt to reconstruct the original IP packet. (It should be noted that in practice, fragmentation is fairly uncommon except with encrypted packets.)

One of the optional variable-length fields in the IP header is for IP Options that were outlined in an earlier chapter. The source IP address, destination IP address, and Protocol field are the primary elements used to:

- Route and deliver the packet to the correct device (destination address)
- Identify the sender or originator of the packet (source address)
- Deliver the contents of the IP packet to the proper upper-layer process or service (Protocol field)

When the IP packet is received at the IP Layer, it is assumed that this information is correct and valid. Further, IP has no mechanism to verify the originating source device, nor perform any integrity check on values in the packet header or data payload. IP, like all Network Layer packet-switching protocols, is considered connectionless.

TCP — The Transmission Control Protocol

The Transmission Control Protocol (TCP) accepts TCP segments from IP and determines the appropriate upper-layer process or application to deliver the contents of the TCP segment. The identity or "process ID" of the upper-layer process is identified in the *destination port* field of the TCP header. The process ID at the originating device is identified in the *source port* field of the TCP header. The combination of *source address* and *source port*, plus *destination address* and *destination port* defines the endpoints of a unique *connection* between any two communicating devices, commonly referred to in Unix terminology as a *socket*.

The *connection* described above is a logic connection, or *virtual circuit*. In addition to the source port and destination port fields, the TCP header also has several other fields. The *sequence* field is filled by the TCP sender and used as a counter for the number of bytes it *sends*. At the receiver TCP layer, this count is used to verify that all segments are received and to resequence them if the segments have arrived out of order. If multiple paths exist through the network, with different delay characteristics, it is possible for some segments to arrive before segments that had actually been sent earlier. The *acknowledgement* field is set by the receiver to inform the sender of the current count of bytes *received*. The normal acknowledgement procedure is to take the incoming sequence number (from the originator) plus one. For example, if the current incoming segment carries a sequence number of 100, implying the last byte sent was the 100th byte, the appropriate outgoing acknowledgement number would be 101, implying that the next byte anticipated by the receiver will be the 101st byte.

The last fields we will discuss are sometimes referred to as the *flag* fields, because they are one-bit fields that may only have the value of one or zero, set or not set, respectively. Four of the six flag fields have special significance for our discussion:

- The SYN or synchronizing bit is used to indicate a connection request, set by the initiator (typically a client), and examined by the responder (typically a host or server).
- The ACK or acknowledgement bit is set in segments sent by the receiver to indicate data has been received, with the byte count of received data contained in the acknowledgement field. The ACK bit also has special significance with respect to a connection request. In response to a connection request, a responder will indicate if the responder is ready, willing, and able to accept a new connection, by setting the ACK bit in the reply segment, even though no "data" has been received that requires an acknowledgement.

- The FIN or final bit is set by either end to indicate a "graceful" close of the connection. Each end should send a segment to the other with the FIN-bit set for a graceful close, but sending the FIN bit is only to show "good manners" and not mandatory to successfully close a connection. If one end drops the connection, the TCP peer at the other end would eventually timeout.

- The RST or reset bit is sent by either end of a connection to indicate an abrupt close of the connection. The term "reset" is an unfortunate choice, since it doesn't necessarily indicate that a new connection will be reformed. It simply indicates that one end is abandoning the connection. The significance is that if the connection simply disappears, each end of the TCP connection will wait for a period of time, in case the connection isn't completely lost. If a segment is received with the RST bit set, the TCP peer at that end will immediately close the connection.

While it may seem that the above discussion is overly tedious detail, it is the bare minimum that will be necessary to understand Cisco's antiflooding features. As we indicated in Chapter 3, a complete discussion of TCP/IP is beyond the scope of this book, and more detailed information is available in *Internetworking with TCP/IP, Volume 1: Principles, Protocols & Architecture,* fourth edition, by Douglas E. Comer (Prentice Hall, 2000).

In the previous chapter we referred to one attack method (also known as an attack *vector*) known as SYN flooding. By monitoring the condition of these flag bits, the Cisco routers and firewalls can make judgments about the connection status or condition. Note that these bits are contained in the TCP header, which is buried within the first 20 or 24 bytes of the IP packet payload. In performing purely routing functions, a Cisco router would not examine the data payload of an IP packet. Access list filtering and antiflooding require a router device to do additional packet analysis beyond the basic routing function.

UDP — The User Datagram Protocol

The User Datagram Protocol (UDP) is an alternative transport-layer protocol, intended for environments that don't require the fuller functionality provided by TCP, or environments where a connection setup is not practical. An example is the Routing Information Protocol (RIP) that uses UDP. RIP routing devices exchange information with other RIP devices via a broadcast mechanism. In this manner, RIP can simply broadcast its routing information out of all its interfaces, thereby reaching any and all RIP-speaking devices with a simple mechanism. Consider the extra steps that would be necessary if RIP needed to set up a TCP connection with each of its peer routers, and send them individual copies of the routing information. RIP also does not require the reliability provided by acknowledged TCP transmissions, instead RIP compensates by repeating the broadcast every 30 seconds. Other UDP-based exceptions include applications and services such as Sun Microsystems NFS (Network File System). NFS prefers to provide the TCP-like functionality as part of the NFS upper layers, doesn't need TCP, and hence uses UDP instead.

There is little similarity between TCP and UDP, and the only common characteristic they share is the concept of port numbers. Like TCP, UDP uses the port numbers to identify the upper layer process, or process ID at each end of a UDP *session*. Please note that the terminology is not always used consistently, and you will sometimes see reference to UDP "connections." The simple fact is that UDP is connectionless, and any references to UDP "connections" are understood to merely signify the relationship and exchange between two partners of a UDP *session* (e.g., client and server). Beyond the port indicators, UDP provides little else; no acknowledgement, no resequencing, no retransmission on error, and no flow control. The UDP header consists simply of source port, destination port, a header checksum, and field indicating the length of the UDP datagram.

TCP and UDP Ports

The length of the port field in TCP or UDP headers is 16 bits, indicating that there are 65,536 different decimal numbers that the field could represent. The convention that has been used is to reserve the port numbers below 1024 for well-known services. Many of these lower port numbers are assigned and registered to specific universal or very common applications, such as SMTP, Telnet, http, and so forth. To reach the Telnet process on a server, the client simply indicates the "well-known" port number for the Telnet host process, TCP port 23. To deliver mail by using SMTP, the request is for "well-known" TCP port 25. If a DNS client needs to query a DNS server to look up an IP address for a given name or URL, the client process requests UDP port 53. The listing of assigned port numbers that is current as of this writing can be found in RFC 1700, titled "Assigned Numbers."

In the case of clients, the port number will be assigned dynamically on an as-needed basis by the client's local operating system. There is no necessity for a client to be well known (i.e., permanent) so long as the client is *currently* known. The client port number is a temporary process ID for a given connection, and once the connection is closed, the port number goes back into the pool of available port numbers. If the client opens a new connection, the client may get a different port number, and the first port number may be reassigned to some other client. This procedure will have significance when configuring access lists and firewalls, since the servers have fixed port numbers while the clients will have randomly assigned port numbers. The server well-known ports are typically 1023 or less, but there are exceptions. Services that are not universal and/or not eligible to be assigned one of the relatively few well-known port numbers (i.e., 1023 or fewer) can use any port number 1024 and above. Product-specific, platform-specific, or vendor-specific servers commonly use higher port numbers, usually well up in the range (e.g., 6000, 8000, et al.). Although there are no guarantees that some other server application may not have chosen the same port number, conflicts are fairly uncommon.

Multimedia applications for audio, video, and teleconferencing typically have high port numbers chosen arbitrarily by the application developer. If an organization must support these through an access list or firewall, the vendor must usually provide information necessary to configure access lists or firewalls.

Now that we have a better understanding of the protocol, we can proceed with the emphasis of this chapter.

What Is a Network Firewall?

Although one may get a variety of differing answers to this question, we will attempt to narrow the range of answers. The term is borrowed from building construction in which a wall is placed or reinforced to prevent the spread of fire, usually fabricated from brick, stone, or some highly fire-resistant material. The term has also been used differently in computer networking. In the late 1980s and early 1990s, the term was used when referring to routers, since they would effectively block broadcast storms that were common on the large bridged networks that were the norm at that time. Bridges and switches always forward broadcasts by default, unless filters are applied. On the other hand, routers never forward broadcasts, and special provision must be made if two devices separated by a router must communicate via broadcast (e.g., a DHCP client seeking an unidentified DHCP server). Cisco implements a configurable feature called **helper address** to address this situation.

Even the current use of the term "firewall" could mean several different things. In the early days of firewalls, routers with simple access lists were described as firewalls, and as a result it is sometimes difficult to determine what functionality is actually provided. The approach we will use here is to define and use the term as it is generally (but not universally) accepted in the networking industry today. We will identify several different firewall architectures that take fundamentally different approaches to securing a site, so that you can evaluate the pros and cons of each.

A simple, broad definition is that a firewall is a device or system of devices that enforce an organization's access control policy between two or more different networks. This is an overly broad definition and could be construed to be a router with simple access lists, a PC with appropriate filtering software, a host or group of hosts collectively, or a specific firewall device such as the Cisco Secure PIX Firewall.

Since that definition is overly vague, we will narrow our discussion to the two primary firewall architectures that are prevalent on today's networks.

If you have done any research on the educational materials that are available, you will find that there are a number of excellent books, articles, white papers, and other materials that specifically cover firewalls. These materials often span a time frame of five to seven years, and circumstances have changed fairly significantly over that time period. If there is a conflict or contradiction in the various materials, they will often be related more to the time that the materials were written, than the substantive issues. What is available today might be considered second-, or even third-generation firewalls, and as such, may not be adequately represented in older materials.

What Kind of Protection Does a Firewall Provide?

The underlying premise behind the justification for firewalls is that an organization is connected to the Internet or some other public network. Most organizations desire protection from both the unknown demons of the public world, as well as the known demons. Many believe that a firewall will fully protect them, but unfortunately that isn't often the case. With the increased usage of Internet technologies comes increased risk. As organizations more fully utilize the available functionality, security is all too often a surprisingly low priority.

Here is a specific case I have witnessed: A rapidly growing company in the financial services industry had a business model that required a high-throughput, high availability connection to the Internet. This company had built a campus LAN environment around Ethernet switches, with a single connecting router to the Internet. At the time, they were in the planning for an upgrade of their Internet connection to T3 speed, and diversifying their risk by having two ISPs.

The campus LAN consisted of 50 to 100 high-end PC workstations, several Web servers, and various WinNT internal servers. The workstations were not used by employees, but, rather, were for the use of the organization's *customers*. These customers were day-traders, and therefore required constant access to the Internet. A group of 50 to 70 customers would arrive each morning, take their assigned station, and begin their stock trading.

The IS manager was a bright, technically capable, but extremely overworked individual who had built the entire network virtually by himself.

At the time I was first introduced to them, they had *no* network security — no access lists, no firewalls, no intrusion detection, no nothing. They relied solely upon simple login passwords and security-by-obscurity.

After giving me an overview of their network, and seeing the surprise on my face, the IS manager explained the reason. He indicated that he was terribly understaffed and his priority was to get things up and running, and keep them running. The organization had taken the first step, and had purchased a PIX firewall, but it was still in the box.

He seemed (fully?) aware of the risk the organization was facing, but top management had a demanding expansion in process, and the IS manager simply didn't have the time to devote to securing the network. As outrageous as this situation may seem, this scenario may be much more common than one would think.

With a firewall in place, an organization will have some degree of protection from the outside, but next to none from the inside. Hostile employees, contract employees, vendor service technicians, and other visitors are on the inside, and may not always have your organization's interests at heart. Although a complete security solution requires more than just a firewall, it is nonetheless a good place to start.

In general, a firewall is similar to a two-way mirror. It lets you see out from one side, but no one on the other side can see in. The underlying premise behind a firewall is to block all incoming traffic originating on the outside, except the replies or responses to traffic that originated on the internal network. To accomplish this, the firewall needs a means to evaluate the incoming packets, and determine if they represent responses to applications initiated from users inside your network, or outsiders attempting to access the internal network.

Protection and Features a Firewall Can Provide

- Attacks against vulnerable services — By shielding your network with a firewall, vulnerable applications or services are protected from attacks, and can be used inside your network. If TCP connection requests from the outside are rejected by the firewall, applications inside the firewall such as Telnet or ftp that pass login information in clear text can continue to be used, protected from outside access. However, the potential still exists for insider abuse.
- Protection from certain specific attacks — Many firewalls, and the Cisco Secure PIX Firewall, in particular, implement specific antiflooding features to prevent certain types of attacks such as SYN flooding.
- Controlled access *into* your site — Network security administrators can control what traffic may *enter* your site. The firewall is an excellent vantage point to observe all traffic entering and exiting the organization's network.
- Controlled access *from* your site — At the discretion of the firewall administrator, access to services *outside* the firewall can be limited if the network security policy requires. The restrictions may be applied by application type, by user, or combinations of the two.
- Isolation of semipublic resources from private resources — With the creation of separate security zones (a semiprotected DMZ and fully pro-

tected internal network), internal resources can be protected from attacks that may originate from compromised hosts in the DMZ.

- Maintain the privacy of network infrastructure — Optional use of NAT can hide details of the internal network from outside view. The common prelude to a network intrusion is address scanning, port scanning, or other forms of surveillance. Like a burglar "casing the joint," this surveillance is commonly the first step in preparing an intrusion. The less information that a potential intruder possesses, the better.

- Audit trail and statistics — By activating the logging of significant events, post event analysis and review of the logged data can provide activity reports and an audit trail. It is crucial that network usage and network intrusion attempts be recorded to verify that network protection is adequate. A site that claims no suspicious activity or attempted breaches probably has not looked very hard. Logging alerts can be tied to various alarm mechanisms to draw attention to active intrusions, so that they can be closely monitored or halted.

- Network policy enforcement — The firewall serves as the checkpoint for analyzing all traffic entering and leaving the organization's network, to verify conformance with established network security policy.

- Confidentiality, Integrity, and Authenticity — With the addition of VPN technology such as IPSec, traffic between inside hosts and trusted remote sites, such as branch offices, can traverse the Internet in encrypted form. Encryption of the data can hide the data from view, verify the authenticity of the remote site, and provide data integrity. Both the PIX Firewall and IOS Firewall can serve as a gateway endpoint for VPN tunnels.

- Advanced authentication — In conjunction with token card or other single-sign-on (SSO) technologies, inbound or outbound users can be authenticated using these more secure authentication technologies.

- Prohibit access to inappropriate sites by your users — The Cisco Secure PIX Firewall can be used in conjunction with a URL filtering server, which can block access to predefined sites that may be prohibited by the network security policy.

What a Firewall Doesn't Protect Against

- Insider misuse and abuse — The firewall only examines data that passes through it and, therefore, is unable to protect internal resources from insiders. Other complementary security products are more appropriate to protect those resources. Although it can be difficult to provide complete protection from insider abuse, intrusion detection systems, logs, stronger authentication (such as one-time passwords or token cards), access control methods, and user education can minimize the occurrences of misuse.

- Data paths that circumvent the firewall — The most common instances of "back door" data paths that bypass the firewall are direct dialup users. With the low cost of dialup modems, users may use a direct dialup connection from the internal network, either for personal convenience, or to intentionally circumvent network security policy. Any data path that circumvents security checkpoints increases risk, and this is a common problem area for most network security administrators.

- Email — While the firewall has some ability to protect the email *system*, many of the widely reported problems are viruses, worms, and Trojan horses included as attachments to email messages. The best current protection method is user awareness of the potential risks of email. A clear, stated email policy describing acceptable security practices, coupled with user education, should reduce the likelihood of problems in this area.

- Viruses — Firewalls typically have no ability to detect viruses. Viruses are often host or operating system specific and various antivirus software packages are available. The network security policy should ensure that they be kept up to date by installing the periodic maintenance updates and releases.

- Features not configured — The firewall has many sophisticated features, but they must be configured properly to be effective.

- There are many operating system and/or application vulnerabilities that the firewall cannot detect. The system administrators of the servers, hosts, and workstations need to be security-conscious, and aware of the necessity to maintain these applications and operating systems with the latest security patches.

As may be evident from the above discussion, a firewall is a very capable device, but it can't do everything. The current thinking is that a layered defense, with the firewall as one of the cornerstones, is the best approach.

Firewall Design Approaches

There are several basic firewall types, but they can typically be grouped into one of two categories: *network gateways or application gateways*. The design layout choices vary slightly between the two fundamental types, with each approach having strengths and weaknesses. Each approach begins with a different underlying design philosophy, but ultimately both types provide comparable functionality.

Network Level Firewalls

Network level firewalls come in two basic forms. One of the legacy firewall approaches was simply a router with packet filters (i.e., access lists). Improvements in packet filtering methods have made the packet filtering router functionally obsolete as a firewall. In its place, a more advanced form of packet analysis and filtering has emerged, commonly described as "stateful" packet filtering.

PACKET FILTERS (STATELESS)

The earlier approach of using packet-filtering routers (access lists) had significant limitations. By today's generally accepted definition, these are no longer considered true firewalls. Stateless packet filters examine the packet at the Network Layer, and make filtering decisions based upon any of the following combinations:

- Source and/or destination IP address (or range of addresses using bitmasking)
- Source and/or destination TCP or UDP port (or range of ports using Boolean operands)
- Protocol type carried inside the IP packet (i.e., TCP, UDP, ICMP, IGRP, et al., as identified by the Protocol field in the IP header)
- Status of the ACK bit in the TCP header

You may recognize that this definition describes Cisco extended access lists. Although stateless packet filters are no longer considered firewalls, there is clearly still a role for router-based access lists. When used in conjunction with a firewall, access lists help to provide a layered network defense. As was described in the previous chapter, they are commonly placed on the perimeter router, outside and in front of the firewall.

One of the primary limitations of access lists and other simple packet filters is that they look at each packet in isolation, one by one. They have a limited ability to see a portion of the upper-layer header that is contained within the first few bytes of the IP packet payload, but they have no ability to evaluate a *sequence* of packets, since they keep no history of previous similar packets. They have a limited ability to distinguish an "established connection" from one that is in the process of being established.

A typical scenario where this is useful would be on an inbound access list at the perimeter router. If we were to take the most secure approach of denying all inbound traffic, we have a small problem. If any of our internal users wants to reach outside services on the Internet, the access list blocking *all* incoming traffic will block the users' return traffic from those Internet servers, as well.

We could define our access lists so that inbound traffic to the destination address of any of our internal user stations was permitted, but that creates an additional problem. That exception will now permit *any* traffic to those same internal destinations, so we need to be more specific. We need to use some method to distinguish the internal user's return traffic from other incoming traffic. The flag bits in the TCP header provide a means to make this distinction.

For example, a TCP connection setup has a clearly recognizable pattern. If one examines the exchange between the initiator and responder, the condition of the TCP flag bits follows a predictable pattern. The pattern for a valid TCP connection setup will look like this:

- Segment #1 — initiator to responder — SYN bit set, no ACK bit (SYN)
- Segment #2 — responder to initiator — SYN bit set, ACK bit set (SYN, ACK)
- Segment #3 — initiator to responder — no SYN bit, ACK bit set (ACK)
- Segment #4 — responder to initiator — no SYN bit, ACK bit set (ACK)
- All subsequent segments exchanged — no SYN bit, ACK bit set (ACK)

We know that any TCP connection initiated by our internal users will set the SYN bit to initiate a connection request, but since we are examining the incoming response from the Internet server, we should notice that *all* incoming traffic *returning* from the external server will have the ACK bit set. The incoming traffic will have the ACK bit set on the connection acceptance from the server, and in all subsequent packets exchanged between the two devices. We also note that any initial connection request from clients on the outside will *not* have the ACK bit set.

This simple test gives us a mechanism to distinguish our users' returning traffic from connection requests that are initiated from the outside. Restating our new rule: Permit inbound traffic from any arbitrary host, if the destination address is an internal host *and* the ACK bit is set. Deny and block all other traffic. In Cisco access list terminology this bit flag test is referred to as the "established" bit.

This may appear to be an acceptable solution, except for a few details. It works for TCP-based applications, such as http, Telnet, passive ftp (to be defined in a later chapter) but is not applicable to UDP, which does not use a connection setup. Many of the common multimedia applications for audio, video, and teleconferencing are UDP-based.

The second issue relates to "crafted packets," that is, packets that are intentionally created to deceive. Consider the following scenario: An incoming packet is really a connection request to an internal server, but the packet has been "crafted" to have both the SYN bit and the ACK bit set. The access list will allow the incoming packet, but the bigger issue is, will the internal host treat this as a connection request or not? The answer: It depends upon the host software.

It is possible that some host software will see a packet with the SYN bit set, and if there is no current connection for this source address, it may not bother to check for the presence of the ACK bit. It may, instead, treat this as a connection request and allow the connection.

While this little scenario may not actually exist, it is representative of the types of programming practices and shortcuts that may be present in any application. These are precisely the type of vulnerabilities that intruders discover and use to their advantage.

If our access list had a "memory," it might have noticed something was wrong and blocked the incoming packet. If this was an "established" connection, the incoming traffic should correspond to a previous outgoing packet (from the originating internal device), but with the source and destination address and ports reversed. That additional functionality enhancement describes what is commonly referred to as *stateful packet filtering*.

STATEFUL PACKET FILTERING

Cisco's firewall products, both the PIX Firewall and the IOS Firewall, implement stateful packet filtering. They maintain internal information about the state of connections that traverse them, and have some limited ability to examine the data inside the packets.

This overcomes the limitations of "stateless" packet filtering that access lists represent. With stateful packet filtering, the firewall keeps track of the current *state* and *context* of a TCP connection, UDP session, or various other types of exchanges between two devices.

For example, when a new connection is initiated from an internal host to an external host that is outside the firewall, the firewall creates a new entry in a "state table." This entry contains such things as the source address and port, the destination address and port, the status of the TCP flag bits (if applicable), TCP segment sequence numbers, and other details.

Upon receipt of an incoming packet, the firewall looks for the applicable entry in the state table. There should be a corresponding table entry with the same IP addresses and port numbers, except with the source and destination reversed, since the incoming packet is the response. In addition, the current status of the TCP flags should be consistent with the sequence of a legitimate exchange, and the acknowledgement number of the returning packet should be consistent with the sequence number that was used in the outgoing packet, as recorded by the entry in the table. This is the "state" and "context."

If an incoming packet is inconsistent with the expected pattern for a TCP or UDP exchange, the packet will be dropped. Likewise, if there is no existing table entry that corresponds to the incoming packet, it will also be dropped.

Stateful packet-filtering firewalls tend to be fairly fast (as compared to application gateway firewalls) due to the fact that packet analysis is a simple "lookup" of an entry in a memory-based cache table. Although the above is a generalized description of the basics of stateful packet filtering, most modern stateful-packet-filter firewalls include several other features. Most firewall vendors, including Cisco, incorporate NAT, VPN functionality (using IPSec and other technologies), URL filtering, and various other features. We will more fully discuss details of Cisco's specific implementation in the sections on the PIX and IOS Firewalls.

Application Layer Firewalls

This class of firewalls has sometimes been referred to by various other names, such as application gateways, proxy gateways, application-level proxies, proxy servers, and other similar names.

The general category also encompasses what is sometimes referred to as *circuit-level gateways*. In general, an application layer firewall is a host running one or more proxy services; however, there are also purely proxy servers that do not necessarily have full firewall functionality, and are instead used in conjunction with a separate firewall.

The strength of this approach is that there is no direct packet flow from one side of the firewall to the other. Instead the proxy function intercepts client requests, and originates its own *new* request on behalf of the client. To the external host or server, the request appears to have been originated by the proxy, and the identity of the real client is hidden. Further, the proxy accepts the responses from the external servers and performs an application layer transfer back to the client.

There are effectively two connections — one between the client and the proxy server, and a second from the proxy server to the external host. There is no direct communication between the client and the external server, and data must be passed from one application to another within the proxy or application level gateway, in order to forward data in each direction. See Figure 4-2 below.

In Figure 4-2, the workstation in the internal network wants to reach the Web server in the Internet. The request is intercepted by the application layer firewall, which initiates a new connection (as a client of the Web server) on

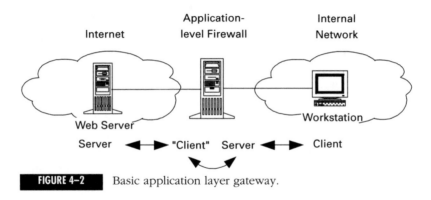

FIGURE 4–2   Basic application layer gateway.

behalf of the workstation. When the firewall receives the response from the Web server, the firewall performs an application-to-application transfer (i.e., from the firewall's client-function to its server-function) and passes the response on to the client workstation.

As a more vivid way to understand the proxy function, we can alter the scenario. Let's assume that the user on the client workstation Telnets into the firewall. As a virtual local user on the firewall, the user opens a client ftp session from the firewall to the external server. The data that is returned by the external server is returned to the ftp client-function on the firewall. Some application-to-application process on the firewall must pipe this ftp data stream onto the Telnet connection. The user receives Telnet-packaged data that carries the ftp response. The firewall performed the ftp to Telnet, application-to-application conversion. Although not exactly the same, the proxy function behaves in a similar fashion, except that in our first example, the firewall performed an http-to-http "conversion."

The second example of Telnet-to-ftp is representative of some legacy implementations of application layer gateway firewalls. These types are not transparent to end-users, since they require a two-step process, and the client must be aware of the proxy to function properly. Some newer variations of application-level firewalls may require a modified client to make this process transparent to the user. Those that use standard clients may require the user to use a two-step process: one to connect to the firewall, and a second to the service that you are trying to reach. Each approach has its pluses and minuses.

There are several points to note here. First, the address of the original internal workstation remains hidden behind the firewall, effectively performing a NAT-like function. Likewise, hostnames and the internal network structure are hidden from view.

Second, when the firewall received data from the external server, it needed somewhere to send the data, that is, on the connection to the workstation. No direct access to the workstation was possible.

If the situation were reversed, with a client on the Internet trying to reach a server on the internal network, the firewall will evaluate the request based upon the security policy it is configured to support. The only way that an outside client can reach an internal server is with the cooperation and assistance of the firewall. The configuration of the firewall will determine what access is allowed, and the firewall will simply not cooperate in relaying the data unless it has been given explicit instructions to do so. This is the nature of the basic firewall functionality of an application gateway.

Also note that the firewall support for the proxy function is specific to each individual application. Most application level firewalls support basic Telnet, ftp, and http, but few other applications. If other applications are required, the firewall may not support those other applications. In contrast, a stateful packet filter firewall has no such dependencies and is essentially protocol independent. With stateful-packet firewalls, standard client software can be used, and nearly all application and protocols are supported. (There are minor exceptions for some multimedia-type applications that *do* require specific firewall support.)

On the other hand, since the application level firewall is protocol or service specific, there is also better granularity of the level of detail on which filtering can be done. Some application level firewalls can filter ftp down to the level of allowing the ftp *get* command, but blocking the ftp *put* command. This has the effect of allowing downloads, but not uploads.

The final point is related to performance. The application-to-application type of firewall is considered to be inherently more secure, but it is potentially more memory and CPU intensive, and also slower than the table-lookup that is characteristic of stateful packet filtering firewalls. This can become an issue in exceptionally high-throughput environments.

Since application gateways are essentially host-based, there is usually extensive logging and auditing functionality available, depending upon the host operating system used. Historically, most application gateways were based on Unix, but other variations currently exist including Windows NT. In many current firewall implementations, the operating system is a specialized, hardened version, although this is not always the case. Some vendors bundle the firewall with a special OS kernel, while others provide only the firewall application to run on standard versions of Unix or Windows NT. Each approach has its pluses and minuses, but the firewall is only as secure as the underlying operating system on which it runs.

The term *bastion host* is often used to describe a host that has been "hardened." This customarily consists of stripping out nonessential services and "beefing up" the security of remaining services to withstand network attacks. A word of caution: The term *bastion host* has had different meanings over time. Some of the earliest application gateway firewalls *were* dual-homed, bastion hosts. Since the introduction of specific firewall products, such as the Cisco PIX, Checkpoint Firewall-1, and others, this practice has become much less common. Instead, the bastion host and firewall are usually separate devices.

Network Design with Firewalls

The Classic Firewall Design

In previous chapters we illustrated one of the possible network designs using firewalls. Even though there can be many variations, we will focus on the smaller number of those combinations that are most commonly used.

The first design is possibly the most common, since it fits application gateway and stateful packet firewall types. As illustrated in Figure 4-3, it con-

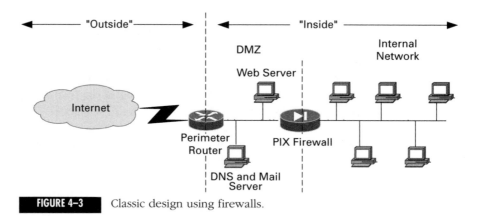

FIGURE 4–3   Classic design using firewalls.

sists of a perimeter router at the outside boundary of the organization's network; a semiprotected zone (i.e., the DMZ) between the perimeter router and the PIX firewall; and the fully protected internal network.

The perimeter router separates the organization's network from the outside world. However, in some instances the perimeter router is provided and controlled by the ISP, blurring the boundary between "inside" and "outside."

The firewall separates the internal network that will be inaccessible from outside the firewall from the DMZ, which is still inside the organization's network but must usually be accessible from outside the organization's network.

The DMZ or demilitarized zone (sometimes referred to as a "screened subnet") is protected only by the limited functionality available on the perimeter router. Similar to the lobby of a building, the DMZ area is "protected" and is inside the boundaries of the organization's network, but must be publicly accessible to deliver email, access the Web server, and translate DNS names or URLs into the IP addresses of the mail and Web servers.

This design might be considered the "classic" design, since most other designs are variations on this basic theme. In legacy firewall designs, the perimeter router and firewall combination is sometimes implemented as a pair of routers, with the "inner" router having more restrictive access lists.

The Contemporary Design

The second design is illustrated in Figure 4-4 and is a variation of the previous example, with the difference being that the DMZ is moved *behind* the firewall, but still isolated from the internal network.

The advantage of this approach is that we can provide a greater degree of protection to the servers in the DMZ than could be provided by the perimeter router alone. The option for a "third" interface has been available in PIX firewalls for several years, and recent versions of the PIX operating system have increased the total maximum number of interfaces even further.

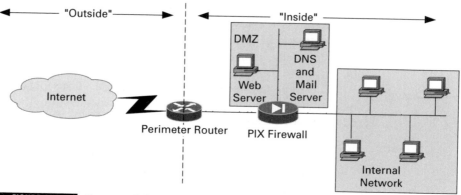

FIGURE 4–4   Improved design using firewalls with additional interfaces.

Depending upon the specific PIX platform and software version, the current maximum can be as high as eight total interfaces, using combinations of 10/ 100 and Gigabit Ethernet interfaces. (Certain nonexpandable, entry-level models are still limited to two interfaces, total.)

Even though the DMZ is "behind" the firewall, it remains isolated from the inside network. In a three-interface configuration, each interface has a name and a security level assigned. The names and applicable security levels are:

- OUTSIDE — As illustrated in Figure 4-4, this is the outermost interface connected to the public network through the perimeter router. This interface is always assigned the lowest security level of zero.
- INSIDE — As illustrated in Figure 4-4, this is the innermost interface that connects to the internal network, and is always assigned a security level of 100.
- DMZ — As illustrated in Figure 4-4, this interface is between the most secure and least secure interfaces and can be assigned a security level ranging from 1 to 99.

The relevance of the names and security levels becomes apparent when we examine the fundamental PIX rules:

- All traffic flows originating on the INSIDE interface with destinations on the OUTSIDE interface will be permitted by default.
- All traffic flows originating on the OUTSIDE interface with a destination on the INSIDE interface will be denied by default.

This rule is enforced by a simple mechanism. When traffic on the INSIDE interface passes through the PIX on its way to the OUTSIDE interface and on to external hosts, an entry is created in the connection table (Cisco's specific term is "translation table," since it is also used for NAT.) When replies return from the applications on external hosts, the reply packets will be compared to entries in the connection table. For most applications, the reply will match the entry made in the table, except with the source and destination reversed, and the packet will be allowed through the firewall.

For traffic that originates on the OUTSIDE, there will be no entry in the connection table that it corresponds to, and the packet will be denied and blocked.

In a three-interface configuration, inside versus outside is not as obvious, but is equally simple. The Outside always has the lowest security level, and the Inside always has the highest. The PIX rule could be restated as:

- For all traffic passing from an interface with a high security value to an interface with a low security value, an entry will be made in the connection table, and the packet will be permitted by default (e.g., Inside=100 to Outside=0)
- For all traffic passing from an interface with low security value to an interface with a high security value, an entry will *not* be made in the connection table, and the packet will be *denied* by default (e.g., Outside=0 to Inside=100)

This more general restatement of the rule can now be applied to configurations that include a third interface. The third interface, DMZ, can only have a security value from 1 through 99. As a consequence it is "more outside" when compared to the Inside interface, and "more inside" when compared to the Outside interface. The relative difference is what determines the flow of traffic. Since traffic flows into one interface and out of another, we only need to look at the security level assigned to each interface to determine which of the two is more inside or more outside, relative to the other.

The end result is that when evaluating packets originating on the Inside interface to a destination on the DMZ, the DMZ is treated as more outside, an entry is created in the table, and the packet is permitted. Conversely, when evaluating packets originating on the Outside interface to a destination on the DMZ, the DMZ is treated as more inside, no entry exists in the table, and the packet is denied by default. To allow access to the DMZ from the Outside interface, a *specific exception* must be made to the default rule. This provides a fail-safe mechanism, since *only traffic that has been specifically permitted* will be allowed into the DMZ from outside of the organization's network.

Figure 4-5 illustrates the basic rule as applied to a three-interface PIX configuration.

Router-Based Firewalls

The final scenario we will illustrate is specific to the Cisco Secure IOS Firewall. The IOS Firewall is an optional software add-on to the IOS of a Cisco router. The IOS Firewall duplicates much of the functionality of the PIX, without requiring an additional device to be added. It is not intended as a substitute for a PIX Firewall, but it is targeted for remote location or branch

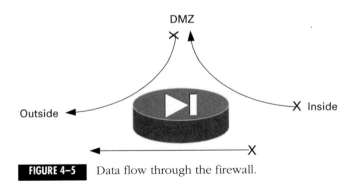

FIGURE 4–5   Data flow through the firewall.

offices where firewall functionality is desired, but a PIX Firewall cannot be cost-justified and where performance is not a significant issue.

Based upon the fact that the IOS Firewall is router-based, our network design layout will change slightly, with the IOS Firewall being superimposed on the perimeter router, as is illustrated in Figure 4-6.

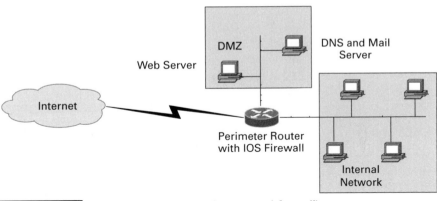

FIGURE 4–6   IOS Firewall (combined router and firewall).

Summary

In this section we compared two fundamentally different approaches to building firewalls; the application gateway and the stateful packet filter. Although each has particular strengths and weaknesses, they provide comparable functionality.

The functionality provided by either of these two approaches to firewall design was shown to be superior to stateless packet filtering, but we also showed how stateless packet filters, as implemented by access lists, can still play a role in secure network designs, even if that role is to supplement and complement the role of the primary firewall.

We also introduced a hybrid in the form of the Cisco Secure IOS Firewall, which is essentially a stateful packet filter applied to a routing platform. In the sections that follow, we will explore the PIX Firewall and IOS Firewall in more depth.

F I V E

The Cisco Secure PIX Firewall

*T*he Cisco Secure PIX Firewall is the flagship firewall in the Cisco product line. The other firewall product in the Cisco line is included in what is currently known as the Cisco Secure Integrated Software (CSIS). This other firewall product will be discussed in Chapter 7. The Cisco Secure PIX Firewall is often described as simply the "PIX," and the acronym PIX refers to Private Internet Exchange, the original name for the firewall product. We will also use this shorter reference, in place of the longer official title. We assume that no confusion is introduced by use of these shorter, simpler references.

A PIX Firewall can be deployed in various design layouts. In simple cases, the PIX Firewall may have only two interfaces, one on the protected internal network (the *inside* interface), with the other on the unprotected side connected to the public network (the *outside* interface), typically the Internet. These references to *inside* and *outside* have special meaning, and the respective interfaces are named "Inside" and "Outside" in PIX Firewall configurations. A representation showing the PIX Firewall employed in a simple, classic design scenario is illustrated in Figure 5-1.

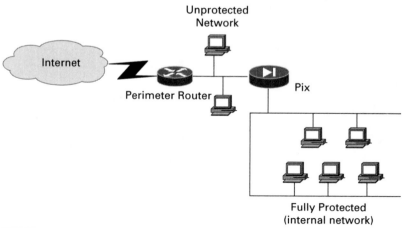

FIGURE 5-1   Classic two interface design.

In Figure 5-1, the Outside, external interface of the firewall is shown connected to the "unprotected" network. This unprotected network is, in fact, protected to a limited degree by the perimeter router, but from the perspective of the PIX Firewall, the network is unprotected. In this context, the reference to "unprotected" is related to the protection afforded by the PIX Firewall, regardless of any other network security protection provided by other devices.

The other PIX interface, the Inside interface, is connected to the internal network. This network is "behind" the firewall and is "fully protected" by the PIX Firewall. In the context of "fully–protected," we refer to the fact that the internal network will be inaccessible from devices connected through the other interfaces, by default.

If we have a simple two-interface PIX Firewall configuration, the rules are simple:

- All connections originating on the Inside interface will be permitted to exit the network, and responses to those packets will be allowed to return through the firewall.

- All connections originating on the Outside interface will be blocked by default.

In a two-interface configuration, the diagram illustrates servers on the network segment between the PIX Firewall and the perimeter router. Cisco and others have traditionally referred to this zone as the "DMZ," but it is also sometimes described as a "screened subnet." (Additional note on terminology: Cisco has also sometimes used the term "dirty DMZ" to describe a DMZ "in front of" and, therefore, not protected by the PIX Firewall.)

For an organization to take advantage of a connection to the Internet, certain servers must usually be accessible to the outside world. These accessible servers include DNS, SMTP, and any public Web servers that an organization may have. The DNS server must be accessible to translate host names, such as those used in the URLs (uniform resource locators) of Web browsers, into an IP address for packet addressing. SMTP servers must be accessible to deliver email to users on the internal network. If an organization has a Web server for public access, this must obviously be accessible, as well. While these servers *could* be located on the internal network behind the firewall, this practice is strongly discouraged, since compromise of any one of those hosts would allow an intruder ready access to a vantage point on the internal network. When these servers are located on the DMZ, the PIX Firewall allows internal users to have unrestricted access to these hosts, while simultaneously limiting access of outsiders to *only* those hosts.

This simple two-interface configuration has commonly been used for PIX-based networks, but Cisco also offers another option that is available on most current PIX Firewall models, except for certain entry-level offerings (e.g., the PIX 506 is limited to two interfaces).

As an option, the PIX Firewall can be implemented with three or more interfaces, with the additional interfaces creating "semisecured" zones. These additional semisecured zones (via the interfaces to which they are connected) are less secured than the internal network zone (connected to the Inside interface), but more secured than the external, public network zone (connected to the Outside interface). Figure 5-2 illustrates a design with a third interface added to the PIX Firewall. In Figure 5-2, the DMZ has been moved "behind" the firewall, but remains isolated from the internal network. This benefit of this alternative design is:

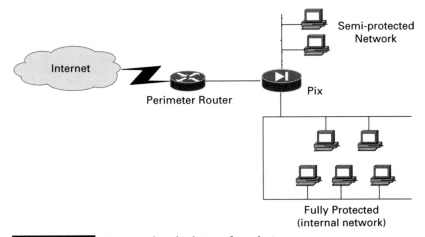

FIGURE 5–2   Improved multiple interface design.

- The publicly accessible servers gain the greater degree of protection provided by the PIX Firewall, in addition to and beyond, than that provided by perimeter router alone.

- The internal network can remain fully protected as before, secure from any compromise of a host in the DMZ, since an intruder would still have to get through the PIX Firewall to access devices on the internal network. The PIX Firewall blocks access to the internal network by connections originating in the DMZ by default.

The DMZ interface is still "more outside" than the Inside interface, and our original PIX Firewall default rule still applies, but with a minor modification. Since the possibility exists that there may be as many as eight total interfaces (one Outside interface, one Inside interface, and as many as six DMZ-like interfaces), we need a method to distinguish which interface is more inside or more outside, when comparing any two particular interfaces. This comparison will be done for each packet that enters the PIX Firewall through one interface and exits the PIX Firewall through another. Fortunately, there is a simple solution. Cisco assigns a value referred to as the "security level" to each interface. This concept was introduced in the last chapter, and will be further clarified here.

Security Levels

All interfaces will have a security level. The interface name and security level values are fixed for the Outside and Inside interfaces. The security level is fixed at 0 for the Outside interface and at 100 for the Inside interface.

The name for the third and any subsequent interfaces, as well as the security level, is selectable. Although these additional interfaces create what has sometimes been described in Cisco documentation as "multiple DMZs," recent Cisco documentation now refers to the multiple "DMZ-like" interfaces as multiple *perimeter interfaces*. Cisco continues to differentiate the *Inside* and *Outside* interfaces from these *perimeter* interfaces. For the sake of clarity, and at the risk of being out of style, we will continue to use Cisco's earlier *DMZ* terminology in our discussions, since we believe the term *DMZ* currently conveys a more precise meaning than the new Cisco-preferred term, *perimeter*.

Names assigned to these interfaces can be any descriptive string of up to 48 characters, but since this name will be entered many times during the configuration and when using various commands, shorter names are recommended since they are easier to type. The security values for these additional interfaces may be any number from 1 to 99, and may *not* be 0 or 100. The security level values of 0 and 100 are reserved for the Outside and Inside interfaces, respectively.

To decide whether the default rule will permit or deny traffic traversing any two interfaces, we simply examine the security levels of each. The interface with the higher security level value will be considered "more inside," the lower security will be level "more outside," and the default PIX rule described earlier will still apply. The only exception is the special case that exists if any two of the other interfaces share the same security value. If the security values are the same, neither is more inside nor more outside than the other. The result is that *no* traffic will flow between these two interfaces. While this may be desirable in some cases, security level values should always be chosen with caution, and with the organization's security policy goals in mind.

The Adaptive Security Algorithm

As described in the previous chapter, the PIX Firewall design uses a form of stateful packet filtering, with extensions to the basic design of a stateful packet filter. Cisco refers to their implementation as the Adaptive Security Algorithm (ASA). The ASA combines Cisco's approach to stateful packet filtering, along with an implementation of NAT, allowing use of private addresses such as those defined in RFC 1918. NAT will be discussed in more detail later in this chapter.

With ASA, each packet entering the router is evaluated according to the following rules:

- If the "conversation" originates on a higher security interface, with a destination reachable through a lower security interface (e.g., internal users traffic to Internet hosts or servers), a new entry will dynamically be created in the "connection table" that is held in memory. Any returning traffic that is part of this "conversation" will be evaluated by the ASA. If the return packet corresponds to an existing table entry, that is, same addresses and port numbers except with source and destination roles reversed, the packet will be allowed back though the PIX Firewall. This temporary, dynamic entry remains in the table for the duration of the conversation; however, once the conversation ends, the table entry is deleted. Special provisions can be made if it is desirable to limit outgoing conversations.

- If the "conversation" originates on a lower security interface, with a destination reachable through a higher security interface (e.g., external user's traffic to internal hosts), the traffic will be denied and blocked by default, since there will be no corresponding entry in the connection table. Special provision can be made to selectively permit the establishment of some conversations that originate on the outside, using a *conduit* which is described more fully below.

- No incoming packets may pass through the PIX Firewall unless they have a corresponding entry in the connection table along with the connection's state information. An exception applies to new entries in the special cases where they are permitted by explicit configuration statements (see reference to *conduits* below). We have generalized the rules to accommodate traffic that crosses any two interfaces. For traffic from a *more* secure zone to a *less* secure zone, new entries are *permitted by default*, but this default can be limited or overridden by explicit configuration statements. For traffic from a *less* secure zone to a *more* secure zone, new entries are *prohibited by default*, but can be overridden and allowed via explicit configuration statements. This one-way data flow through the PIX is assumed, unless explicit configuration statements specify otherwise.
- All attempts to evade the above rules will result in packets being "silently discarded," but with a message generated and sent to a syslog server. With silent discard, the packet is dropped, and no error message explaining the reason is sent to the packet originator.
- All ICMP packets will be blocked unless they have been expressly permitted in the configuration. Note that this rule also applies to the use of Ping, even when the Pings originate on the internal network. This behavior is contrary to behavior of other internally originated traffic. The Ping utility typically sends an ICMP Echo Request and expects to receive an ICMP Echo Reply. ICMP will be permitted only through the use of a *conduit*, described below.

It is important to note that these rules apply in a three-interface configuration, as well. If traffic from external users (low security level) is intended for the servers in the DMZ (higher security level), the traffic will be blocked by default. Similarly, traffic from the DMZ (lower security level) to the internal network (higher security level) will also be blocked by default.

As we stated earlier, the DMZ servers need to be accessible to outside users so we must override this default behavior with specific configuration commands. To make an exception to the default behavior, so that external users can reach our DMZ (Web server, DNS server, mail server, et al.), we must explicitly tell the firewall what traffic to allow. We do this by "hard-coding" a permanent entry in the connection table for this traffic. This permanent, hard-coded entry typically includes the addresses and port number of the applicable servers, but leaves the identity of the address and port number of the external device open.

This permanent, hard-coded entry serves only as a "template" for new entries that can be created in the table, with specific source address and source port information of the originator filled in for each individual external user conversation. As the entry for each new conversation is created, this template is used to spawn the individual entries, which will be tracked individually. It is essential that each new entry have its own record, so that the firewall can evaluate the individual exchanges between these external clients and the organization's servers. This individual evaluation is necessary in order to recognize an inappropriate sequence of packets that are representative of a network attack or intrusion.

Note that this template is *required* if we choose to allow an exception for entries that originate on the outside, since externally originated traffic will otherwise be denied. Cisco has historically used the term "conduit" to describe the exception for this externally originated traffic, and there exists a specific **conduit** configuration command. However, version 5.2 of the PIX operating system introduced new preferred command syntax using access list format that is intended to replace the **conduit** configuration command. For the near term, Cisco's stated position is that either command syntax may be used.

Although Cisco encourages the use of the newer ACL format, we will continue to refer to "conduit" as a descriptive term in this book, since it conveys a specific meaning in PIX Firewall terminology.

This new use of ACL format is part of an ongoing effort by Cisco to improve and promote a greater degree of consistency between similar Cisco products. As will be seen in the Chapter 7, the router IOS-based firewall configuration procedure uses the familiar ACL format as the primary method to configure the firewall component known as Context-Based Access Control (CBAC).

The ASA description above clearly applies to TCP-based applications, with comparable procedures applied to most UDP data exchanges, as well. Certain other application types require special consideration because the exchange of data between devices is slightly more complicated. Multimedia applications, in general, exhibit this behavior, and support for specific applications will be discussed later in this section. For TCP-based applications, the "state" information maintained in the table consists of:

- Source address of the packet
- Source port number indicated in the packet
- Destination address of the packet
- Destination port indicated in the packet
- TCP sequencing and acknowledgement information
- Status of TCP flag bits (e.g., SYN, ACK, FIN or RST; as described in Chapter 4)

The temporary entry for a connection remains in the table until the connection terminates, whereupon the entry is deleted. For UDP-based applications, the "state" information maintained in the table attempts to imitate the above, except there is no sequence or acknowledgement numbers and no TCP flag-bits. Since there is no clear indication of the end of UDP-based exchanges (i.e., no FIN or RST bit to indicate termination), those entries will eventually timeout after a period of inactivity. Applications that are not based upon TCP or UDP will not have port information, but may have comparable characteristics that can be recognized as the exchange between two communicating devices.

A further discussion of terminology is probably appropriate at this point in our coverage. You may have noticed the occasional use of the term "conversation" rather than "connection" or "session." This is an attempt to avoid confusion. The term "connection" is correct when used to describe TCP-based applications, but not necessarily for UDP-based applications. UDP exchanges are connectionless, therefore the term "connection" isn't quite accurate. The other term that is sometimes used is "session," although that term more accurately describes a Layer 5, Session Layer exchange and is also an imprecise term.

You may have also noticed that Cisco uses the term "connection" in their documentation, and this book has also used the same term in several instances. In both cases, use of the term "connection" is merely to illustrate that most Internet applications have a recognizable pattern in the exchange between two devices (e.g., http, Telnet, ftp, SMTP, the ICMP Echo and Echo Reply used by the Ping utility, et al.), and under those circumstances it is considered acceptable to use the term even for applications that aren't TCP-based. We note this apparent contradiction so that the reader does not interpret the loose usage of the terminology to imply TCP-based applications only.

Additionally, we used the term *connection table*. To provide more clarity, we should note that Cisco also refers to a *translation table* or *xlate table* (e.g., the command **show xlate** displays the current contents) because the ASA state table consists of both the connection-state table and the NAT translation table, combined. (Note: This book will refer to this combination as the "state table," since in most cases the table entry includes both the connection state and the NAT xlate information. We hope no confusion will result from the use of the more general term.)

The addition of NAT to the table information requires some refinement and adjustments to the rules we described above, including an additional step that will be performed.

Where reference is made to *incoming* or *outgoing* traffic, we will follow the same convention that is used by Cisco. Use of the term *incoming* refers to traffic entering the PIX from an interface with lower security level, and exiting the PIX through an interface with a higher security level. When the term is applied to simple two-interface PIX configurations, this reference may be clearly understood. However, in situations where there may be from three to eight total interfaces, the reference to *incoming* or *outgoing* is much less obvious.

When outgoing packets arrive at the PIX Firewall (from a more inside interface) the PIX first checks to see if any special restrictions have been explicitly configured that apply to the packet, and if none, uses the ASA to evaluate the packet.

If this is a new connection, the PIX Firewall creates a new entry or *xlate slot* in the translation table. If NAT or Port Address Translation (PAT) is applicable to the packet, the information for this *xlate slot* includes both the real IP address configured on the device, as well as the globally unique NAT or PAT address that is assigned to the device. The PIX Firewall then changes the source address of the packet to reflect the newly assigned NAT/PAT address, modifies the IP header checksum and other fields as necessary, and forwards the packet to the lower security level, outgoing interface.

If this is an existing connection, the ASA updates the current status or "state" information maintained in the xlate slot for this exchange. If NAT or PAT is applicable, the source address of the packet is altered as described above.

When the return traffic for this connection arrives at the lower security level interface (i.e., the more outside), the reply packet will match a corresponding xlate slot entry in the table. The state information will be updated as appropriate, and the incoming packet will be readdressed since it will show the destination address as the *global* NAT/PAT assignment. The PIX Firewall will readdress this packet, changing the address to the *local* IP address that is configured on the device itself. This NAT/PAT function of changing the *local* internal IP address to a *global* external address (and vice versa) is transparent to the host devices for most applications. There are a few applications that don't work with NAT that will be explored later in this chapter.

While the description of NAT contained above is accurate in a general sense, there are fundamentally two methods to assign NAT addresses: dynamic and static.

Network Address Translation

The PIX Firewall includes a Network Address Translation feature that was originally intended to alleviate the problem of IP address depletion. Several years ago, the Internet Assigned Numbers Authority (IANA) stopped their prior practice of assigning IP addresses directly, and instead delegated the authority for address assignment to Internet Service Providers (ISPs). At that time, the assignment of Class B addresses was severely curtailed, since the Class B address space was nearly exhausted. The IANA delegated the assignment of addresses to ISPs, and assigned blocks of Class C addresses to the ISPs for assignment to their customers.

Some pre-Internet organizations had chosen to use TCP/IP and did not bother to apply for a registered address, instead relying upon the fact that their network was isolated. In many cases they simply picked an IP address at random, and assigned their internal network host, servers, clients, and other devices accordingly. So long as they were isolated from other networks this was an acceptable (but shortsighted) practice. Other organizations found that even though smaller blocks of Class C addresses were available, they were sometimes clumsy to use for larger network environments.

With the rapid acceptance of the Internet and its requirement that each device have a globally unique address, the problems described above were simply amplified. As early as May of 1993, this issue was addressed in RFC 1466,[1] "Guidelines for Management of IP Addresses," which stated:

> "The restrictions in allocation of Class B network numbers may cause some organizations to expend additional resources to utilize multiple Class C numbers. This is unfortunate, but inevitable if we implement strategies to control the assignment of Class B addresses. The intent of these guidelines is to balance these costs for the greater good of the Internet."

Although RFC was replaced and updated by RFC 2050, the original point still remains. The issues and policies relating to IP addressing have been the topic of a number of successive RFCs of the years. One of the more significant, RFC 1918,[2] "Address Allocation for Private Internets," (February 1996) makes the further point:

> "With the current size of the Internet and its growth rate it is no longer realistic to assume that by virtue of acquiring globally unique IP addresses out of an Internet registry an organization that acquires such addresses would have Internet-wide IP connectivity once the organization gets connected to the Internet. To the contrary, it is quite likely that when the organization would connect to the Internet to achieve Internet-wide IP connectivity the organization would need to change IP addresses (renumber) all of its public hosts (hosts that require Internet-wide IP connectivity), regardless of whether the addresses used by the organization initially were globally unique or not.

The end result of the above is that, in many cases, an organization will not be able to obtain a globally unique address for every device on their network. However, there are several acceptable alternatives. One of those alternatives is to use different IP address ranges internally, some that are globally unique, with others that are only locally unique. In this same RFC 1918, the Working Group defines three categories of host devices and their respective IP address requirements:

- Category 1: hosts are only reachable by other hosts within the same internal network. Examples of this type would be internal-only servers, clients with no Internet access, and so forth.
- Category 2: hosts that need part-time access to a limited set of outside services that can be accessed through proxy servers. These hosts may use locally unique addresses for internal communications, and proxy servers for Internet communications, since the proxy server inherently hides the internal address of proxy's clients.

---

1. Copyright © The Internet Society, May 1993. All rights reserved.
2. Copyright © The Internet Society, February 1996. All rights reserved.

- Category 3: hosts that need continuous access outside the organization or enterprise. Host devices in this last category require IP addresses that are globally unique.

The RFC refers to the IP addresses on hosts in the first and second categories as *private* (locally unique), and the third category as *public* (globally unique). The RFC further defines a recommended set of addresses for the *private* portion of the address space consisting of the following address ranges that were introduced in Chapter 3, and are repeated here for convenience:

- 10.0.0.0 — 10.255.255.255 (8-bit prefix)
- 172.16.0.0 — 172.31.255.255 (12-bit prefix)
- 192.168.0.0 — 192.168.255.255 (16-bit prefix)

There are, however, several potential implementation problems with the specific approach advocated by RFC 1918 as it is restated and described above.

First, RFC 1918 assumes a differentiated addressing scheme will be used within an organization's internal network, with different devices (hosts, servers, client PCs, et al.) having addresses assigned from two different address ranges: the globally unique address range provided by the organization's ISP, and another address range chosen from one or more of the recommended private address ranges.

This may well require changing the currently assigned IP address of some devices, and may require additional future reassignments if the role of the device changes from *private* to *public* or vice versa. In addition, the use of two different IP address ranges can be problematic in larger organizations, since it may limit the organization's ability to perform route summarization or take fullest advantage of other scalability enhancements. The RFC further assumes the presence of proxy servers to provide the address translation function, by substituting the proxy server's own globally unique address in place of the client's locally unique address. While proxy servers are available for many common applications (e.g., http, ftp, Telnet, et al.) they are not universally available for all applications. If NAT-like functionality, as described in RFC 1918, presupposes the existence of proxy servers, this adds an additional layer of complexity that may not be required or desired.

Fortunately, another alternative exists. If the NAT function can be performed with devices other than proxy servers, a single uniform address space may be used throughout the organization's internal network, with NAT handled on an as-needed basis for any IP device (and any application) that requires a globally unique address for Internet connectivity.

Cisco introduced the PIX Firewall in late 1994, and it included the first commercially available implementation of NAT. Since that time, Cisco has added support for NAT on their router products, beginning with IOS version 11.2 (roughly, late 1997). When implementing NAT for either type of device, Cisco recommends that an organization choose one of the private address ranges defined in RFC 1918. Although any of the address ranges can be used, the network 10.0.0.0/8 provides the largest block of addresses (24-bit), provides the greatest flexibility of the three defined private address ranges, and as a result, it is probably the most common choice for internal network numbering schemes.

For NAT to function properly, some devices, including Web servers, mail servers, DNS servers, or other servers, require a permanently assigned IP address. This *static* IP address is necessary in order to be listed in the appropriate DNS servers. To perform a DNS hostname-to-IP address lookup, the DNS process currently assumes that individual entries have been hand-coded into a text file on the applicable DNS server. (Note: There is a newer standard for Dynamic Domain Name Service (DDNS) that allows dynamic updates to the appropriate text files, but it is not yet widely deployed. There are also security issues with dynamic updates that have not yet been resolved.)

Other devices such as client PCs can usually function adequately with dynamically assigned IP addresses (although there are a few applications that are exceptions) since these devices don't usually need to be listed in the DNS files. These *dynamic* IP addresses can then be assigned from a pool of available addresses on a first-come, first-served basis. With NAT, these addresses are assigned for the duration of the connection. Upon termination of the connection, the address is returned to the pool, and available for other connections or assignment to other client devices.

For those organizations that are unable to secure enough globally unique, registered IP addresses to meet their requirements (a very common situation), Cisco provides an additional feature referred to as Port Address Translation (PAT). In many cases, the number of IP addresses provided to an organization is not enough to support simultaneous access by a large number of users. This situation is becoming more and more common, as Internet access becomes desirable, if not indispensable, for the average worker. According to RFC 1918:

"It has been typical to assign globally unique addresses to all hosts that use TCP/IP. In order to extend the life of the IPv4 address space, address registries are requiring more justification than ever before, making it harder for organizations to acquire additional address space [excerpt from RFC 1466]."

PAT alleviates this problem by taking advantage of an inherent TCP and UDP protocol characteristic. The port number field in a TCP segment or UDP datagram is a 16-bit binary field, allowing the decimal values to range from 1 to 65,536. In theory, this allows an individual host device to support 65,536 simultaneous connections, with each one having a unique port number (i.e., process ID). Port Address Translation (PAT) takes advantage of the generous range of port numbers, and allows one single IP address to be shared by a large number of users.

As we mentioned in an earlier chapter, each connection (including UDP "connections") requires four elements to uniquely identify the data stream or "socket": the source IP address, the source port, the destination address, and the destination port. Even if we assume a hypothetical scenario where all the PAT users shared the same IP address, and were connecting to the same service on the same host, the source port alone would be sufficient to uniquely identify each individual user's TCP or UDP connection or "socket." While the theoretical limit of 65,536 users may not be a realistic scenario, PAT can still easily support tens of thousands of simultaneous users with a single IP address.

Since "there is no such thing as a free lunch" (*tinstaafl*, for those readers who are old enough to remember *Adventure,* the first computer role-playing game from the 1970s), we should add that there are some applications that do not function properly with PAT. Multimedia applications, in general, are problematic because the client implementations sometimes expect that certain client source port numbers will be used. If PAT arbitrarily assigns port numbers, they are likely to be different from the port numbers expected by the servers.

RealAudio Player and RealPlayer are illustrative examples. By default, the RealServer side of the exchange assumes that it can transmit the audio stream to a client UDP port number in the range of 6970 to 7170, inclusive. Although there is a client option to instruct the RealServer to use a specific client port for the audio stream, the client never knows what port number will be assigned by the PAT process at the router or firewall, and the application will usually fail. Multimedia applications for audio and video are also problematic when used behind a firewall, for additional reasons that will be discussed later in this chapter.

PIX Firewall Features

Now that we have a fundamental understanding of how data streams are passed or blocked by the firewall, we can discuss the wide range of features provided by the PIX Firewall.

Stateful packet filter firewalls are the dominant types by market share, with most market surveys placing either the Cisco Secure PIX Firewall or Firewall-1 from Checkpoint® Software in the #1 position. (Firewall-1 is also based upon stateful packet analysis, which Checkpoint calls Stateful Packet Inspection.) Recent studies indicate that these two vendors account for roughly 70 percent of the market for high-end, enterprise-class firewalls.

In the Configuration Guide for the PIX Firewall, Cisco lists approximately 58 "features" of the PIX. While it is not our intention to duplicate that list here, in order to understand what these features are and what they do, a number of them are described below. Some of these features serve an obvious purpose, while others are less obvious. Some features are enabled by default; others require configuring. We have attempted to organize them by function in the section below.

Defense Against Network Attacks

The PIX Firewall includes a number of features that protect the network against specific types of attack. Other features are to protect the PIX Firewall and services that it may host. Most of these features have descriptive names, although the name does not fully describe what the feature is intended to do.

TCP INTERCEPT

Cisco first introduced TCP Intercept in their router products in late versions of IOS version 11.2. This same feature was introduced in PIX Firewall version 5.2. This feature is enabled by default, but some setup is required.

This feature provides protection for host devices behind the firewall from a specific form of network attack known as SYN Flooding. With a SYN Flood, the attacker attempts to deny service to a target host by effectively overloading the victim with connection requests, appearing to come from a nonexistent or unreachable host. SYN Flooding takes advantage of the method used by the operating system to allocate memory and other resources for new TCP connection requests. Even if the host/server can support a large number of connections, it is limited in the number of incomplete connection requests it can handle. In Chapter 4, we briefly described the TCP connection setup, and referred to several one-bit flag fields in the TCP segment: SYN, ACK, FIN, and RST. A device requesting a connection (usually a client) indicates the connection request by setting the SYN bit in the TCP segment that is sent to the desired device (usually a server) along with an initial *sequence* number that will be used to count the bytes of data that it will send. The SYN bit indicates that this segment contains the starting number, and all subsequent segments will increment this base number as data is transmitted. This is a random base number, virtually never zero or one.

When this segment is received at the target device (e.g., server), the responder replies with a segment with the ACK bit set, and an *acknowledgement* number indicating the sequence number it expects to receive next. The acknowledgement number returned is the sequence number received, plus one. This effectively sets up a connection from client to server.

Since TCP is bidirectional and full duplex, it sets up a connection in each direction. To set up the connection from the server to the client, the server sets the SYN and includes his own sequence number requesting a connection from server to client, sending it to the client in the same segment that carries the acknowledgement of the initial connection request from the client. The server then waits for the third step, an acknowledgement from the client, of the connection request from server to client. This procedure is often referred to as the TCP "three-way handshake," since connection setup consists of these three steps.

If the responder server doesn't receive a reply with in a specified TCP timeout interval, the server retransmits the segment with the SYN and ACK. Depending upon the TCP implementation, the typical number of retries is four, with retransmit interval starting at one second, then doubling the waiting time between additional retransmits to two, four, eight, then sixteen seconds. The total elapsed time before the server gives up and abandons the incomplete connection is 31 seconds. Meanwhile, resources that are very limited have been tied up. If a server receives a constant stream of connection requests with no completion, the resources become filled with these *half-open* requests, and no additional incoming requests will be accepted, effectively denying that service.

TCP Intercept solves this problem by intercepting the connection and responding to connection requests on behalf of the host devices it is configured to protect. It opens a second connection from the PIX to the protected host, on behalf of the client. If the client completes the connection normally, the PIX Firewall transparently splices these two connections together, resulting in one connection directly between the client and server.

The PIX Firewall uses more aggressive timeout intervals, and if the connection doesn't complete in this shorter timeout interval, the PIX abandons the incomplete connection with the client and sends a reset (RST bit set) to the protected server, terminating the PIX to server connection, and thereby freeing the server resources. In addition to the more aggressive timeout, TCP Intercept also includes a configurable threshold. This threshold will monitor the total number of connections and the rate during the most recent one-minute interval. If either exceeds the threshold, TCP Intercept will begin dropping half-open connections beginning with the oldest, until the number or rate drops below the threshold.

On the PIX Firewall, the half-open connections are referred to as *embryonic connections*. The threshold is set as an optional parameter of the **static** command, which will be discussed later in this chapter. The default is zero, which effectively disables TCP Intercept, but setting any nonzero value for the embryonic connection parameter enables the feature.

TCP Intercept effectively replaces an older PIX feature called Flood Defender that merely allowed limits to be set on the total number of embryonic connections per host and/or service.

FLOOD GUARD

The Flood Guard feature performs a function somewhat similar to that described for the TCP Intercept. While TCP Intercept provides protection of hosts behind the PIX Firewall that are defined with the **static** command (described later), reachable via a conduit through the PIX, Flood Guard is used to protect host-like capabilities of the PIX Firewall itself.

Specifically, Flood Guard protects the AAA (Authorization, Authentication, and Accounting) function used with Cut-Through-Proxies by freeing resources consumed by incomplete logins. Cut-Through-Proxies allow for user-based authentication, and will be discussed along with AAA later in this chapter.

MAIL GUARD

TCP/IP email service is provided via the Simple Mail Transport Protocol (SMTP), which uses well-known port 25. Mail is delivered in a client-server mode, with the receiver of mail as the server. The "client" could be a terminal user with a Telnet connection to port 25, or it could be a Message Transfer Agent (MTA), for example, another mail server.

The daemon found on most Unix hosts to implement SMTP mail is Sendmail. This particular program/daemon has a long, checkered history, and is often referred to as the "buggiest daemon on earth." There are extensive lists of the known deficiencies that have been discovered. Secure implementations are available for all the variations of Unix-based operating systems, although they are not always included in the standard software distribution.

One of the most notorious of the bugs was responsible for the infamous "Internet Worm attack" by Robert Morris Jr. in 1988. Morris was able to exploit a bug in the DEBUG mode of *sendmail* that allows the recipient of mail to be a program running as "root" or superuser. This allows the intruder to define the recipient as the operating system shell and include shell commands in the body of the message.

Among other problems with the protocol are certain SMTP commands originally defined in RFC 821, that are now considered both passé and insecure, and hence no longer used. The six commands that are rejected by the Mail Guard feature are:

- send — when given a user name, sends a message to the user's terminal
- soml — sends a message to user terminal if user is online; otherwise, delivers to user's mailbox
- saml — send and mail; to user terminal if user is online, *and* deliver to user's mailbox
- verify — when given a user name, replies with full name and email address
- expand — when given a mailing list name, replies with full user name and email address for all members of the list
- turn — reverse the role of sender and receiver; client becomes server and server becomes client

From the description, you may recognize that these commands no longer serve a useful purpose. They may also be misused. Mail Guard scans for the presence of these commands. If Mail Guard finds them used in the delivery exchange, they are treated as *noop* (no operation) and discarded, with an *ok* response to the sender. The only SMTP commands that are supported by the PIX Firewall are MAIL, HELO, RCPT, DATA, RSET, NOOP, and QUIT. These commands are defined in RFC 821, section 4.5.1. All other commands are rejected.

The benefit derived from Mail Guard is illustrated in Figure 5-3.

This design has been common in the past due to the many problems with SMTP-based mail. In Figure 5-3, the mail relay accepts all mail for the organization. The relay function forwards the mail to the real mail server on the internal network. Consider the situation without the mail relay. If the real mail server was in the DMZ, it was vulnerable. If the PIX allowed all outside access directly to the mail server at port 25, anyone on the outside could access the mail server directly. If the intruder could compromise the internal mail server, they could potentially use it as a launching point to attack other hosts.

The PIX Firewall would be configured to allow one specific type of traffic; mail from the mail relay to the mail server at port 25. No other source IP addresses, destination IP addresses, or destination ports would be allowed. In this manner, even a compromise of the mail relay by an intruder would gain little, since all mail resides on the mail server, not the mail relay. Access from the mail relay to the internal network is limited to delivery of mail to a specific device only.

With the addition of Mail Guard, the extra host to serve as mail relay is no longer necessary. In addition, when a three-interface PIX Firewall is implemented, the mail server is often located in the protected, but isolated, DMZ.

The default configuration includes a statement that enables Mail Guard:

```
fixup protocol smtp 25
```

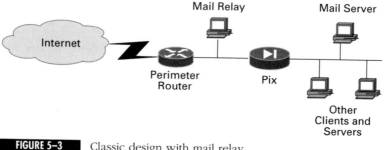

FIGURE 5-3 Classic design with mail relay.

This statement is required for Mail Guard to function, and is included in the default configuration. No other configuration is required to enable Mail Guard other than defining a *conduit* or access list to permit access from external networks. Configuration using **fixup protocol** and **conduit** or equivalent access list statements will be discussed later in this chapter.

DNS GUARD

The DNS Guard feature identifies an outbound DNS request to resolve a name into an IP address, and permits only a single DNS response. A client or other host may query several servers (in case the first server is slow to respond), but only the first response to the query is permitted. Responses from additional servers are discarded.

This feature is an effort to limit exposure to injection of false DNS information, and also limit exposure to *UDP session hijacking*. Since there is frequently no clear indication when exchanges have ended, UDP commonly implements session inactivity timers. If additional UDP data is received before the default UDP timer expires, hijacking may be possible. DNS Guard eliminates this possibility since it can recognize a DNS response, and the PIX Firewall limits additional information that may try to "coat tail" on the first response.

IP FRAG GUARD

The IP specification provides a capability known as *packet fragmentation*. Its purpose is to ensure that IP datagrams (i.e., packets) can travel over various network segments that may support different maximum frame sizes. Fragmentation allows datagrams created as a single IP packet to be split into several smaller packets for transmission across the various LAN and WAN segments, and be reassembled by the receiving host.

For example, Token Ring allows the maximum frame size to be up to 16 kilobytes, while Ethernet limits the data payload of an Ethernet frame to 1500 bytes. Since IP allows the size of a packet or datagram to be up to 64 kilobytes, it is quite possible to create a 3,000-byte packet at a client workstation connected to a Token Ring network segment, with a server on an Ethernet segment as the destination (see Figure 5-4).

To be transmitted on the Ethernet segment, the Router #1 would have to break the original IP packet into two IP *packet fragments* of 1500 bytes each. Router #2 would forward the two fragments to the server, where the two 1500-byte fragments would be reassembled to recreate the original 3,000-byte IP packet.

IP is able to create these fragments by using several fields in the IP header. The header includes:

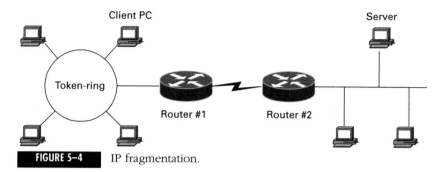

FIGURE 5-4 IP fragmentation.

- Packet ID is a 16-bit field for packet identification. Each original IP packet created will have a unique "serial number" to identify the packet. If fragmentation is performed, this packet ID is copied in the IP header of each fragment created so that a reassembling host will know which fragments are part of the "set" that represents the original IP packet.
- The MF (More Fragments) bit is a 1-bit field. It is set for each of the fragments in the set, except for the last. This alerts the receiving host that reassembly will be required and additional fragments are to be expected. The bit is not set in the last segment in the series, indicating the final fragment in the set. The receiving IP host at the ultimate destination will and must reassemble the IP packet before passing it to upper layer processes such as TCP or UDP, since the upper layer header is carried within the first bytes of the original IP packet, therefore contained in the first fragment (only).
- An *offset* field indicates the position of this fragment in the original IP packet. The offset indicates which byte of the original packet is the first byte in this fragment. The offset starts counting from zero. A fragment offset of zero indicates the first byte of the original packet, and therefore the first fragment in the series.
- Do-Not-Fragment (DF) is a 1-bit field that may optionally be set by the originating device when fragmentation is not desired. If fragmentation is necessary, but this bit is set, the packet will be dropped, with an appropriate ICMP message sent to the originator. (Note: This characteristic is used by the *traceroute* utility to map the path of a packet.)

Under most circumstances, fragmentation will not be necessary, because TCP will usually attempt to avoid IP fragmentation by setting an overly conservative *maximum segment size* (MSS) of 536 bytes whenever the source and destination are not on the same IP network. When a 20-byte TCP header and 20-byte IP header are added to this 536-byte MSS, the total IP packet length will be 576 bytes, and, therefore, small enough to fit into nearly any LAN or WAN frame (although public, carrier-provided X.25 in the U.S. is a notable exception). The magic number of 576 bytes relates to several older RFCs that require all hosts and routers to be able to accept a minimum packet of 576 bytes.

By now you are probably wondering what this has to do with PIX Firewalls. The answer we gave to a similar question in an earlier chapter — everything — also applies here. As stated earlier, most network attacks involve some misuse or abuse of the simple mechanics of various elements of the TCP/IP protocol family. Misuse of IP fragmentation is the basis for a variety of common DoS attacks, including *teardrop.c, boink, bonk, nestea*, and several others.

When an IP host device begins to reassemble fragments, it assigns memory for a "temporary packet buffer," starting with the first fragment. The reassembly process adds additional fragments to their appropriate positions in the reconstructed IP packet using the *offset* to determine their proper location. Once the entire packet is reassembled, it is passed to the upper layers as if it had been received as a single packet. This is crucial since the upper layer header was only present in the first fragment.

In the past, packet fragmentation attacks were able to elude most router access lists and firewalls. They were successful because of the way packets reassembly is accomplished, rather than the way fragmentation is performed. Since reassembly is done at the receiving host, routers will forward the individual smaller IP packets without attempting to reassemble them.

The problem for access lists and stateful packet filters is that the decision to pass or block any packet is often based upon being able to analyze the upper layer header in the first few "data" bytes inside the IP packet. The access lists and their stateful counterparts attempt to match port numbers, et al., in these headers. In the case of a fragmented packet, the header would only be contained in the first fragment and not the others. Since only the first fragment contained the header, it could be blocked but any additional fragments would often be allowed to pass through.

The blocking of the first fragment (containing the upper layer headers) was *usually* sufficient. Since the receiving host would *usually* be unable to correctly reassemble the original packet without the first fragment, reassembly would fail, with the fragments discarded by the host.

The alert reader will notice emphasis on the word *usually* in the preceding paragraph. Once the access list and stateful firewall behavior became known, it didn't take long for "others" to discover a method to misuse that predictable behavior.

Some of the attack programs used overlapping or contradictory *offset* values in the unblocked fragments. Often when a host attempts to allocate buffer space based upon these bogus offsets, the result is often memory allocation errors and system crash. The *teardrop.c* attack program was one cause of the infamous "blue screen of death" on Windows machines.

The IP Frag Guard with Virtual Reassembly provides protection from IP fragmentation attacks, and has been available since version 4.2.2 of the Pix Firewall operating system. Stateless access lists are still vulnerable to these IP fragmentation attacks. Cisco's router-based firewall will be discussed in Chapter 7.

The traditional treatment of fragments has been modified, which permits the PIX Firewall to perform what Cisco refers to as *virtual reassembly*, used in the state table as an integrity check for IP fragments. An *interfragment state* is added to the information maintained in the state table for any IP fragments observed.

Any fragment received will be evaluated against the existing state for that connection.

- There must be a defined conduit or access list that specifically permits this traffic. If none exist, the traffic will be blocked. This is standard behavior for traffic traveling from a low-security level interface to a high-security level interface.
- If a conduit or access list exists and the packet indicates fragment offset = 0, this is the first fragment of a series, and a new entry will be made in the state table, including *interfragment state*. *Virtual reassembly* of the fragments is initiated, and the packet is passed on to the host for actual reassembly.
- If a conduit or access list exists and the packet indicates any fragment offset *other than* zero, there must be an existing entry in the state table for the first fragment (offset=0). The *interfragment state* in the state table is examined to verify that the offset value in the fragment is appropriate and consistent with existing fragments received. *Virtual reassembly* continues until the final segment is received. Upon receipt of the final segment (or a timeout expires), *interfragment state* is "zeroed out," and memory allocated for *interfragment state* is recovered, but the state table remains for the duration of the connection.
- If a conduit or access list exists and the packet indicates any fragment offset *other than* zero, but there is *no* existing entry in the state table for the first fragment (offset=0), *the fragment/packet will be discarded*.

Please note the result indicated by the last point. Although the PIX Firewall will drop packets with fragments that arrive out of sequence, *any* fragmentation is probably rare in today's Internet environment. That opinion is based upon:

- The TCP behavior described above regarding maximum segment size (MSS).
- The increased use of a more recent IP enhancement known as *MTU Discovery*, which is available in some IP implementations. *MTU Discovery* attempts to "probe" the path between source and destination to discover the "maximum transmission unit" (i.e., largest frame size) in order to avoid fragmentation.
- All current LAN and WAN Layer-2 protocols support frames of 1500 bytes or more, with the exception of ATM and some X.25 networks.

Frag Guard is disabled by default. To enable IP Frag Guard, the configuration command **sysopt security fragguard** is used. When enabled Frag Guard applies to all interfaces on the PIX Firewall and cannot be selectively disabled by interface. Various other **sysopt** commands allow a number of system options to be changed, including the TCP MSS. For additional detail, the reader is referred to the appropriate version of the *PIX Firewall Command Reference.*

Special Applications and Protocols

The PIX Firewall supports a number of standard or common applications that require some form of special handling. Some require modification to the information maintained by the ASA state table to work correctly in a stateful packet-filtering environment. Others may require adjustments to one or more of the upper-layer protocol header fields due to modification of IP address by NAT. Another group doesn't follow the expected symmetrical pattern of sender/receiver exchanges that are common. With most applications, the IP packets exchanged between clients and servers have the same source and destination IP addresses and TCP/UDP port numbers, but with the sender and receiver roles reversed in each exchange. These special cases are described in the following sections.

JAVA APPLET BLOCKING

The PIX Firewall allows the network administrator to prevent the downloading of potentially harmful Java applets. The Java filter can be defined by source address of the internal client, destination address of the external server, or both. The command syntax includes a *wild card mask* (similar to the mask used with access lists), which can be used to define an individual address or range of addresses. When Java filtering is enabled, the PIX Firewall searches http packets for the "signature" of a Java applet, the hexadecimal string 0x CAFE BABE.

An example of the configuration command to enable Java filtering is:

```
filter java 80 10.1.1.0 255.255.255 0.0.0.0. 0.0.0.0
```

The interpretation is: When accessing port 80, all clients on subnet 10.1.1.0 (a more-secure interface) will be blocked from downloading Java applets from any hosts (0.0.0.0 0.0.0.0) on a less-secure interface. The 0.0.0.0 0.0.0.0 can also be abbreviated as 0 0.

ACTIVEX

Network security issues with ActiveX are similar to the Java issues. ActiveX controls consist of objects that can be incorporated in a Web page, which are downloaded to the client machine for execution. The ActiveX filter operates by commenting out references to HTML <object> commands. The command syntax is virtually identical to the command for Java except that **filter activex**,,,, replaces **filter java**...

URL FILTERING

Through a partnership with Websense®, Inc., Cisco provides the ability to use the Websense Open Server content-filtering server in conjunction with the PIX Firewall. Websense is used by many organizations to set and enforce Internet Access Policies (IAPs) as an integral part of network security policies. Websense filters Internet content through the use of a master database of over 1.5 million sites, organized in over 60 categories, including MP3, gambling, shopping, adult content, and others. Access can be blocked based upon user, group, or time of day.

URL filtering permits the PIX Firewall to compare the URL requested by outbound users against the IAP defined on the Websense server. The following example filters all outbound access except for users on subnet 10.1.1.0 using a Websense server with an address of 10.2.2.2. The third line is only necessary if exceptions are required; otherwise, it is optional.

```
url-server host 10.2.2.2
filter url http 0 0 0 0
filter url except 10.1.1.0 255.25.255.0
```

THE FIXUP PROTOCOLS

This group of applications requires some additional information or special handling by the state table in order to operate as they are intended. They are enabled in the default configuration, but can be modified or disabled with appropriate configuration commands. The commands, as they appear in the configuration, are shown below, followed by an explanation of their purpose.

```
fixup protocol ftp 21
fixup protocol http 80
fixup protocol smtp 25
fixup protocol h323 1720
fixup protocol rsh 514
fixup protocol rtsp
fixup protocol sip
fixup protocol sqlnet 1521
```

- **fixup protocol ftp** provides for an additional connection in the state table. Most applications use a single, bidirectional, full-duplex connection between a client and server, with the connection request initiated by the client. The client is assigned a random "high" port number (1024 or above) by the local operating system. It sends the connection request to the desired server and indicates the "service" that is desired by specifying the port number for that service. The port number for each different service is usually some *well-known* port number in the range from 1 to 1023. In this example, the client asks for ftp at port 21. At this point, ftp behaves differently than most other applications. The server accepts the connection request but also *initiates* a second connection *to* the client *from port 20.* This is known as *active ftp* or *classic ftp.* An alternative form is available known as *passive ftp or PASV,* in which the client initiates both connections. (Passive ftp was created to work with access lists and older firewalls.) If this was *active ftp* from an internal client to an Internet-based ftp server, this second connection request from the ftp server should fail since PIX Firewall default rule is that *no* connections may be initiated from the less-secure zone. The **fixup** command allows the PIX to make a state table exception so that active ftp is accessible from behind a PIX Firewall.

- **fixup protocol http** — supports URL filtering discussed above.

- **fixup protocol smtp** — enables the Mail Guard that was described earlier.

- **fixup protocol h323** — provides support for the H.323 standard of the International Telecommunication Union (ITU). This set of protocols provides support for a variety of multimedia technologies (i.e., voice and video teleconferencing) including Voice-over-IP (VoIP). These applications have a variety of special needs for call setup and tear down, synchronization and tunneling of multimedia in IP packets. A more complete discussion is beyond the scope of this book.

- **fixup protocol rsh** — provides support for special requirements of Unix remote shell.

- **fixup protocol rtsp** — provides support for the Real Time Streaming Protocol used by RealAudio®, RealNetworks®, RealPlayer®, Quicktime® 4, and Cisco IP/TV®. Multimedia applications typically don't resemble traditional client-server exchanges and the PIX Firewall must be given explicit instructions to deal with the asymmetric exchanges. An illustrative example using RealAudio is provided in a later section of this chapter.

- **fixup protocol sip** — provides support for the Session Initiation Protocol (SIP), and is used by Voice over IP (VoIP). As indicated above, a complete discussion is beyond the scope of this book.

- **fixup protocol sqlnet** — provides support for SQL*Net® (including nonstandard default port number used by SQL*Net).

- **no fixup protocol *protocolname*** — generic form of the command used to disable support for any protocol that is enabled by default.

MULTIMEDIA APPLICATIONS

Multimedia applications, in general, cannot work with most firewalls, unless the firewall vendor offers explicit support for the individual applications, which are sometimes also version-specific. When an internal client initiates a connection to one of these services, there is no simple method to characterize what appropriate replies from the server should look like. In traditional applications, the reply packets sent by an external server bear a strong resemblance to the requests from internal clients, except with IP addresses and port numbers reversed. Other characteristics, such as TCP flags, sequence numbers, acknowledgement numbers, et al., follow a predictable pattern. With multimedia-style applications this is virtually never the case. As an illustrative example, let's look at the traffic between RealPlayer (client) on the organization's network and a RealServer® (server) on the Internet, as shown in Figure 5-5.

Figure 5-5 illustrates two data streams. The TCP connection is initiated by running the RealPlayer application that initiates a connection request to a RealServer *from* the client. In a PIX Firewall environment, this connection would be allowed by default, and the translation table would record the appropriate IP addresses and port numbers. The RealServer response on this connection will be allowed to return through the PIX Firewall, since the response will correspond to the entry in the translation table made when the client request was sent. This TCP connection is used as the "control channel" for communications between the client and server. Once established, the client uses the TCP connection to authenticate to the server, and, during playback, to pass control messages to stop or pause the data stream. RealServer uses this connection to send information to the RealPlayer client about the streamed media, including such things as the name, length, and copyright information of the clip.

However, the UDP data stream carries the audio/video. The RealServer, on the lowest security level interface, initiates it. The UDP stream is addressed

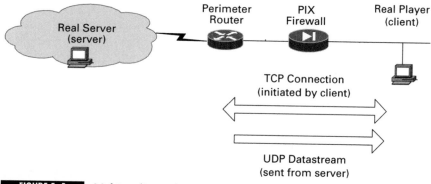

FIGURE 5-5   Multimedia applications with multiple data streams.

to the client IP address, but to a UDP port in the range of 6970 to 7170 (inclusive). Without special instructions, the translation table has no method to correlate the UDP data stream to the established TCP connection, and the UDP data stream will be blocked.

RealNetworks lists the port combinations that are used:

- TCP port for connecting to pre-G2 RealServers
- TCP port 554 and 7070 for connecting to G2 RealServers (two separate TCP connections)
- UDP ports 6970 to 7170, inclusive, for incoming traffic only

A special rule could be added to the PIX that would be applicable if these particular port combinations were observed. Such a rule might read something like this:

> "If a TCP connection is established using port 554 and 7070, then also permit externally initiated UDP packets if the destination port is in the range of 6970 through 7170, and the destination IP address matches the IP address of the (internal client) device that established the TCP connection."

It would not be possible to construct such a rule using any combination of configuration commands. However, it would be fairly simple to encode the rule in the embedded logic of the program or daemon that evaluates packets within the PIX Firewall operating system.

This is essentially what Cisco has done for the following specific applications:

- CUseeMe® (CUseeMe® Networks)
- CUseeMe Pro (CUseeMe Networks)
- MeetingPoint™ (CUseeMe Networks)
- Internet Video Phone (Intel®)
- NetMeeting™ (Microsoft)
- NetShow™ (Microsoft)
- RealAudio (RealNetworks)
- RealVideo (RealNetworks)
- VDOLive™ (VDOnet)
- Internet Phone® (VocalTec®)
- WebTheater® (Vxtreme®)
- StreamWorks (Xing®)

OTHER SPECIAL CASES

PPTP — The PIX Firewall supports the Microsoft PPTP (Point-to-Point-Tunneling-Protocol) to allow remote VPN users to access Windows NT 4.0 servers behind the PIX Firewall. With a PPTP, external users can access internal servers, with the additional level of security provided by VPNs. The PPTP protocol is specific to Microsoft Windows NT 4.0 environments. The PIX Firewall also provides support for two industry-standard VPN technologies: L2TP (Layer 2 Tunneling Protocol, Microsoft's intended replacement for PPTP) and IPSec (the industry standard, Layer 3 protocol suite that provides encryption and authentication services). IPSec and VPNs in general will be covered in later chapters.

NetBIOS Translation Support — Similar to the "fixup" protocols described earlier, NetBIOS has problems when used in conjunction with NAT. Implementation of NetBIOS is not straightforward because of the structure of the NetBIOS header. The NetBIOS header is constructed and applied by the originating device, with a component of the header consisting of the IP address of the originating device. When NAT is applied to the packet, the original IP header is modified to reflect the newly assigned source address. If no other steps are taken, the packet will be forwarded to the Windows NT server. The server will discover that the original IP source address embedded in the NetBIOS header is different from the NAT-assigned source address of the IP packet, and will discard the packet. The PIX support for NetBIOS translation consists of modifying and correcting the NetBIOS header when NAT is applied so that the two address references agree. This functionality is native to the PIX Firewall and no additional action or configuration is required.

Controlling Traffic through the PIX Firewall

In the previous sections, the ASA was described as the fundamental method to evaluate traffic moving through the PIX Firewall from one interface to another. Since the primary purpose of a firewall is to block, or at least control access to the protected networks, we are most interested in *incoming* packets, and defined *incoming* or *inbound* traffic as packets that enter the PIX Firewall from a less-secure interface (more outside; lower security level), and exit through a more-secure interface (more inside; higher security level). We also defined *outgoing* or *outbound* packets as those that enter the PIX Firewall from a more-secure interface (more inside; higher security level) and exit through a less-secure interface (more outside; lower security level).

It was established that the above definition applies to installations that include three or more interfaces, as well. There is only one interface *named* Inside (with security level=100), and one *named* Outside (with security level=0) because these two are always the *most inside* or *most outside* of any of the interfaces. Depending upon their specific security levels, the other DMZ or *perimeter* interfaces may be relatively more inside or more outside compared to other *perimeter* interfaces, but they are always "outside" when compared to the Inside interface and "inside" when compared to the Outside interface.

We will continue to refer to these terms (i.e., incoming, inbound, outgoing, and outbound) when describing traffic flow through the PIX Firewall, and it is, therefore, important to keep the above definitions in mind.

Using those definitions, the PIX Firewall default assumptions are restated as follows:

- Inbound traffic will be blocked by default unless it represents a response to an internal user request, which can be verified by matching the response to an entry in the state table created when the internal user originated the request. Other traffic may be allowed and controlled by configurable exceptions.
- Outbound traffic (connections that originated on a more inside interface with destinations on a more outside interface) will be permitted by default; however, this traffic can be controlled or limited by configurable exceptions.

Controlling Inbound Traffic with Conduits

Earlier in this chapter we referred to a *conduit* as a method to selectively allow inbound traffic that originates on the outside. A conduit is a "static tunnel" that defines the traffic that can be initiated on the outside, using any combination of source and destination addresses, along with upper-layer protocol information. The upper-layer "protocol information" is most commonly TCP or UDP and a specific port number or range of numbers.

There are also a number of applications or services that don't use TCP or UDP (e.g., ICMP, IGRP, OSPF, and others). With these, the "protocol information" will be contained within the first few bytes of the data portion of the IP packet, in the header for the specific protocol. For example, instead of TCP port numbers, we could specify the IMCP message type and code that identify different ICMP messages.

In PIX Firewall versions prior to version 5.2, the command to define the protocol parameters for the permitted traffic was the **conduit** command. The **conduit** command syntax looked very similar to the format used by extended access lists, but with the position of the source and destination inverted in the command syntax. Beginning with version 5.2, the **conduit** command is replaced by a conventional extended access list. For now, both command formats can be used, although Cisco encourages the newer form. However, "conduit" is a more descriptive term, and when used in this book, applies to either command format.

The most common purpose for a conduit is to allow external users to access Web servers, DNS servers, and mail servers located in a DMZ "behind" the PIX firewall, as was illustrated in the three-interface design in Figure 5-2. Since the DMZ or perimeter network is "relatively" inside, we must configure an exception to the PIX default rule that would otherwise block incoming traffic.

To define a conduit for traffic to these servers, we can specify the server's IP address as the destination address, and http, DNS, and SMTP as the destination ports, but we will not usually know the source address and source port. An example access list expression for one server, 10.1.1.1, which hosts all three services would look something like this

```
access-list dmz permit tcp any host 10.1.1.1 eq http
access-list dmz permit tcp any host 10.1.1.1 eq smtp
access-list dmz permit udp any host 10.1.1.1 eq domain
```

The approach illustrated above is probably adequate for the purpose, but opens up a pretty big gap in our security. Since we can't predict in advance what source IP address and source port will be used by an external user, we must permit any source address and source port in our ACL.

What if we had other servers, such as http, ftp, or Telnet, and we wanted to restrict access to individual users? For example, we might need to provide access for senior technical support personnel to access those services from home, using dialup access provided by their local ISP. If that were the case, we have multiple problems.

These users usually receive DHCP-assigned IP addresses, which vary each time they dialup. If we create a conduit to allow them access, the conduit would also permit access to anyone, since the IP addresses for our own external users aren't predictable. Even then, we might prefer to limit access to a specific *user*, instead of a specific *IP address*. Some might argue that the respective hosts provide their own protection by authenticating each user (e.g., username, password), and limiting access through the PIX Firewall is not necessary. On the other hand, some others might question the wisdom of using Telnet or ftp remotely, since login name and passwords are transmitted over the Internet as clear text. Fortunately, Cisco provides another alternative referred to as *cut-through-proxy*.

Cut-Through-Proxy

As discussed in the previous chapter, conventional application gateways or proxy servers provide a very useful access control security function by authenticating users and hiding internal devices and addresses from outside view. However, this protection comes at a cost. Since the proxy function is an application-to-application transfer internal to the proxy, it is resource intensive and limits scalability in large environments. In addition, it is not particularly transparent to the client software, sometimes requiring special client software. At a minimum, it usually requires configuring the client software to recognize and direct its requests to the proxy server.

A cut-through-proxy is fundamentally different. When a user attempts to reach a service protected by cut-through-proxy (only http, ftp, and Telnet are supported), the PIX Firewall intercepts the request and challenges the user for username and password. The PIX Firewall relays the provided username and password to a Cisco Secure Access Control Server (ACS) or other industry-standard RADIUS or TACACS+ server for authentication of the user. Once authenticated (i.e., verified), the ACS responds with the authorization for specific privileges (as defined by the ACS administrator).

Upon receipt of authorization from the ACS, the PIX Firewall "cuts through to transparent mode" (i.e., the PIX Firewall creates an entry in the state table for this new connection), and the connection request is passed on to the appropriate server. All subsequent packets are processed at the Network Layer, without compromising security.

There are a number of interesting points to note in the preceding description:

- No conduit existed, but the ASA created a new entry in the state table for a connection initiated from the outside. This is a *second* way that traffic can be initiated from the outside, and does not rely upon an IP addresses like a conduit does. Instead, the authentication and authorization burden is shifted to the ACS that can provide better granularity, that is, per-user, per-application authentication (see the section below for more details).

- The client addressed the packet to the specific destination host, not the cut-through-proxy on the PIX, making the "proxy" function totally transparent to the client. No special client software and no extra proxy-aware configuration is required.

- Processing of subsequent packets is done at the Network Layer (via the ASA) versus the Application Layer used by conventional proxy servers. This provides high-performance and high-throughput since all subsequent packet "proxying" is performed by fast lookups in the state table, with no resource intensive application-to-application transfer.

- NAT is often used to hide the addresses and identity of internal hosts from outside view.

- Although not stated, two logons may be required of the user. The first challenge is performed by the PIX Firewall, and a second challenge may be required at the individual host (although under some circumstances single-sign-on (SSO) may be possible). With conventional Telnet and ftp client software, user logon is commonly required. Logon requirements for http access are less common, but can be server-configured. Different rules may apply when Web browsers are used for Telnet and ftp access.

In the conventional sense, this isn't really a "proxy," at all. The PIX Firewall uses the ASA, in conjunction with a RADIUS or TACACS+ server to *emulate* the best features of a proxy server, while avoiding the shortcomings.

AAA Support via RADIUS and TACACS+

With a proxy server, conventional username and password logon is commonly used. In addition, "strong authentication" is often available in the form of token cards or other one-time passwords, as were described in Chapter 2.

Likewise, Cisco provides comparable functionality when used in conjunction with the Cisco Secure ACS. The username and password database may be maintained on the ACS, or the ACS may act as a front-end (proxy) to token card servers or other "strong authentication" technologies. The PIX Firewall supports both the RADIUS and TACACS+ protocols to communicate with the Cisco Secure ACS or other RADIUS or TACACS+ servers. The Cisco Secure ACS will be discussed in a later chapter.

FAILOVER

The feature referred to as "failover" provides support for redundant PIX Firewalls. With failover, two identical PIX Firewalls (same model, OS version, RAM memory, and flash memory) may be used in parallel to ensure availability. One unit is designated as the active unit, with the other as the backup. The interfaces on each unit must be connected to the same networks, but with the primary and secondary PIX firewalls having different IP addresses on those networks. The IP address and MAC address of the primary will always be used. In the event of failure, the primary and secondary swap IP addresses to maintain transparency.

Communication between the two units is accomplished by messages exchanged over a *failover cable*, a modified RS232 cable that can operate at 115kb (versions prior to 5.2 are limited to 9600 bps). Other than the redundant PIX Firewalls, this cable is the only hardware required to support failover.

The data exchanges over this link consist of identification of each unit, power status of the other unit, and various status messages that are exchanged. The two units exchange *keepalive* or *hello* messages over this cable (and all interfaces) every 15 seconds by default, but can be configured to any value from three to fifteen seconds.

Upon startup, the configuration of the active (primary) unit is replicated to the standby (secondary) unit. In addition, any configurations made on the active unit will automatically be written to the memory of the backup unit. Changes made on the backup unit are *not* replicated on the active unit. The replication and modifications are memory-to-memory transfers. A **write memory** command on the active unit is required to save the configuration into flash memory on the standby unit.

Basic failover does not maintain the state information between the active and backup unit, but beginning with version 5.0 the PIX Firewall supports an option for *stateful failover*, with initial state table information and changes (except for http) on the active unit automatically copied to the backup unit.

This ensures that existing connections will be maintained during transition from the active unit to the backup unit, upon failure of the active unit. In addition to the failover cable, *stateful failover* requires that a 100 mbps Ethernet connection exists between the units in order to transmit updates of the state information.

Differences exist in the specific procedures used by different versions of the PIX Firewall operating system, and the appropriate PIX Firewall Configuration Guide should be consulted for a more complete description.

Summary

In this chapter we described a wide range of features supported by the PIX Firewall, and introduced the terminology used to describe the operation of these features. The key element of a PIX Firewall, the ASA, was explained, along with its interaction with the NAT function. In the next chapter, we will discuss how to apply some of these features in a basic PIX Firewall configuration.

Configuring the PIX Firewall

In This Chapter

*T*he last chapter described a wide range of features offered by the PIX Firewall, and attempted to explain how those features can be applied to provide a greater degree of network protection. This chapter will focus on the configuration rules and command syntax to apply the feature set to manage, enforce, and monitor an organization's network policy.

Before proceeding, it is important to recognize that installation and configuration of a PIX Firewall requires a complete understanding of the organization's network topology and security policy. There are many details of the configuration that relate to specifics of the network topology, such as the identification of servers and services, IP addressing strategy, routing protocol in use, and others. Likewise, choices will be required that directly relate to the organization's network security policy, and definition of the acceptable behavior that is expected of the users. Network security policies can range from very strict to very permissive depending upon the circumstances, and will vary greatly from one organization to another.

For this and other reasons, most texts on network security begin by emphasizing the necessity of a formal Network Security Policy as a major component of the comprehensive planning stage that *must* precede the installation and configuration of sophisticated tools like the PIX Firewall. The extensive feature set of the PIX Firewall includes features that are required and others that are optional. In many cases, the decision to activate some of the optional features will depend upon the organization's expectations, attitudes, and security goals as defined in their Network Security Policy. Certain features may be crucial for one organization, but may be totally unnecessary for another.

For example, the PIX Firewall begins with a basic premise that internal users are permitted free access to all resources outside the organization's network. While this is the default assumption, the PIX Firewall provides several optional features that can be enabled to limit this access. The outgoing traffic can be filtered by source and/or destination address, and by protocol or application types (e.g., by source and/or destination port number) using access lists. A different feature allows certain outbound access selectively by user, by requiring that each user authenticate at the PIX Firewall before outbound access is permitted (e.g., AAA applied to outbound traffic). Still another feature provides for filtering by destination URL, so that access to individual servers or services can be permitted or denied based upon a specific file or directory. Finally, access can be allowed but monitored by logging inbound or outbound ftp commands entered by users, as well as the URLs they use to access other sites.

In the case of features such as those described above, each organization must decide if any or all of these features are desired or required, in order to meet the organization's policy goals. This further underscores the necessity to have a clearly stated Network Security Policy that will serve a guideline and reference document when choosing various configuration options of the PIX Firewall.

Getting Started

The discussion of configuration that follows assumes that the PIX Firewall has been physically installed and cabled, and has a current operating system. If you are upgrading an existing configuration, see the *Release Notes* and *PIX Firewall Configuration Guide* specific to your version. Recent releases of the PIX Firewall may require changes in the update procedures since the operating system no longer fits on a single floppy disk, as it has in the past. This requires that the new operating system be downloaded from a TFTP server, rather than loading from a floppy. Likewise, some commands have been added or changed in the more recent versions. This book assumes version 5.3, so adjustments may be necessary if you are using another version.

It is also assumed that an appropriate terminal device is attached to the console. For details on configuring Windows workstations using HyperTerminal, see the *PIX Firewall Configuration Guide* for instructions to configure HyperTerminal. Cabling details can also be found in the *Configuration Guide*. A PIX Firewall Setup Wizard is also available, but will not be discussed here.

Provision for Routing

Before we begin the configuration of the PIX Firewall, we need to prepare other network devices that will be impacted by the addition of the PIX Firewall into the network topology. Since the PIX Firewall is *not* a router, some adjustments will be required to any routers and hosts that are on network segments that are directly connected to the PIX Firewall. As indicated in Figure 6-1, the directly connected networks may include the perimeter router, any internal routers, the hosts on perimeter networks (i.e., DMZ hosts), and any internal host devices that are on segment directly connected to the PIX Firewall.

Each of the indicated devices must have "forwarding information," sometimes referred to as "next-hop" information. In the case of hosts, a default router or default gateway is defined as part of the IP addressing information. Hosts that are on network segments directly attached to the PIX Firewall should indicate the PIX as the default gateway. Although the PIX Firewall is not a router, its configuration will include forwarding instructions in the form of static and default routes, and, therefore, can relay packets to a router for further forwarding. In the case of routers connected through the PIX Firewall (e.g., the perimeter router and internal routers), static or default routes will be required to forward packets since the PIX Firewall should not allow routing protocols (e.g., IGRP, OSPF, or EIGRP) to be exchanged through the PIX. Although the PIX Firewall can run RIP version 1.0 or 2.0 in passive mode, this is not commonly done in Cisco environments since use of RIP is relatively uncommon.

The DMZ host(s) and internal host(s) will point to the PIX as their default gateway or default router, as part of the IP address configuration for those hosts. The DMZ host will refer to the IP address of the PIX Firewall's

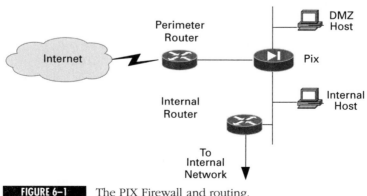

FIGURE 6-1   The PIX Firewall and routing.

DMZ (perimeter) interface, and the internal host will refer to the Inside interface. Refer to IP address configuration details in the documentation for your specific host.

The internal router should have a *default route* specifying the PIX Firewall as the next-hop for unknown destinations not found in the routing table for the internal network. These unknown destinations will include the DMZ and any Internet destinations, since neither will be learned and known to the internal routing protocol. On Cisco routers, the global configuration command to define a default route is in the form:

```
Router(config)# ip route 0.0.0.0 0.0.0.0 a.b.c.d
```

where *a.b.c.d* is the address of the Inside interface on the PIX Firewall.

The perimeter router should have static routes defined specifying the PIX Firewall as the next-hop for internal destinations. Note that in cases where NAT is used, these static routes will specify the *public* (or global) assigned network numbers, rather than the *private* (or *local*) real network numbers. The NAT function will convert the destination address on incoming packets, and forward them to the appropriate *local* network segment. From the public side of the PIX Firewall (the Outside interface), the internal network numbers are hidden, and all references must be to the publicly known or *global* addresses. Once the default routes have been configured, it is a good idea to clear the ARP cache.

Static or default routes must be configured on the PIX Firewall in order to move packets through the appropriate interface and on to the correct destination. From the vantage point of the PIX Firewall, all destinations must be defined in the configuration, except for those network segments that are directly attached to the PIX Firewall. Although details will vary from installation to installation, the considerations may be summarized as follows:

- Networks directly connected to PIX Firewall interfaces — The PIX will discover these networks by examining its own interface addresses. For example, if the interface address is 10.1.1.1/24, the PIX Firewall will conclude that hosts on subnet 10.1.1.0/24 are directly reachable through that interface.
- Internal subnets that are not directly connected — These networks must be defined in static route statements. If private addressing is used (such as 10.0.0.0), the static route to all internal subnets should point to the nearest internal router that will know how to reach all internal subnets.
- External destinations (e.g., the Internet) — a default route pointing to the perimeter router for all unknown or undefined destinations outside the organization's network.

With multiple perimeter interfaces, and/or subnets reachable through routers attached to perimeter interfaces, the steps are less obvious. The important point to remember is that the PIX Firewall must have one unambiguous place to relay packets arriving on any interface, and some combination of static or default routes must be provided for any destinations that are not directly connected to the PIX Firewall's interfaces.

Configuring the PIX Firewall

The command line interface (CLI) of the PIX Firewall is very similar to the CLI interface on Cisco's router products, and uses some of the exact same commands. Other commands that are PIX-specific bear a strong resemblance to router commands. A few are deceptively similar except with the syntax inverted from their router counterparts.

Like the routers, the PIX Firewall has two primary modes: basic user and privileged user, and the PIX CLI prompts follow the same convention as the routers. The privileged used mode is activated with the same **enable** command. Configuration mode is activated with the same **configure terminal** command, after which the prompt changes to "(config)#", preceded by the PIX hostname. For example, if the host name was Pix1, the command line prompt would read:

```
Pix1(config)#
```

Disable, **quit**, and **exit** all work the same as they do on the router IOS. The PIX Firewall shares the older router IOS commands (prior to version 11.0):

- **write terminal** — display the running configuration on the screen.
- **write memory** — save configuration to *flash* memory (not NVRAM). Unlike the routers, both the configuration and operating system are stored in flash memory.
- **write erase** — erase the configuration stored in flash memory.
- **write net** [[*tftpserver_ip*]:[*filename*]] — copy configuration to the named file on the TFTP server at IP address *tftpserver_ip*. If the full path name is specified, only the colon is required.

There are also two additional commands that are PIX Firewall-specific:

- **write floppy** — saves configuration to floppy disk.
- **write standby** — when failover is used, copies the configuration to the standby PIX Firewall; memory-to-memory.

Likewise, there are a set of **configure** commands similar to the router IOS commands:

- **configure terminal** — enter the configuration editing mode from this "terminal."
- **configure memory** — reload configuration from flash, and merge with the running configuration in memory (if any).
- **configure net** [[*tftpserver_ip*]:[*filename*]] — merge the configuration file named *filename* located on a TFTP server at IP address *tftpserver_ip* into the configuration in RAM memory.
- **show config** — display configuration stored in flash memory.

Other commands specific to the PIX Firewall:

- **configure floppy** — copy configuration to RAM from floppy disk.
- **clear configure primary | secondary | all** — **primary** resets the **interface, ip, mtu**, and **route** commands in the configuration held in memory to the default values, and removes interface names. The **secondary** option removes the **aaa-server**, **access-list**, **apply**, **conduit**, **global**, **outbound**, **static**, **telnet**, and **url-server** commands from the configuration in memory. The option **all** combines both the **primary** and **secondary** options. Use the **write erase** command to delete the entire configuration from flash memory.

If the PIX Firewall has not yet been configured, enter the **enable** command. When prompted for the password, press the Enter key. The prompt (Pixfirewall#) will indicate that privileged user mode is active, and the default host name is "Pixfirewall." This behavior is the same as the router IOS. To set a privileged user password, use the command **enable password** *textstring*. Unlike the router IOS, this command will automatically encrypt the password on the PIX Firewall. With the router IOS, this same command is used to set an unencrypted password, and there is a different command (**enable secret** *textstring*) to set an encrypted password. The PIX Firewall provides no option for an unencrypted password.

The PIX Firewall default configuration allows incoming Telnet, and uses a default password of **cisco.** You should promptly change the password using the global configuration command:

```
Pixfirewall(config)# passwd textstring
```

This command also allows access by the PIX Firewall Manager GUI software (which actually uses a Telnet connection). This password is also automatically encrypted. To reset the password back to the default password of "cisco," use the command **clear passwd**.

The above commands provide a working vocabulary for basic housekeeping chores. Additional commands will be introduced later in the material. For a complete listing of all PIX Firewall commands, refer to the *PIX Firewall Configuration Guide* for your specific version.

Identifying the Interfaces

To configure the interfaces on a PIX Firewall, a set of three commands is required for each interface. The first command in the set establishes names and security levels for each of the interfaces. The default configuration provides names for each interface: Inside, Outside, and each perimeter interface. The security level for Inside is 100, the security level for Outside is 0, and any others will have a value in between, that is, 1 to 99. You may change the default names and security levels for perimeter (i.e., DMZ) interfaces, but not Inside or Outside. In older versions, the port or slot position on the PIX Firewall chassis dictated that the first interface must be Outside, the second interface Inside, and so on. Beginning with PIX Firewall version 5.3, any interface may be Outside or Inside, and chassis position of the interface is no longer a determination. Any interface may be Inside, Outside, or any of the perimeter interface names, so long as they are properly identified in the configuration; however, security levels and names are still fixed at 0 and 100 for Outside and Inside, respectively.

The second command in the set defines the interface hardware parameters and speed. Although automatic speed sensing is applicable to some interfaces (e.g., Ethernet at 10 or 100 mbps) Cisco currently recommends that you specify the speed (and duplex, if applicable) for each interface.

The third command in the set establishes the IP address and subnet mask for each specific named interface.

By default, each interface in a PIX Firewall is shut down. After configuring each interface, the **no shutdown** command will be required. A representative example of the applicable set of three configuration statements is as follows:

```
nameif ethernet0 outside security0
nameif ethernet1 inside security100
nameif ethernet2 dmz security50

interface ethernet0 100basetx
interface ethernet1 100basetx
interface ethernet2 100basetx

ip address outside 171.70.1.1 255.255.255.0
ip address inside 10.2.2.1 255.255.255.0
ip address dmz 10.1.1.1 255.255.255.0
```

Note that the Outside interface has a registered IP address (171.70.0.0 is registered to Cisco Systems), while the others use addresses reserved for private internetworks by RFC 1918.

Permitting Access from the Inside

Although reference has been made to a default configuration, it might more properly be described as a configuration "template," since no traffic will flow through the PIX Firewall in any direction until at least a minimal configuration has been created. Since the default configuration provides no IP address on any interface, the PIX Firewall CLI is initially reachable only through a terminal directly connected to the console port. In addition to interface names, security levels, IP addresses, et al., there are other elements required for a functioning PIX Firewall. To allow internal users to establish connections to less secure outside interfaces, NAT must be configured. The configuration of NAT is a two-step process. A **nat** command is required to define the internal user IP addresses that will be allowed to initiate connections, and a companion **global** command is required to define the public, registered IP addresses that will be applied to all packets originating on the private network.

There are several terms that Cisco uses to refer to NAT-oriented addresses:

- *local* — refers to *internal* addresses, often from the address pool reserved for *private* addresses, and used on an organization's internal network.
- *global* — addresses that are registered and unique to the organization. These are the addresses that identify a device visible to the outside, *public* network; the end result of the NAT process.
- *foreign* — these are IP addresses of other organizations, as seen outside on the public network.

We will follow the Cisco convention when discussing these addresses.

The **nat** and **global** statements are a complementary set used to define the *local* addresses to be translated, and the *global* addresses to which they will be translated. NAT is always assumed as a native element of a PIX Firewall. If NAT is not required, the PIX Firewall treats it as a special case, described later.

The basic format of a **nat** statement is as follows:

```
nat(if_name) pool_id local_ip netmask mask
```

where *if_name* is the name of the more secure interface, *pool_id* identifies the NAT "pool," *local_ip* and *netmask* define the internal private IP address, or range of addresses, to be translated.

A **nat** statement is always required to allow connections from a higher security level interface to a lower security level interface. With two-interface configurations this is easy to understand; however, addition of a third interface or more makes the logic less obvious. Figure 6-2 illustrates our example.

In Figure 6-2, NAT will be used to translate the private, local IP addresses from the 10.0.0.0/8 range into global, public addresses in the 171.70.0.0/16 range. (Note: Per the Internet Assigned Numbers Authority

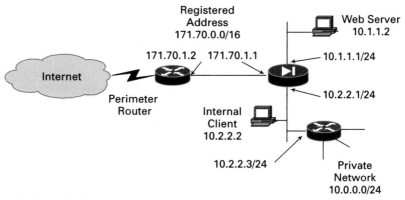

FIGURE 6-2   NAT with the PIX Firewall.

[IANA], the Class B address of 171.70.0.0 is registered to Cisco Systems.) It may be obvious that internal clients need a **nat** statement defining some or all of the 10.0.0.0 addresses that will be translated and assigned addresses in the global range 171.70.0.0, in order to access Internet hosts. What is less obvious is that those same clients will require NAT in order to reach their *own* Web server that *also* has a local address in the 10.0.0.0 range. The **nat** command on the inside interface would be:

```
nat(inside) 1 0.0.0.0 0.0.0.0
```

This can also be abbreviated as:

```
nat(inside) 1 0 0
```

The significance of the NAT pool ID of 1 will be explained below. The reference to 0.0.0.0 0.0.0.0 implies all addresses, and can be abbreviated as 0 0, as shown above. This command syntax presents us with the first of several opportunities we have to limit connections originating on the "inside." In previous discussions, we indicated that all connections from the "inside" would be allowed by default. More correctly, we should have added that all connections *having an address defined in a **nat** statement* would be allowed by default. One method to limit connections originating on the inside is to use the masking in the **nat** statement to exclude certain internal IP addresses. Other methods to control outside access by inside users will be discussed in subsequent sections.

Since we stated that all connections originating on a more secure interface for destinations reached through a less secure interface require a **nat** statement, we also need a **nat** statement for any connections that may originate on the DMZ with destinations on the Internet. Specifically:

```
nat(dmz) 1 0 0
```

The counterpart to the **nat** statement is the **global** statement. As an example:

```
global(outside) 1 171.70.1.11-171.70.1.255 netmask 255.255.255.0
```

There are several items to note in this example command. First, the pool ID correlates to the pool ID used with the NAT statement. If we have multiple individual local address ranges (**nat** statement), we could associate them with individual global pools (**global** statement). For example, if we had two local pools, 10.1.1.0 and 10.2.2.0, and we wanted each to be assigned to their own separate pools, 171.70.1.0 and 171.71.9.0, we can use the pool ID to specify which local addresses are to be translated using which global pool. In many cases this option will not be necessary, since separate pools may not be required. A special case exists for addresses that are already registered addresses, are globally unique, and therefore do not require NAT. The NAT pool ID of 0 (zero) is reserved for this purpose and indicates that no NAT is to be performed. This case will be considered later in this section.

- Define a **nat** statement and range of allowed addresses for each higher security level interface that will initiate connections to a lower security level interface.
- Define a **global** statement and address pool for each lower security level interface to translate addresses originating on a higher security level interface.
- Global address pools defined in a **global** statement must not overlap address pools defined in other **global** statements on other interfaces.

Tying the pieces together, our matched set of **nat** and **global** commands will consist of the following:

```
nat(inside) 1 0 0
nat(dmz) 1 0 0
global(outside) 1 171.70.1.11-171.70.1.255 netmask 255.255.255.0
global(dmz) 1 171.70.2.11-171.70.2.255 netmask 255.255.255.0
```

Although not perfectly obvious from casual observation of the above, we have defined a **nat** and **global** set for each combination of more secure to less secure interface combinations:

- Inside to Outside
- Inside to DMZ
- DMZ to Outside

With multiple perimeter interfaces the configuration logic is even less obvious. It may be easier if you sketch a simple diagram to verify your logic, showing the flow of traffic that is desired, to serve as a double check for your configuration statements.

One result of the configuration rules that seems to create the most confusion is the fact that NAT is performed when connections are initiated from the internal network to devices in the DMZ. It seems unnecessary and even counterintuitive to translate internal client address in order to access a Web server in the DMZ, since both devices have addresses from the same internal private address space. This is a byproduct of the configuration rules and useful if the Web server is ever compromised, since the internal addresses are still hidden, even from the Web server. Similarly, internal users will be assigned a global IP address when accessing the Web server in the DMZ, which is from a different IP address range than those assigned when accessing the Internet. This makes troubleshooting network problems more complicated, since the same "traffic" through the PIX Firewall will have a different source or destination addresses on opposite sides of the NAT function. Diagnosing network problems will require extensive use of the **show xlate** command referred to in the previous chapter, since this is the only place that dynamic address translations are listed. Documentation becomes confusing since the internal devices will have both a real *local* address and an assigned *global* address.

Remember that NAT is *always* performed when connections originate on *any* and *all combinations* of higher security-level (more secure) interfaces with a destination on a lower security-level (less secure) interface.

Also note that we have not yet made any provision for connections originating from the following interface combinations. Based upon the "default rule" discussed in the last chapter for traffic originating on a lower security level interface, these connection combinations will be blocked by default, but can be permitted with configuration statements that will be discussed in the next section.

- Outside to Inside
- Outside to DMZ
- DMZ to Inside

The last item to note regards the use of Port Address Translation (PAT). Since most organizations will not enjoy the luxury of one-to-one mapping of internal addresses to registered, global addresses, PAT may be a necessity. To modify our configuration statements to accommodate PAT, a simple adjustment of the **global** command is all that is necessary. Rather than specify a range of addresses with corresponding mask in the **global** statement, simply specify a single host address, with mask of 255.255.255.255. This informs the PIX Firewall to use PAT rather than NAT. We could add another **global** statement after the first. Our new configuration statements would look like this:

```
nat(inside) 1 0 0
nat(dmz) 1 0 0

global(outside) 1 171.70.1.11-171.70.1.255 netmask 255.255.255.0
global(outside) 1 171.70.1.10 netmask 255.255.255.255

global(dmz) 1 171.70.2.11-171.70.2.255 netmask 255.255.255.0
global(dmz) 1 171.70.2.10 netmask 255.255.255.255
```

For Internet access, the PIX Firewall would first assign dynamic NAT addresses from the 171.70.1.11 to 171.70.1.255 pool. Once those addresses were exhausted, PAT would assign any additional addresses needed, using the address 171.70.1.10 with varying source port numbers. For access from the internal network to the DMZ, the PIX Firewall would first assign dynamic NAT addresses from the 171.70.2.11 to 171.70.2.255 pool. Once those addresses were exhausted, PAT would assign any additional addresses needed, using the address 171.70.2.10 with varying source port numbers. It is important to note that the sequence of the statements is significant.

If we reversed the sequence of the statements, the PIX would use PAT first, then NAT. Since PAT can provide approximately 64,000 addresses, the additional addresses provided by NAT may never be used. It is also critical to verify that various **global** statements do not contain overlapping address ranges.

Establish PIX Firewall Routes

Since we established earlier in this chapter that the PIX Firewall is not a router, it may sound like an oxymoron to refer to "firewall routes." However, since the PIX Firewall sits in the direct path from router-to-router, we are obligated to provide a method to relay packets from router-to-router, host-to-default gateway, and router-to-host, while maintaining some transparency to the routing process. In the first part of this chapter we described setting the default gateway for directly connected hosts to the PIX Firewall for destinations outside the organization's internal network (e.g., the Internet). We now have to instruct the PIX Firewall what to do with those packets it receives.

Any host-like device can relay packets, as long as we provide explicit "forwarding information." The reason for the awkward terminology is simple. The PIX Firewall doesn't participate in the traditional routing process and is relatively transparent. The PIX Firewall does not exchange routing information, doesn't decrement the time-to-live field in the IP header, doesn't perform fragmentation, and often doesn't generate ICMP error messages and other actions that are common with routers. The PIX Firewall is the classic "black box" that operates in "stealth mode," intercepts packets, and decides whether to permit or deny their passage.

For traffic that is to be allowed to pass, the PIX Firewall must imitate some of the router functionality, such as relaying packets that have been permitted. Therefore, we will need to configure some combination of default and/or static routes to instruct the PIX Firewall where to relay the packets it permits to pass.

The first step is to create a default route to the "outside" (e.g., the Internet). The default route is the catchall for all destinations not otherwise specified. Since specific information listing outside networks is not made available to routers "inside" the PIX Firewall, they will have incomplete routing information for unknown destinations. However, the internal routers will have a default route to the PIX Firewall, and the PIX will have a default route to the outside via the perimeter router. From the vantage point of the PIX Firewall, an administrator with knowledge of those "inside" networks may configure static routes for "inside" destinations. In the case of all undefined, unknown locations, the PIX Firewall must have a "router of last resort" (i.e., the default route) to forward packets for unidentified destinations. In most cases, the perimeter router will have either a default route "upstream" to their ISP, or exchange BGP information with upstream neighbors, and have a complete or partial listing of external destinations. In either case, the PIX Firewall relies on the perimeter router as the next-hop for destinations unknown to the PIX.

The PIX command to defined the default route is:

route outside 0 0 *perimeter_router*

where "outside" is the Outside interface on the PIX, 0 0 is "any network," and *perimeter_router* is the IP address of interface on the perimeter router that connects it to the PIX Firewall. This command is very similar to the router command for the default router, except that the interface name (i.e., outside) is a required part of the syntax, and 0 0 is a PIX-specific abbreviation for 0.0.0.0 0.0.0.0 that is used with the router IOS.

In the special case of a two-interface PIX Firewall, a comparable statement can be configured for undefined inside networks. For that special case, the equivalent command is:

route inside 0 0 *internal_router*

where "inside" is the Inside interface on the PIX, *0 0* is "any network," and *internal_router* is the IP address of the interface on an internal router that is directly connected to the PIX Firewall. Used together, these commands may seem ambiguous, since there are conflicting directions to reach unknown destinations. However, it is applicable to two-interface configurations (only), since any packet entering the Outside interface will be directed towards the "inside" and, conversely, packets arriving at the Inside interface will be directed towards the "outside."

For configurations with more than two interfaces, multiple default routes are problematic. For packets entering from a perimeter (DMZ) interface, the PIX Firewall will not know which default route to use, and packets will not be forwarded properly. As a result, only a single default route can be defined for configurations with three or more interfaces.

For multiple (more than two) interface configurations, static route statements can provide the additional detail. In the case of the example in Figure 6-2, a static route statement is not required for the DMZ. Once an IP address is entered for the DMZ interface, the PIX Firewall applies the subnet mask to its own address, determines the subnet number that is connected to that interface, and creates a route entry for that subnet. In Figure 6-2, the address of the DMZ interface is 10.1.1.1 with a mask 255.255.255.0 (/24). The PIX Firewall applies the mask to the address and concludes that it is directly connected to subnet 10.1.1.0/24 through the DMZ interface.

The PIX Firewall will repeat the process for the internal interface and conclude that it is connected to subnet 10.2.2.0/24, but there are other subnets and routers on the internal network. Therefore, we need to supplement the default route and PIX-learned routes with additional information for other subnets of 10.0.0.0/24 attached to unidentified routers on the internal network. In the case of Figure 6-2, we see an internal router that would have knowledge of other unknown subnets of 10.0.0.0/24. With regards to the undefined internal subnets, we can simply forward packets to the internal router, for further forwarding to other routers that may exist. If we can correctly assume that all "hidden" internal subnets are from the 10.0.0.0/8 range, we can configure a static route to them with the following global configuration command:

```
route inside 10.0.0.0 255.0.0.0 10.2.2.3
```

The syntax is interpreted as follows: For destinations where the best match is 10.0.0.0/8, send packet to 10.2.2.3 via the Inside interface. Although we could have listed the internal subnets individually, the above is sufficient for our purposes. The PIX Firewall will attempt to the packet's destination to one of the entries in its table. The best (longest) match will be to match the directly attached subnets 10.1.1.0/24 and 10.2.2.0/24. The next best match would be 10.0.0.0/8 and, ultimately, 0.0.0.0/0; the gateway of last resort is the perimeter router. These configuration statements, like those for **nat** and **global** emphasize the need for careful planning by someone with detailed knowledge of the overall network. Simply memorizing the commands is not sufficient to configure a PIX Firewall. The technician or administrator needs to fully comprehend the flow of packets through the entire network. Planning before configuration and verifying and/or troubleshooting after configuration is the biggest part of the job. Many would say, perhaps correctly, that a PIX Firewall can be "configured" in minutes, but that assumes that the "configuration planning worksheets" are fully filled out. Except for very simple networks, the most understated portions of the task are the preconfiguration and postconfiguration stages. Cisco provides fairly thorough sets of configuration forms in the *PIX Firewall Configuration Guide* that proceed step-by-step through the planning process. It is highly recommended that they be used as a planning tool to ensure a complete and thorough configuration.

Permitting Access from the Outside

Although the fundamental premise of the PIX Firewall is to block access originating from the "outside," there are obvious situations where this is not feasible. In the case of SMTP-based or other mail servers, DNS-based name servers, and public or semipublic Web servers, outside users must be able to initiate connections through the PIX Firewall in order to deliver mail, translate host names or URLs into IP addresses, and access the Web servers.

As indicated in the previous chapter, these connections will be blocked by default, but we can allow selective access through the PIX Firewall, limited to these or other specific devices in several ways. The primary method is via "conduits," and older versions (prior to 5.3) used a **conduit** statement, which defined the parameters of allowable access by any combination of source IP address, destination IP address, TCP/UDP source port, TCP/UDP destination port, or other protocol parameters identifiable in the first few bytes of the data payload of an IP packet (e.g., ICMP header, IPSec header, et al.). Beginning with version PIX Firewall version 5.3, Cisco introduced new command syntax to replace the **conduit** command. The **conduit** command includes many of the same parameters that are used by extended access lists, except with their order inverted. The "new" command syntax uses extended access list statements, in place of **conduit** statements.

Although these statements appear nearly identical to the extended access list statements used on the router line and the configuration commands used on the IOS Firewall, their meaning is different on the PIX Firewall. With routers, these ACL statements are simple stateless packet filters, applied to a specific interface, to analyze packets entering or exiting the router.

On the PIX Firewall, these ACL-like statements effectively create a "template" in the translation/state table. Connections originating on the outside will be allowed if they fit the parameters as defined in the ACL statements, effectively creating a "conduit" to permit *some* connections originating on the "outside." We will continue to refer to this process as a "conduit" due to the term's descriptive value, but will illustrate the newer, preferred ACL command syntax to implement these "conduits."

To allow connections originating on the outside to access the mail server, DNS server, Web server, or other internal hosts, we need to override the default behavior of the PIX Firewall. We do so by defining a conduit, which typically defines the destination address and destination port of the applicable servers. Although other parameters can be defined, we usually can't predict the source IP or source port in advance for many of the common services we want to allow. For example, if we have a public Web server or mail server, the client IP address and source port can't be predicted with any degree of accuracy. Likewise, we want to restrict outside connections to specific servers and services, and, therefore, want to be very specific when defining the destination address and destination port. For each conduit we define, we are creating an opening in the firewall, and need to minimize our exposure to connections that originate on the outside.

Since, in most cases, the server is behind the PIX Firewall, the servers will usually have an address from the internal network number space, and therefore we need to use NAT. In the case of servers and services, the global addresses must be fixed and statically assigned. Since access to these servers will most often be by host name and/or URL, the servers must be listed in the Domain Name Service, to allow lookup of their IP addresses. Since the DNS tables are still based primarily on static text files, dynamic address assignment would require constant modification of those text files, and is not acceptable. We can, however use NAT to assign a permanent, static IP address that would solve the problem. We accomplish the assignment of static global address via NAT with a **static** command.

Like our previous examples of **nat** and **global** statements as a set, we find that conduits and static addresses are also a set. We first define a static command to map a global address to be used in place of the local address, and then define a conduit to reach the global address. Notice that the conduit will refer to the global address since that will be the address visible on the outside. Incoming packets on these conduits will have a destination address of the server's global address, and the NAT function on the PIX Firewall will change the packet's destination address to the real, local address in the translation table.

In the NAT example earlier in this chapter, we reserved some addresses from the dynamic NAT pool for "special purposes." One was used for PAT and the other addresses are available for static assignment to individual hosts, and, hence, unavailable to the dynamic pool. The basic format for the **static** global configuration command is as follows:

```
static(more_secure, less_secure)global_addr local_addr netmask
mask
```

where:

- *more_secure* — name of the higher security level interface.
- *less_secure* — name of the lower security level interface.
- *global_addr* — the NAT-assigned, global IP address; an alias for the device. This address should be on the same subnet as the lower security level interface.
- *local_addr* — the local IP address; the real address of the device.
- *mask* — subnet mask used with both the global and local addresses. In most cases the mask will be 255.255.255.255. Other masks can be used to described *net statics,* which will be discussed later in this section.

Figure 6-3 shows an illustration for the example commands that follow:

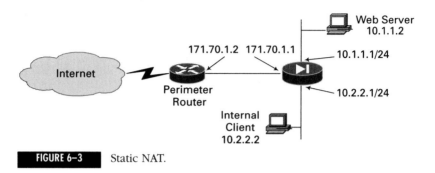

FIGURE 6-3   Static NAT.

The example showing use of **static** command:

```
static(dmz,outside)170.70.1.3 10.1.1.2 netmask 255.255.255.255
```

The Web server has an actual address of 10.1.1.2, but appears to be 170.70.1.3 when viewed from the outside. Incoming packets arriving at the Outside interface will have a destination address of 170.70.1.3 for the server. The NAT function of the xlate table will change the packet's destination address to the actual address and forward it to the Web server. This process is transparent to both the client and server. The client never knows the real address of the server, and the server never even knows it has another "alias" address.

Note that the order of the interface names inside the parentheses is always specified as more secure than less secure, but the addresses are entered as *global address*, then *local address*. This makes the command syntax seem inverted. A common mistake is to assume the order of the names inside the parentheses is the same as the order of the addresses in the rest of the command.

Now that we have an address assigned for outside clients to use, we still need to allow packets through the PIX Firewall to reach the Web server. Previously, the **conduit** command provided this exception handling, but the preferred method is now to use the familiar **access-list** command. For our example shown in Figure 6-3, the statements would look something like this:

```
access-list outside_access permit tcp any host 170.70.1.3 eq http
```

Since access-list statements are rules applied at an interface, we also need an **access-group** statement. The format of PIX Firewall access-group statements is slightly different from router **access-group** statements:

```
access-group acl_name in interface interface_name
```

where:

- *acl_name* — the name of the access list
- **in** — interpreted as "inbound at" or "into"
- **interface** *interface_name* — name of the interface (e.g., inside, outside, dmz, etc.)

The alert reader may notice that the PIX Firewall **access-group** statement is slightly different from the similar router command. On the router, the interface is identified as e0, e1, s0, et al., since router interfaces do not have names. The other subtle difference is in the placement of the **in** parameter, which on the router follows the interface number, and can be applied either **inbound** or **outbound**. The PIX Firewall only uses **in** (i.e., inbound); outbound has no relevance with the PIX Firewall.

Most other characteristics of router access-list also apply on the PIX Firewall:

- The syntax for both allows use of the numeric 0.0.0.0 0.0.0.0 or the word **any** when specifying the source or destination address, although **any** is the preferred.
- A host-specific address may be configured as **host** *a.b.c.d* or the host address followed by a mask, although **host** *a.b.c.d* is preferred.
- There is a presumption that all packets will be denied, unless specifically permitted by an **access-list permit** … . statement.
- Both allow the option to specify mnemonics instead of numbers for TCP/UDP ports, ICMP message types, and codes, et al., although mnemonics are preferred.

However, a more significant and subtler difference was not apparent from our example **access-list** statement above. PIX Firewall command syntax uses a *network mask* not a *wild card mask*. For example, if we wanted to permit all IP packets from any source address, and with a destination of all hosts on subnet 10.1.1.0, the router **access-list** command syntax using a *wild card mask* would be:

```
access-list router_style permit ip any 10.1.1.0 0.0.0.255
```

The equivalent command syntax on a PIX Firewall using a *network mask* is:

```
access-list pix_style permit ip any 10.1.1.0 255.255.255.0
```

In the PIX Firewall syntax we revert back to a "normal" mask format. For those who had difficulty understanding the rationale for the wild card mask used by the router IOS, this may be a welcome relief (although the router IOS still uses wild card masks).

For others, this is simply one more "exception" to remember (or forget). When the command syntax is *almost* identical, there is a much greater likelihood of mistakes in configuring either device. The PIX Firewall CLI won't allow errors in *syntax*, but may allow errors in *logic*: Be on your guard, since simple typographical errors can have significant consequences.

In an earlier paragraph we referred to *net statics*. This term simply describes an option that may be convenient when configuring multiple static addresses. Rather than list each **static** command statement individually, it may be possible to cover multiple static statements with a single statement. For example:

In Figure 6-4, there are three hosts in the DMZ that require static NAT addresses, in order to be accessible from the Internet. The global address pool will consist of 171.70.1.3/24 – 171.70.1.255/24, the subnet number of the network segment connecting the PIX Firewall's Outside interface to the perimeter router. The addresses for the PIX and perimeter router are not included in the pool, but all other addresses are available. We need create a dynamic pool with appropriate **nat** and **global** statements to allow internal users to access the Internet. We will carefully choose the range from 171.70.1.10 – 171.70.1.255 for our global addresses. We still have available the addresses from 171.70.1.3 – 171.70.1.9 for static assignment to the three DMZ hosts, in order to allow Internet access to those hosts.

We could just configure three individual **static** commands to assign addresses to those hosts; however, we notice that the individual host portion of their actual addresses (10.1.1.**3** – 10.1.1.**5**) corresponds to the first three available host addresses in our static pool (171.70.1.**3** – 171.70.1.**5**). This stroke of luck allows us to take advantage of the **netmask** parameter in the **static** command. Using this option to our advantage we can assign **net static** addresses as follows:

```
static(dmz,outside) 171.70.1.0 10.1.1.0 netmask 255.255.255.0
```

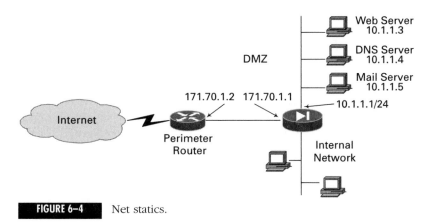

FIGURE 6-4   Net statics.

The effect of the mask is that the host portion of the actual addresses in the DMZ subnet (.3 / .4 / .5) will map onto the equivalent host addresses in the global pool. The global addresses for each will be:

- 10.1.1.3 → 171.70.1.3
- 10.1.1.4 → 171.70.1.4
- 10.1.1.5 → 171.70.1.5

The effect is as if we simply changed the 24-bit network prefix and kept the remaining 8-bit host portion. This simple shortcut avoids the necessity of configuring individual **static** commands for each host. This type of "luck" doesn't happen very often, but it could be *planned*. Some organizations choose their addresses carefully so that the host portion *does* map one-to-one, because it makes correlation of actual-to-translated addressing easier to remember, especially for diagnostics and troubleshooting.

The last item to be discussed relates to circumstances where NAT is not required. If your organization is fortunate enough to have IANA-registered addresses for all of your hosts, NAT is not necessary.

Even when there are not enough for all hosts, an organization may choose to configure registered addresses on certain hosts, with NAT for the others. For example, if an organization has sufficient addresses, they may choose to configure hosts in the DMZ with the globally unique, registered addresses. Under these circumstances, we make some simple adjustments to the **nat** statements, the **static** statements, or both.

To allow users on more secure interfaces to access destinations through less secure interfaces (e.g., Inside to Outside) we use a **nat** command, and specify a NAT pool identifier of 0 (zero). The formal command syntax is:

```
nat(interface_name) 0 [access-list listname]
```

To disable NAT for all inside addresses, use the command *without* the optional [**access-list** *listname*] modifier. For example, to allow internal users (on Inside interface) to access the Internet (via the Outside interface), and NAT disabled for all addresses, the command syntax is simply:

```
nat(inside) 0
```

To selectively disable NAT for individual source and/or destination addresses, use the **nat 0** command *with* the optional [**access-list** *listname*] modifier, where the named access list defines the source and/or destination addresses *exempt* from NAT. If NAT is selectively disabled for certain addresses, conventional NAT must also be configured for the remaining *non-exempt* devices using the **nat** command with a nonzero pool number.

To allow connections from a less secure interface to a more secure interface (e.g., Outside to DMZ) and NAT is not required, we adjust the **static** statement. Rather than specifying the local address and the global address, we will effectively use the local address *as* the global address, since they are one and the same. For Internet access to a Web server on the interface named *dmz* that has an actual IP address of 171.70.44.9, the static command would look like this:

```
static(dmz,outside)171.70.44.9 171.70.44.9 netmask 255.255.255.255
```

This is an otherwise conventional **static** command, except that the local IP address is also the global IP address.

Testing and Remote Administration

ALLOWING PINGS THROUGH THE PIX FIREWALL

Now that we have covered the steps required for a basic configuration, we should configure additional features that will be useful to test and verify the operation of our basic configuration. Although a live network test is more thorough, we should perform at least some preliminary tests of the basic operation of the PIX Firewall. While this preliminary testing is not very comprehensive, it will provide some indication that the PIX Firewall is functional.

The single most common IP troubleshooting tool is the Ping utility included with all IP devices. The limitation of this simple program is that, while it may tell you that something is wrong, it doesn't tell you *what* is wrong, or how to correct the problem. If you can ping another IP device successfully, it is simply verification that you have "IP connectivity" from one device to another, and through all the cables and network devices in between. If pings fail, there is often no indication what failed or where.

In a security environment, Ping may even be less useful, because the failure may be an intentional part of the security configuration. If you try to ping from host to host through the PIX Firewall, the ping will fail unless you have specifically configured the PIX Firewall to pass ICMP Echo Requests and ICMP Echo Replies, the two protocol messages that constitute the Ping utility. This applies to any combination of interfaces, including pings from hosts on the internal network to hosts on the Internet.

Although we have stated that all connections from more secure interfaces to less secure interfaces (e.g., internal network to the Internet) are permitted by default, this general rule does not apply to Ping "connections." The ICMP Echo Requests will be permitted from more secure interfaces to less secure interfaces, but the ICMP Echo Replies will be blocked on the return from less secure to more secure interfaces.

To permit pings through the PIX Firewall, an **access-list** statement must be defined to specifically permit ICMP messages. You will also need an **access-group** statement on each interface that the pings will enter.

If you are getting the impression that this process is burdensome, you are correct. However, it is Cisco's position (and others who are security conscious like this author) that pings through the PIX Firewall should only be activated for troubleshooting, then disabled. There are few good reasons to allow pings to originate on the outside. Allowing pings to originate outside the PIX Firewall gives intruders an opportunity to probe your network. The "righteously paranoid" attitude is that the less information provided to outsiders, the better.

Some would argue that outsiders might need to ping your servers to determine reachability. The "security response" is that the potential risks outweigh the minimal benefits. Since ICMP is ubiquitous on all IP networks, there are a dozen or more network attack methods that use ICMP messages as the carrier, that are very difficult to distinguish from harmless or useful ICMP messages.

The general form of an **access-list** statement to permit pings through the PIX from any interface to any other interface is:

```
access-list listname permit icmp any any
```

An **access-group** statement is required on all lower security interfaces where ICMP messages will enter. Since different **access-group** statements may be required on different interfaces, referring to different access lists, it may be appropriate to include a line similar to the above in each access list defined. Adding and deleting individual lines in different access lists can be accomplished with a small "batch" text file that can be cut and pasted to add and delete a group of statements when needed.

If it is determined that *some* pings are necessary (e.g., Inside to DMZ, Inside to Outside, et al.), the access-list statements can be "tightened" by more precise specification of allowed ICMP messages by type. For example, if pings are desired from Inside to Outside, but not from Outside to Inside, we can more precisely define the allowed message types that will be allowed in from the less secure Outside interface.

```
access-list listname permit icmp any any echo-reply
```

If this access-list statement is bound to the Outside interface by an appropriate access-group statement, ICMP Echo Replies to pings initiated on more secure interfaces would be allowed. Pings originating from the Outside interface (ICMP Echo Requests) would still be blocked.

PINGING THE PIX FIREWALL INTERFACES

When pinging is disabled, the PIX Firewall cannot be detected on the network, and will not respond to pings directed at its interfaces. The **icmp** command introduced with version 5.3 provides this capability, which is referred to as *configurable proxy pinging*.

This command provides for selective ICMP responses based upon source address. To use this feature (i.e., disable pinging) an **access-list** command must be defined to permit or deny traffic that terminates at the PIX Firewall interface(s). Once this step has been accomplished, the **icmp** command must be added to the configuration. The format for the **icmp** command is:

```
icmp permit|deny src_addr mask msg_type interface_name
```

where:

- *src_addr* — IP source address permitted or denied the ability to ping
- *mask* — applied to *src_addr* to specify a host or subnet/network range; when specifying an individual host, another option is to precede *src_addr* with **host** and omit the mask
- *msg_type* — ICMP message type (by number or mnemonic)
- *interface_name* — interface where pings are to be permitted or denied

CONFIGURING REMOTE TELNET ACCESS

As indicated earlier in this chapter, the default configuration contains the default password "cisco" for Telnet access. However, Telnet access is not allowed until permission for Telnet from specific hosts is defined in the configuration. Further, Telnet access is only permitted only from "internal" interfaces (i.e., not from the Outside interface). Since Telnet requires a login name and password that are sent in clear text, Telnet access from the Outside interface is susceptible to eavesdropping.

Since Telnet is considered a nonsecure application, Telnet access from the Outside interface is available only if the connection is secured via an IPSec-encrypted VPN or "tunnel". IPSec will be discussed in a later chapter, and will not be considered here. Once the IPSec tunnel is established, the PIX Firewall configuration statement for access from the Outside interface is similar to access from other interfaces, described below.

To allow Telnet from "internal" interfaces, the configuration must list the host addresses of permitted hosts for each interface from which access is to be permitted. An example statement allowing Telnet access from host 10.20.30.40 via the Inside interface is:

```
telnet 10.20.30.40 255.255.255.255 inside
```

The mask in the **telnet** command may also be used to indicate a network or subnet range, in which case all hosts in that range will be permitted access via Telnet. The changes are very subtle. The comparable statement to include all hosts on the subnet 10.1.1.0/24 through an interface named "research_dept" would be:

```
telnet 10.1.1.0 255.255.255.0 research_dept
```

Notice that the interface name is part of the command syntax, and additional statements would be required to allow Telnet access via any other interfaces. After the IPSec VPN is setup (discussed in a later chapter), access via the Outside interface from host 170.71.6.13 the command would be:

```
telnet 170.71.6.13 255.255.255.255 outside
```

SECURE SHELL (SSH)

As an alternative to Telnet, the PIX Firewall also supports Secure Shell (SSH) version 1.x (not 2.x). SSH is a program that provides remote terminal access, remote command execution, and file transfer over unsecured networks. It provides strong authentication and encrypted communications, and is intended as a replacement for Telnet, rlogin, rsh, and rcp. The basic functionality of SSH provides application-layer encryption for remote terminal access.

The PIX Firewall SSH implementation provides secure (encrypted) remote shell session, without requiring IPSec. The PIX Firewall provides server functionality (only) for up to five simultaneous SSH client sessions. Outgoing SSH connections from the PIX Firewall are not supported. The PIX implementation supports both DES and 3DES encryption, and therefore requires an activation key for DES or 3DES to function.

The command syntax for SSH is similar to the command syntax for Telnet except **ssh** is substituted for **telnet**. Using the first example for the Inside interface from above:

```
ssh 10.20.30.40 255.255.255.255 inside
```

For more information on SSH, see the Secure Shell Community Site at http://www.ssh.org. The site provides information on SSH versions 1.0 and 2.0, FAQs, and links to sites to download both free and commercial versions of SSH.

Controlling Outbound Access

As indicated earlier, the PIX Firewall administrator has the optional ability to limit outbound access. In this context, "outbound" is defined as access from any higher security level interface to any lower security level. Also, as indicated earlier, once the appropriate **nat** and **global** statements have been configured, outbound access is permitted by default.

We have several optional methods to restrict, limit, and/or control outbound access if appropriate for our circumstances and/or required by the organization's Network Security Policy. Some organizations will not choose to enable these optional features at all, while other organizations will use them extensively. The Network Security Policy for each organization will determine the extent to which they are used.

The ability to control outbound access consists of several parts. The first consists of conventional access lists, except with the PIX Firewall-specific syntax for **access-group** statements and network mask rather than a wild card mask.

Except for the syntax changes, these behave like traditional access lists, and, therefore, serve a slightly different purpose than the **access-list** statements applied to inbound connections that we described earlier in this chapter.

Like conventional access lists, those applied to outbound traffic serve the traditional purpose — compare packets to a set of predefined rules that permit or deny traffic based upon any combination of source address, destination, source port, destination port, and other upper-layer specific parameters.

The following chapter on the IOS Firewall will provide a more extensive review of access lists since they make up the major portion of the configuration statements required to configure the IOS Firewall.

Java Applet Filtering

Java, developed by Sun Microsystems, is a programming language similar to C. The special difference with Java is its native ability to create *applets*. When a client or user runs a Java-based program, applets are downloaded for execution on the client or user platform. Downloading of applets serves two purposes. First, the server can support more users and more sophisticated applications, with fewer server resources and less communication bandwidth. Graphics and other compute-intensive applications run on the client host, with each client having their own copy of the application.

If extensive graphics, calculation, or other resource intensive applications run on the client platform, fewer resources (CPU, memory, etc.) are need on the server to support any given number of users. In addition, the applets can take advantage of specific hardware or software that may be available on the client that might not be available on the host. Java applets can be relatively platform independent and still provide comparable functionality across different client platforms that support Java (e.g., Unix, Windows, Macintosh, et al.).

The host application is typically written so that some simple mechanism (e.g., point-and-click) activates the applet download, with minimal effort on the part of the client. A client may even trigger a Java applet download without realizing it.

That is where the risk lies. Hostile applets can easily be written, downloaded to clients, executed locally on the client machine, and perform nearly any function desired by the applet developer. Current Web browsers provide options to block or warn the user that they are about to download a Java applet, but this relies upon user awareness of the potential risk, ability to configure the browser properly, and often, the user's discretion whether to configure the Java-specific features at all.

To provide a security "overlay," the PIX Firewall can monitor the traffic entering the organization's network and recognize the unique Java "signature" in the packet header. The PIX Firewall can't distinguish between good and bad Java applets, but can be configured to permit or deny their entry into the organization's network, based on the server's source address and/or client's destination address.

The format of the Java filtering statement is:

```
filter java port# inside_client_addr addr_mask
outside_server_addr addr_mask,
```

where:

- *port#* — the port number of the outside servers' http service; usually 80
- *# inside_client_addr* — the address of the inside host or range of hosts
- *addr_mask* — mask used to determine whether *inside_client_addr* is a specific host or network range
- *outside_server_addr* — the address of the outside host or range of hosts
- *addr_mask* — mask used to determine whether *outside_server_addr* is a specific host or network range

The example used in the last chapter is repeated here for convenience:

```
filter java 80 10.1.1.0 255.255.255 0.0.0.0. 0.0.0.0
```

The statement is understood to mean: Any packets containing java applets from source port 80 to all clients on subnet 10.1.1.0 (a more secure interface) will be blocked from any hosts (0.0.0.0 0.0.0.0) on a less secure interface. The 0.0.0.0 0.0.0.0 can also be abbreviated as 0 0. This example command statement will block inbound packets (less secure to more secure) that contain a java signature, a source address of any host (0 0), a source port of 80, and destination address of any client devices on network 10.1.1.0.

ACTIVEX FILTERING

In slightly oversimplified terms, ActiveX is Microsoft's answer to Java. ActiveX controls consist of "objects" that can be incorporated in a Web page, and are then downloaded to the client machine for execution. These objects can be forms for gathering or displaying information or other functions. The ActiveX filter operates by commenting out references to HTML <object> commands in the copy of Web pages that the client receives. The command syntax is virtually identical to the command for Java except that **filter activex** replaces **filter java**.

```
filter activex port# inside_client_addr addr_mask
outside_server_addr addr_mask,
```

where:

- *port#* — the port number of the outside servers' http service; usually 80
- *# inside_client_addr* — the address of the inside host or range of hosts
- *addr_mask* — mask used to determine whether *inside_client_addr* is a specific host or network range
- *outside_server_addr* — the address of the outside host or range of hosts
- *addr_mask* — mask used to determine whether *outside_server_addr* is a specific host or network range

URL FILTERING

As was described in the previous chapter, the PIX Firewall can be used in conjunction with a Websense Open server to permit or deny access to specific URLs as defined on the Websense server. The administrator can customize the URL lists provided with the server to conform to the organization's Internet Access Policy (IAP). Version 4.0 of the Websense protocol allows the PIX Firewall to perform authentication based upon username or user group.

The command syntax consists of identifying the Websense server, defining the source address of clients, and/or destination address of the server that the URL represents. The command syntax also includes an **allow** option that may be used. When the optional **allow** parameter is included, the PIX Firewall will allow all access without filtering if the Websense server is unavailable. If the option is not included, all access will be denied for all traffic to destination port 80, until the Websense server is once again available. The basic command syntax is one of two forms:

```
filter url port client_addr mask server_addr mask [allow]
```

where:

- *port* — destination http port ; usually 80
- *client_addr* — the address of the inside host or range of hosts
- *mask* — mask used to determine whether *client-addr* is a specific host or network range
- *server_addr* — the address of the outside host or range of hosts
- *mask* — mask used to determine whether *server_addr* is a specific host or network range
- [**allow**] — option; allow all access if Websense server is unavailable

The other form of the command is to create an exception to a **filter url** statement.

```
filter url except client_addr mask server_addr mask [allow]
```

where:

- **except** — the indicated addresses are an exception to the previous **filter url** statement

- *client_addr* — the address of the inside host or range of hosts
- *mask* — mask used to determine whether *client-addr* is a specific host or network range
- *server_addr* — the address of the outside host or range of hosts
- *mask* — mask used to determine whether *server_addr* is a specific host or network range
- [**allow**] — option; allow all access if Websense server is unavailable

  Using the example from Chapter 5, but adding the **allow** option:

```
url-server host 10.2.2.2
filter url http 0 0 0 0 allow
filter url except 10.1.1.0 255.25.255.0 allow
```

The example defines the Websense server address as 10.2.2.2, and filters all outbound access except for users on subnet 10.1.1.0. If the Websense server is unavailable, allow all http traffic without filtering.

Authentication and Authorization

Another of the methods to control outbound access can be used to more tightly control inbound traffic, as well. The PIX Firewall support for AAA service can be used to authenticate and authorize users for Telnet, ftp, and http, only. It can be applied to inbound connections from external users, outbound connections from internal users, or both. Although the PIX Firewall configuration steps are the same, we will discuss inbound and outbound access separately, since their purposes are slightly different.

Inbound Connections

Occasionally, inbound access is required, but IP addresses do not provide the degree of granularity required to identify specific users from their IP address. AAA may provide a solution. When used in conjunction with an appropriate access control server (ACS), the PIX Firewall uses either the RADIUS or TACACS+ protocols to *authenticate* user credentials with the ACS.

We can require that the user initiating an inbound connection must *logon* at the PIX Firewall, in order to establish the inbound connection. The ACS will look up the user in its database, and will respond with the *authorization* defining access that is permitted for the specific user. The CiscoSecure ACS, along with RADIUS and TACACS+ protocols, with be covered in a later chapter. This chapter will focus on functionality and configuration steps required on the PIX Firewall.

AAA applied to inbound connections requires a preexisting **conduit** or **access-list** statement describing the service or services that will be authenticated (Telnet, ftp, or http). Rather than allowing inbound connections based solely upon source or destination IP address information, the PIX Firewall overlays the address specification with an additional check, the authentication credential. Although the PIX Firewall AAA configuration statements provide the ability to specify the source and/or destination addresses, Cisco recommends that they not be specified, instead letting the ACS server supply the required address parameters as part of the authorization response. The reason is to eliminate possible configuration conflicts between the PIX Firewall and the ACS server's authorization definitions of specific hosts or services that are authorized. The configuration steps of the PIX Firewall consist of defining the following:

- ACS server *group* name and protocol (i.e., RADIUS or TACACS+). Since backup ACS servers may be required for redundancy, multiple servers can be referenced by their group name.
- Identification of the ACS servers (by IP address) that are members of the specified server group
- Definition of the secret key used for encrypted communications between the PIX Firewall and the ACS server
- Definition of the service or services to be authenticated — Telnet, ftp, or http. The command parameter ***any*** implies any combination of the three.

The four steps are illustrated by the following example:

```
aaa-server Inbound_Auth protocol tacacs+
aaa-server Inbound_Auth host 10.1.2.3 sanfran
aaa authentication include any inbound 0 0 0 0 Inbound_Auth
aaa authorization include any inbound 0 0 0 0
```

The first statement creates a server group named Inbound_Auth and specifies that the TACACS+ protocol will be used for communications between the PIX Firewall and any servers in this group.

The second statement identifies host 10.1.2.3 as a member of the group Inbound_Auth, and specifies the encryption keyword "sanfran" will be used to encrypt communications between the PIX and ACS server.

The third statement defines that authentication is required for any of the three services (i.e., Telnet, ftp, and http), from any source address (0 0), to any destination address (0 0), and with authentication to be verified with a server in the group Inbound_Auth. If multiple servers are defined, the PIX Firewall will try each one in the sequence listed in the configuration, until a pass or fail response is received. If no response is received, it will try the next server in the group, and so on.

The fourth statement defines that the ACS will provide authorization for any Telnet, ftp, or http service, with any source or destination address.

We could have been more specific in defining the source and destination IP addresses, but since the ACS server responds with an authorization that *can* include a user-specific or *user group-specific* ACL, defining duplicate logic in the above command syntax is often unnecessary. If the ACS server does provide an ACL name or number, that ACL would also be defined on the PIX Firewall as part of the configuration, but has been omitted from the above description. More details will be provided in the chapter on the CiscoSecure ACS server.

Outbound Connections

AAA can also be applied to outbound connections, as another mechanism to limit outbound access in addition to the NAT and access-list controls, or Java, ActiveX, and URL filtering discussed earlier in this chapter. We can require that outbound users *login* at the PIX Firewall before an outbound connection will be allowed. As with other statements that are ACL-like, we can specify source or destination addresses, but outbound AAA is limited to Telnet, ftp, and http applications, as was the case for inbound AAA.

The command statements are identical to those used for inbound AAA, except **outbound** is substituted for **inbound** in the command syntax. If we used the above example for outbound connections, the statements would look very similar.

```
aaa-server Outbound_Auth protocol tacacs+
aaa-server Outbound_Auth host 10.1.2.3 sanfran
aaa authentication include any outbound 0 0 0 0 Outbound_Auth
aaa authorization include any outbound 0 0 0 0
```

The same servers can be used for both inbound and outbound AAA, but we have created different *group* names for convenience. If we add servers, change servers, or separate inbound and outbound AAA to different servers in the future, we simply need to redefine which servers are in which groups, with the balance of the configuration statements unaffected.

Logging Events

Logging of significant events is a critical element for the administration and management of the organization's network health and network security. The PIX Firewall can log events to a console screen, a Telnet session, or PIX Firewall buffers for troubleshooting and diagnostics. However, due to the time duration, volume, and audit-trail value, most logging will be to a syslog server.

The severity or "significance" of events on the PIX Firewall range from critical to informational and debugging, and are organized by "levels," numbered 0 to 7. The **logging** command defines the level in order to view syslog messages from the console or a terminal during debugging and troubleshooting. Similarly, the logging command is also used to define the level of message sent to a syslog server.

Message Level	Mnemonic	Message Type
0	emergencies	System unstable
1	alerts	Immediate action required
2	critical	Critical condition
3	errors	Error messages
4	warnings	Warning messages
5	notification	Normal, but significant condition
6	informational	Informational messages
7	debugging	Debug messages, plus logging of ftp commands and URLs

The level is set with a parameter in the **logging** command. The number or mnemonic is used to specify logging of messages of the indicated level or lower. For example, the following command sends syslog messages for level 3 and below to local buffers on the PIX Firewall:

```
logging buffered errors
```

or

```
logging buffered 3
```

When messages are sent to buffers, they may be viewed with the **show logging** command. The local buffers are fixed in size, and only limited amount of information can only stored. Once the buffers are full, newer information replaces older information.

To send information to the console, the command is **logging monitor** *level*. To redirect the **logging monitor** *level* output to a terminal device, Telnet into the PIX Firewall then enter the **logging monitor** *level* command followed by the **logging monitor** command. For example, to send all messages of level 7 (debugging) and below to a Telnet connection:

```
logging monitor debugging
terminal monitor
```

Syslog

Most commonly, messages are sent to a syslog server. To direct the messages to a syslog server, the syslog server must be specified, the desired level set with the **logging trap** *level* command, and logging must be enable. To send all message levels to a syslog server at address 10.20.30.40, the configuration commands would be:

```
logging host 10.20.30.40
logging trap 7
logging on
```

The sending device uses a "facility" number to identify the source of the messages sent to the syslog server. The facility number can range from LOCAL0 (16) through LOCAL16 (23). Syslog uses the facility number to identify the device that sent the message. The default facility number for the PIX Firewall is LOCAL4 (20). If that facility is being used by another device, the facility number of the PIX Firewall can be redefined with the **logging facility** command. To redefine the facility number used as an identifier by the PIX Firewall to LOCAL5(21) the configuration command would be:

```
logging facility 21
```

Since syslog is an application that is included on most Unix systems, but is not common on Windows systems, Cisco provides a syslog server application known as the PIX Firewall Syslog Server (PFSS) that runs under Windows NT. This application is available at no cost from the Cisco Web site. Configuration instructions for the PFSS are included in the *PIX Firewall Installation Guide*. For more details, see the *Installation Guide*.

Standby PIX Firewalls with Failover

The PIX Firewall provides redundancy via the *failover* feature. With failover, two identical, units are used; an *active* unit and a *standby* unit. The more recent versions of the PIX Firewall provide the ability for this to be a *hot standby,* with the translation table on the active unit backed up and synchronized with the table on the active unit. In the event of failure of the active unit, the standby unit takes over almost immediately. Since it has a mirrored copy of the translation table, the users are subject to only minimal disruption, although some connection states are not updated and would have to be restarted.

Cisco has made numerous changes in the support for *failover* in the last several releases of the PIX Firewall. As a result, the capabilities and implementation details vary by platform, operating system, and version. The details of various combinations are beyond the scope of this material, and the reader is referred to the appropriate *PIX Firewall Configuration Guide* for further detail.

Summary

In this chapter we discussed the wide range of configuration statements available. Although some detail was omitted, most of the commonest implementations can be accommodated with the range of configuration statements covered. As with many Cisco products, there are more combination and permutations that could exist, but are difficult to generalize. We attempted to show the baseline commands that are required in a simple, minimal configuration, and the purpose and context for the more advanced capabilities.

For the reader attempting to gain basic understanding of the PIX Firewall features and their application, we hope this level of detail has been sufficient.

For those who will perform the actual PIX Firewall, we believe that any additional detail would *still* be insufficient, and probably only cause more confusion. Since no two configurations are ever quite the same, some improvisation is required when applying the PIX Firewall "rules" to an organization's specific environment. We would encourage those readers to read the *PIX Firewall Configuration Guide*, which includes a step-by-step approach to configuring the PIX Firewall, and details on the command syntax. We would encourage those implementing a PIX Firewall to avail themselves of the abundant configuration examples for different feature combinations available on the Cisco Web site.

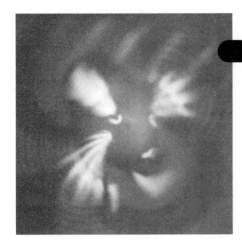

Router-Based Firewalls

In This Chapter

- ◆ Access Lists
- ◆ Cisco Secure Integrated Software
- ◆ Other Considerations
- ◆ Summary

*T*he alternative to a dedicated firewall like the Cisco Secure PIX Firewall is to add appropriate firewall software to an existing router. Although this option is not 100 percent equivalent to a dedicated firewall, router-based firewalls may be appropriate for environments where performance is not an issue.

When we talk about router-based firewalls, we differentiate between stateless packet filters, also known as access lists, and stateful packet filters. Cisco provides a stateful packet filtering firewall that has been known by several names. When initially introduced for some platforms with late versions of IOS version 11.2, it was known as the *Firewall Feature Set*. The Firewall Feature Set is based upon Context-based Access Control (CBAC), and is an implementation of *stateful* packet filtering, which builds upon the grammar and syntax used for the *stateless* access control lists (ACLs). The primary difference is the additional information maintained in a state table, and various **inspect** commands that activate the CBAC functions. This functionality has also been referred to as the *Cisco Secure IOS Firewall*.

More recently, Cisco has included a subset of the intrusion detection capabilities from the Cisco Secure Intrusion Detection System (formerly known as Net Ranger). The resultant product is now known as the *Cisco Secure Integrated Software* (CSIS) and includes both the functionality of the IOS Firewall, as well as limited intrusion detection. This chapter will focus on the firewall functionality, and, hence, we will continue to use the older name, *IOS Firewall* (which uses CBAC) when describing the firewall-specific functionality, despite the fact that the preferred Cisco nomenclature now refers to the product by the broader name, *Cisco Secure Integrated Software* (CSIS).

Since this is a router-based product and builds upon the existing access list commands, we will begin our discussion with a review of access list command syntax and rules.

Access Lists

For filtering IP traffic, Cisco defines two primary types of access lists: standard and extended. Standard access lists allow only the source address (or part of the source address) to be specified when defining the match criterion. Extended access lists allow combinations of source and destination addresses (or partial addresses), along with additional protocol information. The reference to partial match means that we may specify some portion of the address (subnet prefix, et al.) using a *wild card mask*. However, once defined, the match must be exact for every bit of the address we specify. We could specify the subnet portion, ignoring or masking off the host-specific bits in order to indicate all hosts on the specified subnet.

For purpose of discussion in this chapter, we will consider access lists that permit or deny traffic through an interface, although the same access list command syntax has other applications, as well. The access list command syntax is also used in a different, more general context to define the profile of *traffic of interest*. The command syntax is used to define packets that may initiate a dialup connection (dialer lists), filters on routing updates (route lists), and other purposes that will not be discussed here. In later chapters, we will also see the same command syntax used with IPSec to specify which packets are to be encrypted.

Access lists perform a filtering function by specifying which packets will be allowed to pass (permit) or blocked and dropped (deny), at a specific interface.

Standard Access Lists

Standard access lists are numbered in the ranges 1 to 99 or 1300 to 1999. The second range 1300 to 1999 has recently been added to allow for more than the original 99 standard access lists that could be defined. Standard ACLs can also be *named* access lists, as long as the name correlates to a numbered list in the appropriate number range. The numbered or named ACL is created with one or more global configuration statements and applied to an interface with an interface-specific **ip access-group** statement.

All access lists of this filtering type are directional in that they only examine packets that *either* enter the router through a specific interface (inbound), *or* exit the router from a specific interface (outbound), and are *not bidirectional*. Note that the direction is specified relative to the router, rather than to the specific networks attached. This is different than was the case with the PIX Firewall, where inbound and outbound referred to the more protected network. This difference should be noted in order to properly apply access lists via **ip access-group** statements, as well as the **inspect** statements that will be discussed later in this chapter. The format to define a standard access list consists of one or more global configuration statements in the form:

```
access-list list_# {permit|deny}{src_addr mask|any}
```

To apply a list of statements (as a group) specify the following as an interface-specific statement:

```
ip access-group list_# {in|out}
```

As an example of the global configuration statements from above:

```
access-list 10 deny 10.20.30.40 0.0.0.0
access-list 10 permit 10.20.30.0 0.0.0.255
access-list 10 deny any
```

Applied to interface s1

```
ip access-group 10 in
```

The example blocks any packets that contain the specific source address of 10.20.30.40, but will allow packets from any other hosts on the subnet 10.20.30.0. The last statement is optional, since the command syntax assumes that anything not specifically permitted will be blocked by default. The group of statements will examine only packets entering the router (inbound) through interface serial 1.

If we chose to use named access lists for convenience and clarity, the syntax changes only slightly, in that we would need to identify the chosen name as a standard access list. The additional global configuration statement to associate a list name with either a standard or extended access list is:

```
ip access-list {standard|extended} list_name
```

Modifying our previous example to accommodate a named list with the name *mysample*:

```
ip access-list standard mysample
access-list mysample deny 10.20.30.40 0.0.0.0
access-list mysample permit 10.20.30.0 0.0.0.255
access-list mysample deny any
```

Applied to interface s1:

```
ip access-group mysample in
```

Extended Access Lists

Extended access lists are full supersets of standard access lists, in that any standard access list could also be expressed as an extended list, by simply not specifying the destination address. As with standard access lists, they may be named or numbered. The number ranges applicable to extended access lists are 100 to 199 and 2000 to 2699. As with standard access lists the second range 2000 to 2699 allows additional access lists to be defined beyond the original 100.

Extended access lists are generally more useful as security filters since they can be more specific as to the source *and* destination, with the additional benefit of being able to examine protocol-specific values that are either in the IP packet header, and/or within the first few bytes of the data in the IP packet. By looking at the *protocol* field in the IP header, one can determine if the IP packet is carrying data intended for TCP, UDP, or other higher layer protocols. The *protocol* field is sometimes referred to as the *next-header field*, since it carries a numeric value that identifies the next header contained within the first few bytes of the IP data. While the protocol field often indicates TCP or UDP, some services or protocols do not use TCP or UDP, and therefore the *protocol* field indicates those other protocols, as well.

Common examples in this category include most routing protocols (IGRP, OSPF, or EIGRP) and ICMP. Similarly, IPSec includes additional headers that may be inserted between the IP header and any upper layer headers, and hence any IPSec headers are also defined in the *protocol* or *next-header field*. Other valid protocols identifiers could include any integer in the range 0 to 255 representing an IP protocol number.

The command syntax for extended access lists is similar to that for standard access lists, with provision for the additional fields that are included in extended access lists. The basic format for extended access list statements is:

```
access-list list_number {permit|deny} protocol {src_addr
src_mask|any}{operator}{src_operand}{dest_addr dest_mask|any}
{operator dest_operand}
```

where:

- *list_number*— is the number (or name) assigned to the list
- *protocol* — is the protocol identified; generic IP; or, more specifically, TCP, UDP, ICMP, IGMP, IGRP, OSPF, EIGRP, and others
- *src_addr*— the source address to match (or **any** address)
- *src_mask* — the wild card mask identifying the number of source address bits to match
- *operator*— a Boolean expression; e.g., equal to, greater than, less than, not equal to, et al. (optional)
- *src_operand* — used with Boolean expression to define any optional protocol specific parameters
- *dest_addr*— the destination address to match (or **any** address)
- *dest_mask* — the wild card mask identifying the number of destination address bits to match
- *operator*— a Boolean expression; e.g., equal to, greater than, less than, not equal to, et al. (optional)
- *dest_operand* — used with Boolean expression to define any optional protocol specific parameters

When IP is specified as the *protocol*, the Boolean expression (*operator*) and protocol-specific parameters (*operand*) are not used. For other more specific protocol definitions (e.g., TCP, UDP, ICMP, et al.) the *operator* and *operand* are optional but frequently used. When used, the *operand* identifies applications by their TCP/UDP port numbers, ICMP messages by message code, and/or type. Cisco also provides a list of mnemonics or keywords that may be used in place of port numbers, type codes, etc.

Since the optional parameters vary for different protocol definitions and can be very confusing, we have listed the most common combinations below.

IP

```
access-list list-number {permit|deny} ip {src_addr src_mask|any}
{dest_addr dst_mask|any} [log]
```

Only the source address with mask (or **any** address) and/or the destination address with mask (or **any** address) are specified. No protocol specific options are included.

TCP

```
access-list list-number {permit|deny} tc p{src_addr  src_mask |
any} [operator [src_operand]] {dest_addr  dst_mask | any}
[operator [dest_operand]][established][log]
```

The operator parameter is a Boolean operator; e.g., EQ (equal to), GT (greater than), LT (less than), NE (not equal). The *src_operand* is the source port number or mnemonic, and the *dest_operand* is the destination port number or mnemonic. The optional **established** parameter checks for the presence of the ACK bit in the TCP header, indicating an established connection. The optional **log** parameter will log any occurrences that match criteria contained in this statement. In place of the port number, the following mnemonic keywords may be used:

bgp	lpd
chargen	nntp
daytime	pop2
discard	pop3
domain	smtp
echo	sunrpc
finger	syslog
ftp	tacacs-ds
ftp-data	talk
gopher	telnet
hostname	time
irc	uucp
klogin	whois
kshell	www

UDP

```
access-list list-number {permit|deny} udp {src_addr src_mask
|any}[operator[src_operand]]{dest_addr dest_mask
|any}[operator[dest_operand]][log]
```

This is fundamentally the same as the syntax that is used for TCP, except that there is no **established** option, since UDP is connectionless. In place of the port number, the following mnemonic keywords may be used:

biff	rip
bootpc	snmp
bootps	snmptrap
discard	sunrpc
dns	syslog
dnsix	tacacs-ds
echo	talk
mobile-ip	tftp
nameserver	time
netbios-dgm	who
netbios-ns	xdmcp
ntp	

ICMP

```
access-list list-number {permit|deny} icmp src_addr src_mask
dest_addr dest_mask [icmp-type|[[icmp-type icmp-code]|[icmp-
message]][log]
```

This format is similar to TCP and UDP except that in place of an option for source and/or destination ports, we can optionally specify ICMP messages types. In place of ICMP message type number and code number, the following mnemonic keywords may be used:

administratively prohibited	net-tos-unreachable
alternate-address	net-unreachable
conversion-error	network-unknown
dod-host-prohibited	no-room-for-option
dod-net-prohibited	option-missing
echo	packet-too-big
echo-reply	parameter-problem
general-parameter-problem	port-unreachable
host-isolated	precedence-unreachable
host-precedence-unreachable	protocol-unreachable
host-redirect	reassembly-timeout
host-tos-redirect	redirect
host-tos-unreachable	router-advertisement
host-unknown	router-solicitation
host-unreachable	source-quench
information-reply	source-route-failed
information-request	time-exceeded
mask-reply	timestamp-reply
mask-request	timestamp-request
mobile-redirect	traceroute
net-redirect	ttl-exceeded
net-tos-redirect	unreachable

There are several points that should be made here. First, the mask is unlike subnet masks with which the reader may be familiar. Cisco refers to this mask as a *wild card mask,* to differentiate them from subnet masks. Wild card masks are the inverse of subnet masks. For example, when expressed in binary format, 255.255.255.0 is a string of 24 ones followed by 8 zeros.

```
11111111   11111111   11111111   00000000
```

In subnet masks, the presence of a one indicates that the bit position is part of the subnet, while a zero indicates that the bit position in not part of the subnet number and should not be included when matching entries in the routing table.

With wild card masks, the logic is inverted. A zero in the mask indicates "match this bit position," while a one indicates "ignore this bit position" when attempting to match addresses. The wild card mask to match the first 24 bits, while ignoring the remaining 8 bits of an address, would be:

```
00000000   00000000   00000000   11111111
```

When we reexpress the binary as a decimal number, the result is 0.0.0.255.

If we look at other examples, the results become even more unfamiliar. To specify a wild card mask to match the first 12 bits of an address the binary mask becomes:

```
00000000   00001111   11111111   11111111
```

When we restate this binary representation in dotted decimal notation the result is 0.15.255.255.

The second point to be made is that it is not always necessary to specify both a source and destination address. In fact, in many cases where access lists are used to evaluate packets, one or the other will not be predictable. This is where the option **any** comes in handy. While there is a numerical expression that means the same thing (address 0.0.0.0 with wild card mask of 255.255.255.255), it is much simpler and more obvious to use the **any** parameter. In fact, if the numeric format is entered into the configuration, the router will convert it to the keyword **any** when it interprets the command and builds the resulting configuration file.

In addition, there will be cases where a specific IP host address is part of the configuration. The numeric expression to match all 32 bits exactly would carry a wild card mask of 0.0.0.0. For example, if the specific host address 10.20.30.40 (wild card mask of 0.0.0.0) is desired the command syntax indicates that it would be represented numerically as:

```
10.20.30.40 0.0.0.0
```

An alternative is to specify the word **host** in front of the address and drop the 0.0.0.0. mask. The resulting portion of the expression would be:

```
host 10.20.30.40
```

An example illustrates the above points. If we want to allow IP packets from any source address, to the destination address of 10.20.30.40, the access list statement would be:

```
access-list 100 permit ip 0.0.0.0 255.255.255.255 10.20.30.40
0.0.0.0
```

An equivalent expression (and the one written by the router IOS) would be:

```
access-list 100 permit ip any host 10.20.30.40
```

Guidelines for Access Lists

Several additional general rules apply to access lists:

- Top-down processing — access list statements are interpreted in the order that they are listed in the configuration. Once a match is made, no additional statements are evaluated. More specific (longer) matches should be towards the top of the list so that they are evaluated first.
- New statements are always added to the bottom of the list — the IOS command line interface is a single-line editor and hence does not allow for insertion of new lines in a particular position.
- Selective deletion — in general, selective deletion of individual list items is not possible. An exception exists for named access lists. Selective deletion is possible; however, selective insertion is still not possible.
- Editing of access lists — Cisco recommends that access list modification and editing be done off-line with a text editor or word processor of your choice, in order to allow for more flexible editing. If the resulting file is saved as text and located on a TFTP server, the IOS commands can be used to download the partial or complete configuration containing the changes. There are three variations of the command syntax that can be used, depending upon the IOS version being used. The original command **config network** (IOS 10.3 and older) and the newer **copy tftp running-config** (version 11.0 and newer) are probably the two most commonly used.
- The router always inserts a hidden "deny everything else" statement at the end of all configured statements. For extended access lists, this means that that there is an implied statement that is effectively interpreted as **access-list *name* deny ip any any** added to all configured lists. However, to log matches to this statement requires that it be explicitly configured and include the **log** option.
- Access lists have no effect until they are applied to a specific interface with an **ip access-group [in|out]** statement. If not specified, outbound is assumed by default, however it is strongly recommended that **in** or **out** be explicitly stated in order to make the configuration more readable, understandable, and verifiable. Access lists are directional and only evaluate packets flowing in one direction.
- Only one access list of any type, per protocol, per direction can be applied on any interface. A standard and an extended access list are different types and are allowed. An inbound and an outbound access list

are different directions and are allowed. However, two extended IP access lists cannot be applied in the same direction on the same interface. One set of rules per protocol, per type, per direction, per interface is all that is allowed.

- With more sophisticated access lists, the logic can be difficult to verify and test. Access lists are often more a test of one's power of logical reasoning and knowledge of the TCP/IP protocol suite, including the behavior of various applications and services. If one is not thoroughly familiar with the pattern of packets exchanged by different applications, creation of sophisticated access lists will not be possible.

- Stateless packet filters are of limited security value. Since they evaluate packets individually, there are numerous methods that may be used to deceive them. They have no ability to recognize patterns of activity that are often the "signatures" of malicious activity. As a result, stateless packet filters may be appropriate as a first line of defense (such as a perimeter router) but should be backed up by a firewall for more complete protection. When used in this fashion, the combination of router access lists coupled with a firewall can provide a very effective layered defense.

It should be noted that the above section is intended as a review and refresher for those readers familiar with access lists, and a solid introduction for those unacquainted with access lists. The balance of the chapter will focus primarily on the IOS Firewall, which uses the same command syntax, builds upon the same principles, but does so in conjunction with additional Context-based Access Control (CBAC) commands that turn a *stateless* access list into a *stateful* firewall.

We did not attempt to cover all of the options that are available, nor every consideration that should be made when implementing access lists. In addition, there are additional IP access list types that we did not discuss, specifically *dynamic access lists* (also referred to as Lock and Key Security) and *reflexive access lists*. The primary reason for their omission was the fact that these other types were introduced into the router IOS as intermediate steps between conventional access lists and the IOS Firewall, with the firewall providing the highest level of functionality.

If the IOS Firewall (as implemented within the CSIS) is not being implemented, these other access list types may warrant your attention. For further information on these, or more detailed information regarding syntax options, please refer to the appropriate *IOS Configuration Guide* and/or *IOS Command Reference Summary* for your particular version.

Cisco Secure Integrated Software

In Chapter 1 we outlined a variety of network hazards and attacks. The router IOS can provide protection from some of these since the basic router functionality incorporates the following security oriented features:

- Standard and extended access lists — provide basic stateless packet filtering as defined in the beginning of this chapter.
- Dynamic access lists — provide temporary access through router access lists. Dynamic access lists are activated upon authentication of user via user name and password. They dynamically create a temporary **permit** statement as an exception to the existing access list rule set. The temporary entry is deleted after a configurable idle-timeout, or configurable total-elapsed time has been reached.
- Encryption capability — using either proprietary Cisco Encryption Technology (CET) or industry-standard IPSec (to be covered in a subsequent chapter).
- VPN capabilities — using Generic Route Encapsulation (GRE), Layer 2 Forwarding Protocol (L2F), Layer 2 Tunneling Protocol (L2TP) or IPSec (to be covered in a subsequent chapter).
- Network Address Translation — as discussed in an earlier chapter, NAT provides the ability to hide the details of an internal network and, thereby, limit access to or from internal hosts.
- Peer Router Authentication — this functionality is available when using OSPF, EIGRP, or RIPv2, and provides verification of the identity of the peer router for routing information that is received.
- Event Logging — provides logging of "significant" events to the router console, internal buffers or a Syslog server.
- Encrypted passwords are provided for router access using an MD5 keyed-hash.
- AAA — Authentication, authorization, and accounting of administrative access to the router. AAA is also applicable in instances where the router is also acting as network access server.

With the addition of CSIS, the security feature set is greatly expanded to include:

- Context-Based Access Control — The IOS Firewall implements stateful packet filtering with capabilities beyond what is available from stateless access lists. The mechanism used to provide stateful information is referred to as context-based access control.
- Java blocking — provides protection from malicious Java applets (comparable to the protection afforded by the PIX Firewall) as described in Chapter 6.
- Denial of Service Detection and Prevention — provides protection from SYN flooding attacks.

- Audit trail — more comprehensive logging to include time stamps, source, and destination addresses, source, and destination ports and total byte counts.
- Real-time alerts — are generated in the event of denial-of-service attacks or other "suspicious" activity.
- Intrusion detection — including a subset of the full intrusion detection capabilities of the Cisco Secure Intrusion Detection System (CSIDS). CSIS includes 59 of the most common attack "signatures" with reporting/logging to Syslog server or CSIDS Director console.

CSIS, in conjunction with existing router capabilities and other router options (e.g., IPSec), provides a full-featured firewall system, which rivals the features available from dedicated, stand-alone firewall systems, such as the PIX Firewall.

It should be noted that although a router with CSIS approaches the functionality of a PIX Firewall, the performance might be dramatically different. There are two primary reasons for the difference in performance. First, the router has additional routing tasks to perform, which require CPU and memory resources — a PIX Firewall has no such additional duties. In addition, the PIX Firewall hardware and operating system are optimized to provide the highest level of firewall performance, while CSIS is implemented on top of an architecture and operating system that is optimized for routing.

As a result, a router with CSIS is practical only for those environments where high performance and high-throughput are not required. However, CSIS can provide an affordable, full-featured firewall for smaller sites or other situations where a dedicated firewall is not cost-justifiable.

Cisco Secure Integrated Software Architecture

The CSIS is not a mini-PIX Firewall. While it provides nearly all of the features of a PIX Firewall, is does so in a manner that is conceptually similar, but architecturally different from the PIX Firewall. Although the end result is similar, the mechanics of the implementation are different. As a result, the command syntax, nomenclature, and assumptions are borrowed from the router conventions, which are not necessarily the same as those used by the PIX Firewall. This may lead to some confusion when comparing the two, since the same terminology may be used in a slightly different manner.

For example, with the PIX Firewall, the interfaces have a name and a security level that defines their respective roles (i.e., Inside, Outside, more secure, less secure, et al.). As a result, the term "Inside" or "more secure" has special meaning in the PIX environment. Likewise, there is an assumption that connections or "sessions" originating on the Inside interface, with destinations on the Outside interface, will automatically create entries in the state table, regardless of the application. Neither of these assumptions is valid for the IOS Firewall.

With CSIS, the procedure for creation of state table information is known as CBAC and is fundamentally different from the ASA used by the PIX Firewall. To create an entry in the CBAC state table, there must be an **inspect** command applied to *outgoing* sessions (i.e., those originating on the internal network) that creates the entry. Return traffic for these sessions will be evaluated against an *incoming* access list (i.e., an access list that evaluates packets arriving from an external network). If an entry exists in the state table (created by the **inspect** command), a temporary access list statement is placed at the top of the *incoming* access list.

Confused? It may depend upon your perspective. If you are accustomed to the way that this process is implemented by ASA on the PIX Firewall, the CBAC method will probably seem clumsy and counterintuitive. If you are familiar with router access lists, this may not seem so awkward.

To better understand the CBAC procedures and naming conventions, we need to redefine several terms. Figure 7-1 illustrates the basic conventions: In Figure 7-1, we have defined one interface as internal, and the other external. The term *incoming* and *outgoing* refer to the internal network, not any individual interface. When configuring CBAC, we must declare what we want to inspect with appropriate **inspect** commands applied to *outgoing* sessions (i.e., those initiated from the internal network). The inspection rule can be applied to either the e0 or s0 interface.

The inspection rule set will be inbound if applied to e0, or outbound if applied to s0, since outgoing packets will flow into e0 and out of s0 when exiting the internal network. When *outgoing* sessions match an **inspect** criterion that we have defined, this will trigger an entry to be made in the CBAC state table.

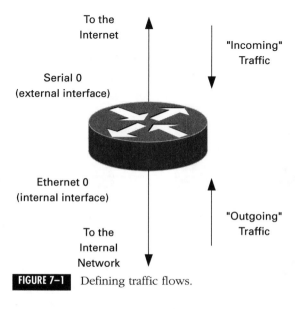

FIGURE 7-1 Defining traffic flows.

We also need to create an *incoming* access list. This access can be configured to block all incoming traffic or permit any selective external access as may be appropriate. This *incoming* access list will evaluate all packets arriving from the external network, and can be applied inbound at s0 or outbound at e0, since packets arriving from the external network will flow into s0 and out of e0 on their way to the internal network. The inspection rule set will create exceptions to this access list for traffic that matches an entry in the state table.

When the return traffic for *outgoing* sessions arrives at the *incoming* access list, the CBAC table will be checked to see if the packets correspond to an existing entry. If they correspond to such an entry, an additional temporary **permit** statement will be added to the *incoming* access list, and the packets will be allowed to pass on to the internal network. Any sessions initiated on the external network will not have an entry in the CBAC table, and will be evaluated against the *incoming* access list as it was configured. In the simplest of cases, all sessions initiated on the external network could be blocked; however, in practical situations some packets will probably be allowed.

Figure 7-2 illustrates the possible combinations for *outgoing* inspection lists and *incoming* access lists.

As can be seen in Figure 7-2, all of these are acceptable combinations. However, some are "better" than others. For a simple two-interface configuration, the first combination on the left might be preferred since 1) both *incoming* access list and *outgoing* inspection list are applied to the same interface, making a slightly more logical appearance, and 2) the *incoming* access list is evaluated before any packets enter the router, providing a slightly more secure approach. If three or more interfaces are involved, other combinations might be preferred, depending upon the logic necessary to achieve the security objectives.

In the simplest cases the *outgoing* inspection lists would inspect all applicable traffic. The corresponding *incoming* access list would deny all traffic, except the returning traffic for sessions that have an entry in the CBAC state table.

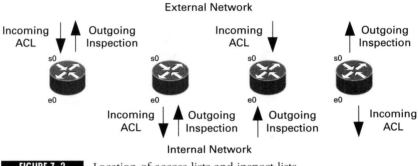

FIGURE 7-2   Location of access lists and inspect lists.

An additional point to remember is that if there are any *outgoing* access lists, they must permit the traffic that will be inspected by the *outgoing* inspection list. Also, be aware that not all applications are supported by CBAC. For applications not covered by CBAC (see details below), a **permit** statement in any *outgoing* access lists and complementary **permit** statement in the *incoming* access lists may be required. (Remember that the source and destination address and ports will be reversed for returning traffic.)

Any permitted *incoming* sessions (i.e., those initiated on the external network) must have a conventional access list **permit** statement, and CBAC does not apply. Similar to conduits and access list statements on the PIX Fire-wall, these result in permanent openings in the organization's security perim-eter and should therefore be as specific as possible to minimize exposure to external threats.

As you can see, implementing a router-based firewall is potentially more complicated than an equivalent PIX Firewall, and may require considerable planning to perfect the logic. Now that we have a fundamental understanding of how CBAC works, and how it is different from conventional access lists and the PIX Firewall, we can discuss some of the features that are provided and applications that are supported by CBAC.

CBAC and Stateful Packet Filtering

In Chapter 4 we introduced the concept of stateful packet filtering as one approach to building a firewall. In Chapter 5, we discussed how this is achieved with the PIX Firewall, using the ASA. In this section we will attempt to point out the similarities and differences with CBAC. Since ASA and CBAC are similar but different processes, one should expect that each approach would result in slightly different features and limitations.

In our earlier discussions of various applications, we noted that some applications are "well-behaved," in that exchanges between client and server, or between two hosts, are often predictable. The source and destinations address and ports are fixed once the session or connection is established. The addresses and port numbers remain constant for the duration of the exchange, except that the source and destinations are reversed in exchanges from client-to-server and server-to-client. In most cases, the server uses a "well-known" port for the majority of common applications, further adding to the predictability. This category of applications is sometimes referred to as *single-channel,* since in most cases there is a single TCP connection, or with UDP-based sessions, a single "connection-equivalent" (i.e., each device uses a single port number).

There are, however, a growing number of applications that use *multiple-channels.* File Transfer Protocol (ftp) is an excellent example, since it uses two connections and two well-known port numbers, port 20 and 21. In classic ftp, the client makes a request to port 21 on an ftp server, and provides two client port numbers. The first port number is the client-end of connection to server port 21(ftp-control). The second port number is provided so that the server can initiate a second connection *from* port 20 (ftp-data) back to a "known" client port. (Note: There is another alternative known as Passive FTP, where the client initiates both connections; one to port 21 and the other to port 20.) In either case, the exchange has a pattern that can easily be recognized when building a state table entry.

A number of other multichannel applications do not exhibit this same degree of predictability and, therefore, special provisions must be made case-by-case. These multichannel applications are essentially unsupportable with conventional access lists, since overly permissive access lists statements would be necessary to cover the range of ports that an individual application might choose. In Chapter 5, we discussed RealNetworks products as an example of a multichannel application, and it is representative of other similar applications.

CBAC shares a similar limitation with the ASA on the PIX Firewall, in that there are a number of applications that require special handling and support. For that reason, Cisco provides a list of supported applications, with the caveat that other applications may not work correctly through the PIX Firewall. Similarly, there is a list of supported applications for the router-based IOS Firewall, as well.

However, the IOS Firewall has some other subtle limitations that the PIX Firewall does not share. When defining applications or protocols to inspect, the choices are limited to generic (single-channel) applications based upon TCP or UDP, and approximately 14 other specific applications. No stateful support is available for ICMP (or any other protocols other than TCP or UDP) and, therefore, ICMP can only be accommodated with stateless access lists. The common Ping utility is a vivid illustration of the consequences. If a user on the internal network needs to ping an address on an external network, two **permit** statements may be required. The first would be required on any *outgoing* access list (if configured) to allow the ICMP Echo Request (or all ICMP messages) to traverse the router to reach the external network. More importantly, a permanent **permit** statement must be configured on the *incoming* access list allowing the ICMP Echo Reply (or all ICMP messages) to get back to the initiator, since CBAC only supports TCP or UDP-based application.

Since it is considered bad security practice to allow all ICMP packets from the outside, care must be taken to specify only the "right" ones (e.g., Echo Replies, MTU Discovery, and possibly a few others). A more complete discussion of the issues with ICMP is beyond the scope of this material.

CBAC Supported Applications

In addition to single-channel TCP and UDP-based applications, the list of supported applications (at the time of this writing) includes, and is limited, to:

- CUseeMe (White Pines version, only)
- ftp
- H.323 (used by many audio/video application, such as NetMeeting and ProShare®)
- http (with Java blocking)
- NetShow (Microsoft)
- The Unix r-commands (rlogin, rexec, and rsh)
- RealAudio
- Real Time Streaming Protocol (RSTP)
- rpc (Sun RPC only)
- SMTP (with functionality comparable to PIX MailGuard)
- SQL*Net
- StreamWorks
- tftp
- VDOLive

Other Restrictions of CBAC

In addition to the restrictions mentioned above, there are a few incidental points that warrant mention.

- CBAC will not inspect packets where an interface on the router/firewall is the source or destination address.
- ICMP Unreachables messages are ignored by CBAC.
- H.323 version 2.0 and RTSP protocol inspection is limited to Cisco IP/TV, RealAudio G2 Player, and Apple® QuickTime 4.
- ftp — CBAC does not support three-way ftp transfers. CBAC will not open the data channel (port 20) if client server authentication fails, and only allows data channel port numbers in the range from 1024 to 65535.
- IPSec — CBAC can only inspect packets where the router/firewall is the endpoint of the encrypted tunnel. If the tunnel endpoint is elsewhere, the protocol ID in the IP header will indicate IPSec (specifically AH or ESP), not TCP or UDP.
- Memory and performance — each connection/session requires approximately 600 bytes of memory, either limiting the number of connections or requiring additional RAM memory on the router/firewall. Depending upon the environment, additional processing required for CBAC may negatively impact router performance.

CSIS — Other Features

Although we have focused upon the stateful packet filtering and firewall capabilities provided by CBAC, the CSIS includes several other significant security features. Like our earlier discussion of the PIX Firewall, denial-of-service protection, Java applet blocking, SMTP protection (like MailGuard), and other features are necessary in a full-featured firewall. While the CSIS does not include every feature included in the PIX Firewall, such as support for URL filtering, it does provide an intrusion detection capability that is not (at the time of this writing) included in the PIX Firewall.

JAVA APPLET BLOCKING

For reasons that were discussed in the PIX Firewall section, it may be desirable to block the downloading of Java applets at the firewall. Although this can also be blocked by proper configuration of client Web browsers, the firewall provides a convenient, central point to enforce the organization's network security policy if desired. Support for Java blocking is comparable to support on the PIX Firewall; however, ActiveX, VB Scripts, and URL Filtering are not currently supported on the CSIS product. For more complete Java content filtering, ActiveX, and/or virus protection, Cisco recommends that an organization consider a dedicated content-filtering product.

SMTP

CSIS incorporates a SMTP protection function comparable to the MailGuard feature discussed in the PIX Firewall section. This feature accepts only the SMTP application commands addressing the problem sometimes found with older versions of the Unix Sendmail application.

DENIAL-OF-SERVICE

In addition to the TCP Intercept feature inherent in the router IOS, the CSIS incorporates its own protection against SYN Flood types of attacks, as well as certain fragmentation attacks. SYN flooding protection consists of configurable thresholds and timeouts to limit the impact of DoS attacks.

The router/firewall compares the rate at which new connection requests arrive and the total number of half-open connections to a configurable threshold. If the router/firewall detects abnormal volumes or rates of arrival, it will revert to one of two (configurable) courses of action.

- Drop old half-open connections to avoid depletion of resources. The system administrator may set threshold levels and timeout values for half-open connections via configuration statements. This method is preferred for lower speed connections (i.e., 128kbps or lower).

- Temporarily block all incoming connection requests sent to a host under attack, which will also protect the router. However, this is often the goal of DoS attacks, and may not be the best course of action. The administrator can configure an automatic timeout period after which new connections can again be sent to the host, or the router may be manually restarted. (This method is better for connections of more than 128 Kbps.)

All TCP connections are monitored to determine if TCP sequence numbers are within reasonable ranges to eliminate the injection of bogus packets. If the sequence numbers are not within a reasonable range, the packets are dropped.

AUDIT TRAILS

CBAC information detail allows enhanced audit trail capabilities, by using Syslog servers to record time stamps, source and destination host addresses, source and destination port numbers, and the total bytes transmitted.

REAL-TIME ALERTS

Real-time alerts and/or syslog messages may be sent to centralized network management platforms upon detection of abnormal or suspicious activity. The default settings provide for alerts to be sent upon DoS attacks, denied Java applets, illegal SMTP commands, and intrusion detection.

INTRUSION DETECTION

The CBAC functionality incorporates a minor degree of intrusion detection, specifically for SMTP-based attacks. In addition, the CSIS incorporates the IOS Firewall Intrusion Detection System, which results in an inline intrusion detection "sensor." The IDS sensor function analyzes packets and sessions passing through the router/firewall, scanning for any one of 59 individual attack "signatures." The 59 signatures were chosen from a larger set supported by the Cisco Secure Intrusion Detection System, and represent the most serious security breaches and/or the most common attack types and information gathering scans. The IOS Firewall IDS can be configured to take the following courses of action, upon intrusion detection (i.e., match an intrusion detection signature):

- Send an alarm to a syslog server or Cisco Secure IDS Director (the central collection platform for the CSIDS)
- Drop the packet
- Reset the TCP connection

AUTHENTICATION PROXY

In conjunction with an appropriate RADIUS or TACACS+ server, the IOS Firewall permits security policies to be set on a per-user basis rather than a one-size-fits-all policy. Access privileges can be tailored per user. This topic will be covered further in a later chapter.

PORT TO APPLICATION MAPPING

The IOS Firewall support for this functionality allows standard applications to be remapped to nonstandard ports, allowing the CBAC function to be tailored to environments that use nonstandard port numbers for otherwise standard applications.

Configuring CBAC

There are several fundamental steps to configuring an IOS Firewall. Some steps may not be required for some implementations, as will be indicated in the discussion of the configuration steps.

CHOOSE THE INTERFACE FOR CBAC INSPECTION

The choice of interface where inspection occurs may depend upon various factors. Cisco defines an internal interface as one that connects to the internal, protected network, and an external interface as one that connects to the external, unprotected network, such as the Internet. In a situation where three or more interfaces may be involved, the concept is similar to the Inside, Outside, and perimeter (or DMZ) interfaces that are defined for the PIX Firewall. We will consider the simpler, two-interface configuration first.

If the router/firewall has only two interfaces, one internal and one external, the choice of which interface to apply CBAC inspection is arbitrary, although common practice suggests that it be placed on the external interface. It is also common practice for the *incoming* access list to be applied there also, so that packets are filtered before reaching the router/firewall. This is illustrated as the first combination in Figure 7-2. If there are any *outgoing* access lists, they could be applied to either the internal or external interface, but care must be taken to ensure that packets that are to be inspected are also permitted by any *outgoing* access list, applied to either interface.

If more than two interfaces are involved, the choice may be influenced by other factors, as is illustrated in Figure 7-3.

In Figure 7-3, we have an *incoming* access list applied to s0 (inbound) and an inspection list applied (inbound) at e0. We also see additional access lists applied to e0 (inbound) and to e1 (inbound). The inspection list at e0 will create state table entries that will create exceptions to the *incoming* access list at s0, and the "other" access list at e1, so that any traffic originating on the internal network will allow returns from either the Internet or the DMZ.

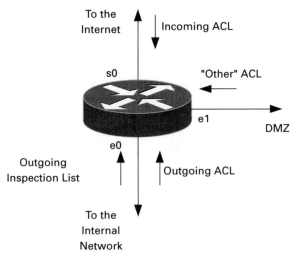

To the
Internet

Incoming ACL

s0

"Other" ACL

e1

DMZ

e0

Outgoing
Inspection List

Outgoing ACL

To the
Internal
Network

FIGURE 7–3   Access list location with multiple interfaces.

The access list applied to e1 could be used to protect the internal network in the event that a DMZ host is compromised, by allowing all return traffic to the Internet, but blocking access to the internal network, initiated from the DMZ. This can easily be accomplished by denying all packets with a destination on the internal network. Any traffic initiated on the internal network will creat an *exception* to any access list applied to e1 (as a result of the ipspect statement), and *allow* returning packets with to destinations on the internal network. As a result, an access list (as described) applied to e1 would prevent only connections or sessions that might be *originated* on the DMZ, destined for the internal network. Notice this is only possible if the inspection takes place on e0, rather than s0, making e0 the appropriate location for the inspection rule for this particular situation. If the inspection rule had been applied at s0 outbound, it would not create the exception need for traffic returning to the internal network from the DMZ.

The *outgoing* access list is shown applied to e0 (inbound) and might be used to verify that all addresses being used by internal devices are authorized addresses (and thereby preventing IP address spoofing by users on the internal network; the "good network citizen" approach) or impose any other restrictions that might be placed upon internal users. If an access list is applied here, remember that it must permit any traffic that will be inspected.

This example illustrates the flexibility of the command syntax; however, one must be fully familiar with its application to use it properly. As is probably evident, it is very easy to misconfigure access lists and/or inspection rules. Careful planning, along with thorough understanding of the environment, is a minimum requirement for success.

CONFIGURING IP ACCESS LISTS

Access lists must be defined and applied to each *applicable* interface, either inbound, outbound, or both, depending upon the result you are trying to achieve. This is probably the most difficult part of the process since it can quickly become complex if multiple interfaces are involved. Additionally, access list construction requires a fairly thorough understanding of TCP, IP, and the various protocols and applications to properly implement the desired level of security. *There is no simple formula.*

Even if you take the approach of blocking all sessions initiated on the "outside," you will discover that this may not be practical. ICMP is one particular example. CBAC does not support ICMP, but there are certain ICMP messages that may be required or desired that come from external networks. Some of the more notable examples are:

- Echo Reply — the response to an Echo Request as part of a Ping initiated on the internal network.
- Time-exceeded — traceroute commands initiated by internal users required these messages to return.
- Packet-too-big — MTU Path Discovery requires that these messages be returned to internal applications.
- Unreachable — various "unreachable" messages can provide valuable diagnostic information to internal users. Variations include Network Unreachable, Host Unreachable, Port Unreachable, and others.
- Other general guidelines as discussed for perimeter routers in Chapter 3 are also applicable on the IOS Firewall (e.g., no directed broadcasts, no packets with reserved addresses as source or destination, etc.).

CONFIGURING GLOBAL TIMEOUTS AND THRESHOLDS

This step is not mandatory, and the default values may be used. The timeouts and thresholds that may be modified consist of the following global configuration commands:

- **ip inspect tcp synch-time** *seconds* — sets the time to wait for a TCP connection to be established before abandoning the connection attempt (default 30 seconds)
- **ip inspect tcp finwait-time** *seconds* — length of time that a TCP connection will be managed after FIN exchange has been detected (default 5 seconds)
- **ip inspect tcp idle-time** *seconds* — length of time a TCP connection will be managed after expiration of TCP idle-timeout (default 3600 seconds; 1 hour)
- **ip inspect udp idle-time** *seconds* — length of time a UDP session will be managed after expiration of UDP idle-timeout (default 30 seconds)
- **ip inspect dns-timeout** *seconds* — length of time a DNS name lookup session will be managed after no activity (default 5 seconds)

- **ip inspect max-incomplete high** *number* — number of existing half-open connections that will cause the router to begin deletion of oldest half-open connections (default is 500 half-open connections; "high-water mark")
- **ip inspect max-incomplete low** *number* — number of existing half-open connections that will cause the firewall to stop deletion of half-open connections (default is 400 half-open connections; "low-water mark")
- **ip inspect one-minute high** *number* — one-minute rate of new connections that will cause the firewall to start deletion of half-open connections (default is 500 half-open connections per minute; "high-water mark")
- **ip inspect one-minute low** *number* — one-minute rate of new connections that will cause the firewall to stop deletion of half-open connections (default is 400 half-open connections per minute; "low-water mark")
- **ip inspect tcp max-incomplete host** *number* **block-time** *minutes* — number of existing half-open connections to the same host that will cause the firewall to start dropping half-open connections to that host. If the *number* is 0, one half-open connection will be dropped for each one new connection request. If the number is nonzero, all half-open connections will be dropped and new connection requests will be refused for the number of minutes indicated by the value in *minutes*. (default is 50 existing half-open connections; 0 minutes).

DEFINE THE INSPECTION RULE

The inspection rule is defined by a *named* list of global configuration **inspect** statements, which lists the applications to be inspected. The rule "set" is then applied by name to a specific interface, indicating outbound or inbound. As with access list statements, *inbound* and *outbound* refer to the individual interface.

The global configuration command syntax for single-channel TCP and UDP-based applications is as follows:

```
ip inspect name list-name tcp [alert {on | off}] [audit-trail {on
| off}] [timeout seconds]

ip inspect name list-name udp [alert {on | off}] [audit-trail {on
| off}] [timeout seconds]
```

Other specific inspect statements exist for the 14 supported applications listed earlier in this chapter. For specific syntax and additional details, see the appropriate *IOS Configuration Guide* or *IOS Command Reference Summary* for your version.

The inspection list is applied to an individual interface with the following interface-specific configuration command:

```
ip inspect list-name {in | out}
```

LOGGING AND AUDIT TRAIL

By activating logging and audit trail, a record can be maintained of access through the firewall, which includes failed attempts along with inbound and outbound services. The following global configuration commands activate and configure logging and audit trails.

- **serviced timestamps log datetime** — adds the date and time to all syslog and audit trail messages (strongly recommend).
- **logging** *host* — identifies the host name or IP address where syslog messages are to be sent.
- **logging facility** *facility-number* — defines the facility number used to identify the source of syslog messages sent.
- **logging facility trap** *level* — limits messages to the severity level specified or higher (i.e., lower number = more severe). The default is set to level 7 (informational).
- **ip inspect audit-trail** — enables CBAC audit trail messages.

Other Considerations

In Chapter 3 we discussed a variety of considerations that consisted primarily of "good practices" and configuration options that should be enabled or disabled to provide a more secure environment. Since the IOS Firewall will most likely act in a dual role as perimeter router and firewall, those considerations are applicable. Rather than repeat the material here, the reader is referred to Chapter 3 for additional information.

Summary

In this chapter we introduced the CSIS and emphasized its primary function as a router-based firewall. As a firewall, its feature set compares favorably with the PIX Firewall; however, the CSIS does not share the same high performance and high-throughput that is characteristic of dedicated platforms such as the PIX Firewall.

Likewise, we attempted to highlight the similarities and differences between the CSIS and the PIX Firewall. As was demonstrated, the configuration process is considerably different between these two functionally similar devices.

We also illustrated that the IOS Firewall incorporated within the CSIS has extremely strong roots in conventional Cisco access lists, and the configuration procedure is, in many ways, comparable to configuring advanced access lists, but with the additional benefit of having more sophisticated stateful inspection or stateful packet filtering as the foundation.

Introduction to Encryption Techniques

*T*he subject of encryption is fundamental to a complete network security strategy. With increased use of public facilities such as the Internet comes a need to guarantee message confidentiality and integrity for many applications. In the past, security was a matter of physically securing the data and limiting access to the data. Where data communications was involved from site to site, the data often traveled over point-to-point dedicated circuits, which afforded a reasonably degree of privacy and integrity since the actual path traveled by the data was fixed and determinable, and relatively secure from casual eavesdropping.

Encryption has primarily been used to prevent the disclosure of confidential information, but can also be used to provide authenticity of the source of the message, verify the integrity of received data, provide the digital equivalent of a handwritten signature, and nonrepudiation. Nonrepudiation assures that a transacting party cannot deny that the transaction took place.

Cryptography is the name for the study of procedures, algorithms, and methods to encode and decode information. *Cryptanalysis* is the study of methods and means to defeat or compromise encryption techniques. *Cryptology* is the study of both of cryptology and cryptanalysis combined, and is derived from the Greek *kryptos logos*, which translates into "hidden word."

Encryption usually requires the use of a hidden transformation that requires a *secret key* to encrypt, as well as to reverse the process or decrypt. With some encryption methods, the same key is used to both encrypt and decrypt the information. This form of encryption is known as *symmetric* encryption, which is also known as *single-key* or *secret-key* encryption. Another form of encryption uses two keys: one key to encrypt and a different key to decrypt. These systems are referred to as *asymmetric* encryption, also referred to as *public-key* encryption, since one of the two keys is publicly known (and the other is kept secret).

Messages or data are referred to as *clear text* or *plain text* before encryption is applied, and *cipher text* to describe text or data that has been encrypted. When the key is used to reverse the process (i.e., transform cipher text back to the original clear text), the decoding process is known as *decryption*.

Symmetric Key Encryption

Symmetric or *secret-key* systems have been around for a very long time. Caesar used one of the earliest known single-key systems when communicating with his generals. The Caesar code used a key of three, that is, each letter in the alphabet was shifted by three positions.

a=d, b=e, c=f, d=g, and so on

With the Caesar code, the word c-a-t would be transformed into f-d-w. For letters at the end of the alphabet, the code would wrap around to the beginning of the alphabet:

s=v, t=w, u=x, v=y, w=z, x=a, y=b, z=c

The Caesar code is easy to "break" since the key is a single digit from 1 to 9. While this code may be confusing, with paper and pencil, a little trial and error and a lot of patience, this code is breakable by mere mortals. Puzzles using a similar "code" are often included as brainteasers in popular magazines.

We could make the process a little more difficult by making the key a two-digit number (e.g., 1 to 99) and successively cycling multiple times through the alphabet, making it approximately 10 times more difficult. A third digit would make it approximately 100 times more difficult, with each additional digit increasing the number of possible combinations by a factor of 10. While this would make it much more difficult to try all the combinations by hand, this is a trivial exercise for a modern computer. The method of attempting all possible combinations is referred to as the *brute force* method. If all possible combinations of the key are attempted, eventually a message that makes sense will appear. We need some method of increasing the complexity beyond what is possible to defeat by use of brute force methods and state-of-the-art computers.

These more complex code systems will require computers to encrypt and decrypt, so we will need a method of describing our code as a mathematical expression. Fortunately, the field of mathematics has such an expression using *modulus* arithmetic. The above Caesar code can be expressed in modulus arithmetic as:

x+3 modulo 26 (where x is the character in plain text, before transform)

The limitation with simple codes like the Caesar code is not only the key length, but also the algorithm it is based upon. There is a higher frequency of occurrence for certain letters in most languages. This fact suggests a shortcut might be found using statistical analysis of individual letter frequencies, so that it might not even be necessary to attempt all possible combinations. What is also need is a method to randomize the distribution, so that these patterns are disguised. Any encryption algorithm that we chose must randomize the data so that the encrypted result (i.e., *ciphertext*) appears random, so that statistical analysis of word and grammar patterns is not possible. When brute force is the only method available to perform *cryptanalysis* (i.e., break the code), the length of the key becomes the critical issue. Key lengths that were once assumed to result in "unbreakable" code may now be considered inadequate.

Data Encryption Standard

The Data Encryption Standard (DES) was formulated by the U.S. Government in the late 1970s, and uses a 56-bit (binary) key. The standard is defined in Federal Information Processing Standard (FIPS) 46.

The clear text is processed in blocks of 64 bits (therefore, DES is considered a block-cipher) and subject to various permutations involving the key. The algorithm used is an improvement of the Lucifer algorithm developed by IBM, with enhancements done by the National Security Agency (NSA) and National Institute of Standards and Technology (NIST). The NIST (formerly known as the National Bureau of Standards) is a division of the U.S. Commerce Department, and is the author of various FIPS publications. NIST issues the standards that are used by all nonmilitary federal agencies, and many private sector organizations choose to follow their lead, as well. NIST declared DES the official standard in early 1977, and it soon became the de facto standard in the private sector, as well.

As has been the practice of NIST, the DES standard is reassessed on a periodic basis. In 1994, NIST recertified DES for an additional five years. The

DES standard has been considered adequate until fairly recently when a collaborative effort, involving numerous machines, proved that brute force attacks can be successful against 56-bit DES, if the attacker can harness sufficient computing power (well within the affordable reach of any sufficiently motivated organization such as a national government).

The "breaking of DES" came as a result of a challenge issued in January of 1997 by RSA® Laboratories that offered a $10,000 reward. The challenge was to discover the 56-bit DES key used to encrypt a message. An independent consultant, Rocke Verser, developed a program that used the brute force method, and made the program available on the Internet, along with a request for volunteers to join in a collaborative effort to discover the secret key. The effort received wide support involving over 70,000 individual machines, with each volunteer assigned a portion of the 2^{56} number range. Over a period of slightly more than three months, the group had searched approximately 25 percent of the possible combinations when they "hit pay dirt." Although this took a relatively long time, with a large number of machines, it did reaffirm the use of modest computing platforms operating in a distributed computing environment to solve large-scale problems.

Bear in mind that this was not a trivial exercise, since even when one combination results in a clear text message from the cipher text, someone or some process must recognize that it is in fact readable clear text, which assumes that 1) the language of the clear text is known and/or 2) the clear text had not been compressed before being encrypted, thereby obscuring the clear text message.

Since DES had been proven to be inadequate for at least some application environments, the NIST began a search for a new standard algorithm to replace the aging DES. The replacement has been named the *Advanced Encryption Standard* (AES), and has been in the works for nearly four years.

Advanced Encryption Standard and Others

The AES standard defined multiple key lengths of 128, 192, and 256 bits, in order to provide some longevity to the standard as computing technologies constantly improve. The NIST criteria had several objectives, including flexibility, ability to implement in hardware and software, and various other factors. They invited proposals and went through a series of evaluations of the various proposals before deciding upon one.

In late 2000, the NIST tentatively selected the Rijndael (pronounced like rine doll) algorithm as the basis for the new standard that should be ratified sometime in 2001. Until the AES standard is finalized, DES continues to be adequate for many applications. Where there is concern regarding the strength of DES, triple-DES (3DES) is a more than adequate substitute, in that 3DES is significantly stronger. (Cisco currently supports both DES and 3DES and will likely support AES once the standard has been ratified).

Although "triple" sounds like it is three times stronger, it is many orders of magnitude stronger. With 3DES, data is encrypted three times, with a 56-bit key applied each time, for an effective key length of 168 bits. The total number of combinations with 56-bit DES is 2^{56}, while 3DES increases the total number of combinations to 2^{168}. This indicates that 3DES is 2^{112} times (168-56=112) stronger than DES, and is considered "unbreakable."

A footnote is in order when we use the term "unbreakable." Mathematicians consider an encryption algorithm unbreakable when there is "no known method other than brute force," and the brute force method is not feasible with known computer technologies. There is always a caveat that unpublished methods that are unknown in the academic community, could be theoretically possible. (Note: The U.S. National Security Agency [NSA] may be the world's foremost authority on encryption, but obviously do not publish all of their research.)

Bear in mind that this does not mean that 3DES is always warranted. The computing power necessary to perform encryption and decryption is always significant. With 3DES, the computational power required is approximately three times that required by DES. For many applications it is not always necessary that encryption be unbreakable, only that it be infeasible. Infeasibility implies that the time and/or effort to apply brute force to break the code exceeds the timeliness or value of the information. Even if it only took one day (24 hours) to brute force a 56-bit key, if the key were changed once per hour, the decoding process would always be behind, since the 24 keys used during any one day would take 24 days to break. If the value of intercepting the data decreases over time, the information may be "secure enough." Common symmetric encryption methods and their key lengths are:

- DES — 56 bit
- IDEA — 128 bit; the International Data Encryption algorithm, developed by Lai and Massey of the Swiss Federal Institute of Technology. This encryption algorithm is included in PGP (Pretty Good Privacy), and has therefore been widely distributed.
- 3DES — 168 bit
- AES — 128/192/256 bit

In Chapter 7 of *Applied Cryptography* by Bruce Schneier (2nd edition, John Wiley & Sons, Inc., 1996), the author provides a thorough discussion of the computational effort required to perform a brute force attack on various key lengths, along with estimates of equipment cost. The author also provides a very comprehensive view of various other encryption methods and algorithms that are beyond the scope of this book.

DES and the other encryption methods listed above are described as *block-ciphers*, meaning that the clear text data (transformed into binary format) is encrypted in blocks of a given length (commonly 64 bit blocks) and produces a cipher text message of approximately the same length. Another excellent text that describes the detailed internals and mathematical foundation of various encryption methods is *Cryptography and Network Security* by William Stallings (2nd edition, Prentice Hall, 1999). The interested reader is referred to either or both of these texts for a very thorough, detailed discussion of encryption techniques, algorithms, and methods.

Key Management

One of the drawbacks with symmetric encryption is key distribution and management. For each pair of encrypting devices, a separate key should be used. If a given device has many encryption partners, distribution of the keys becomes logistically inconvenient. For each pair of devices, a key must be generated then transported via some secure means to each device. Even if one device generates the key, the problem remains of delivering or communicating the key to the companion device via special courier or other secure transport method. When large numbers of devices are involved, this burden becomes unwieldy very quickly. Consider the case where it might be desirable to encrypt email to multiple parties or casual parties on a one-time basis, but key distribution must be performed first.

The Kerberos protocol partially solves this problem by using the concept of a key distribution center (KDC), but Kerberos is more appropriately used for a distributed computing environment that has a central management. Kerberos is also notorious for the administrative effort required to manage and maintain the environment. A complete discussion of Kerberos is beyond the scope of this material, and will not be presented here.

Fortunately, there is another solution to the key distribution dilemma in the form of asymmetric encryption, as will be explained below.

Asymmetric Key Encryption

As described above, asymmetric encryption involves a two-key set. Data encrypted with one key can only be decrypted with the other in the set. This type of encryption is often described as *public-key* encryption, to emphasize that one of the keys is made publicly available. Even though the other remains secret, this fact should not be confused with the single secret key that is used in symmetric encryption, which we have also referred to as *secret-key* encryption, since the single key is always kept secret. When describing the undisclosed, nonpublic key used with public-key systems, we will refer to it as the *private* key to differentiate from the *secret* key associated with symmetric encryption.

The asymmetric method of encryption has only been around for a short time, when compared to classical symmetric encryption that predates the Romans. Public-key encryption was "discovered" by mathematicians Whitfield

Diffie and Martin Hellman of Stanford University, and described in a paper they published in 1976. It evolved as a direct result of work done in search of a better method to manage key distribution for classic secret key environments. The result of that research is covered in more detail below.

The primary difference between asymmetric (public key) and symmetric (secret key) encryption is that public-key encryption is based upon mathematical functions. By contrast symmetric encryption relies upon clever rearrangement of the bits through successive substitutions and permutations. In layman's terms — the bits are "scrambled." The fact that two keys, one public and one private, are used allows public-key encryption to be applied in creative ways to provide additional functionality beyond the fundamental confidentiality associated with encryption.

Various forms of *asymmetric* or *public-key* encryption exist that serve different purposes, including the Diffie-Hellman method, named after the creators, and the RSA method, named after mathematicians Ron Rivest, Adir Shamir and Leonard Adelman of MIT.

The two keys are used in different ways to achieve different purposes. Used in one fashion, they can provide confidentiality, and in another can provide authentication of the sender. A by-product of public key systems can also be nonrepudiation, by proving that one party *did* send a communication even though they may claim that they did not.

In a public-key system, each individual party generates two related keys: a *private key* and a *public key*. They keep the private key secret, but publish or otherwise make the public key readily available to anyone who needs it. This eliminates one of the shortcomings of symmetric key systems, namely that of secure key distribution. The individual public keys can be obtained by anyone who has a need for them from a conveniently located (public) server, eliminating the necessity for a secure means to deliver the keys, and without compromising the private key in any way. Although the public and private keys are mathematically related, it is not possible to determine one key of the set from knowledge of the other key.

The administrative burden to establish and maintain public key distribution is minimal when compared to the comparable process for symmetric key methods, especially the KDCs used by Kerberos. Further, the function can be distributed across multiple servers, if desired. There is also no requirement to send the public key any individual encryption partner; instead, the partner can the key from a server on an as-needed basis.

How Public-Key Encryption Works

Public-Key encryption proves a number of capabilities, depending upon how it is applied. The major features that are most commonly sought are discussed in the sections that follow.

CONFIDENTIALITY

The relationship between the two keys (private and public) is that whatever is encrypted by one key can only be decrypted by the other key of the set. To illustrate their use to provide confidentiality or authenticity or both, consider the following case.

Alice and Bob each generate a set of keys. Alice generates keys A_{Public} and $A_{Private}$, while Bob generates B_{Public} and $B_{Private}$. Each party keeps their private key, and they exchange their public keys. The only requirement for exchange of public keys is that each party be assured that the public key they receive is, in fact, the true public key of the other party (more on this aspect later).

The end result is that Alice now possesses $A_{private}$ and B_{public}, while Bob has $B_{private}$ and A_{public}. If Alice wants to send a confidential message to Bob, she will use Bob's public key, B_{public}, to encrypt the message and send it to Bob. Since only Bob has the companion private key, $B_{private}$, only he will be able to successfully decrypt the message. This solves the problem of confidentiality between these two parties, without requiring that they share a common key, and is illustrated in Figure 8-1.

However, if we add a third-party, Carol, things get a little more complicated. Carol generates her own set of keys, $C_{private}$ and C_{public}, and each of the three parties receives the appropriate public keys from the other parties. Each party will now have the following keys:

- Alice $A_{private}$, B_{public}, C_{public}
- Bob $B_{private}$, A_{public}, C_{public}
- Carol $C_{private}$, A_{public}, B_{public}

FIGURE 8–1   Public key exchange.

Using the same scenario described earlier, Alice sends a confidential message to Bob encrypted with Bob's public key, B_{public}. Only Bob will be able to decrypt the message, since he has the complementary private key, $B_{private}$. Carol will still be unable to decrypt the message since she has the same key (B_{public}) that was used to encrypt, and only the companion key ($B_{private}$) can be used to decrypt the message.

Bob now has a confidential message that he is able to decrypt, claiming to be from Alice; *however,* Carol could also have created the message, pretending to be Alice, since she also has Bob's public key, B_{public}. Although we have solved the confidentiality problem, we now have an authenticity problem, since anyone with Bob's public key could have generated the message.

Before we solve this particular problem, let's see how public-key systems might be used alternatively to provide authenticity, alone.

AUTHENTICITY

If the communication from Alice to Bob did not require confidentiality, but did require that Bob be assured the message genuinely came from Alice, we can alter the scenario slightly. Alice would now encrypt the message with her *own private* key, $A_{private}$. Anyone who possesses Alice's public key (including Bob) can decrypt and read the message, but Bob (and any others) would know that *only* Alice could have sent the message, since only Alice has the appropriate companion private key. We have now solved the authenticity problem, but we still have not solved the confidentiality problem, since anyone with Alice's public key can decrypt the message she sent encrypted with her private key.

COMBINING CONFIDENTIALITY AND AUTHENTICITY

The challenge is to simultaneously provide confidentiality and authenticity. A little bit of creativity, patience, and logic provides us with an answer.

For Alice to send a confidential message to Bob and provide assurance that the message really came from Alice, we apply a double encryption.

Alice encrypts the message by first using her private key, then encrypts the result using Bob's public key. No matter who receives this double encrypted message, only Bob can decrypt the contents.

To make this procedure easier to understand, think of an envelope inside of an envelope. The inner envelope is the message encrypted with Alice's private key. This inner envelope is then encrypted using Bob's public key, B_{public}, creating the outer envelope.

Only Bob can "open" the outer envelope since only he has the companion key, $B_{private}$, Bob's private key. Any others who may intercept the message will be unable to open the outer envelope, since they could only have Bob's public key, B_{public}, which was used to encrypt the message, and, therefore, cannot also be used to decrypt the same message. As stated earlier, anything encrypted with one key can *only* be decrypted with the other from that public/private "set." Public-key methods never allow the same key to be used for both encryption and decryption.

Bob now has received a confidential message, but the contents and authenticity are not yet determined. If Bob now applies the second stage of decryption to the "inner" envelope, using Alice's public key, he can read the message. If he can successfully decrypt the inner envelope using Alice's public key, he also knows that only Alice could have generated the message with her own private key, providing the authentication of the sender.

In addition, Alice cannot deny sending the message since only Alice could have encrypted the message with her own secret key, $A_{private}$, which also provides nonrepudiation. This procedure could be generalized by rephrasing the steps:

- First, encrypt the message with your *own private* key, providing the authentication and nonrepudiation since only you possess your secret key.
- Second, encrypt the message using the *public key of the recipient* since only the recipient will be able to decrypt the received message, providing confidentiality.
- Send the message.
- The recipient (only) can decrypt the received message with his or her *own private key*, maintaining confidentiality.
- The recipient can then decrypt the contents using the *sender's public key*, verifying the origin of the message.
- If either party doesn't have the other's public key, it must be obtained before the procedure can be completed.

HASHES AND MESSAGE DIGESTS

Although the procedure outlined above would work in theory, in practice a modified approach is used. As described, the procedure consists of two encryptions and two decryptions of the entire message. Since encryption, especially using asymmetric methods, is a very compute-intensive process to begin with, it would be desirable to reduce the volume of data that needs to be encrypted. Compression of the data before encryption would be one means, although it not often used. A simpler process could be achieved through the use of an algorithm known as a *one-way hash* or *message digest*.

A message digest is a short, unique representation of your message; a fingerprint. A message digest (sometimes also referred to as a one-way hash or cryptographic checksum) does not, by itself, require an encryption key. Instead, it is a computation or formula performed on the message, treating the message as a long string of bits representing a very large binary number. The resulting output is a *digest* of a predictable fixed length. The important characteristic of a one-way hash or message digest function is that each message produces its own unique digest.

The digest may be transmitted along with the message as an integrity check or error detection mechanism. However, if the message is intercepted and intentionally altered, a new digest could be computed and delivered with the message. To provide the authentication function and integrity check on the message, the *digest* may be encrypted using the sender's private key. This digest is calculated before any encryption is applied to the message.

Rather than encrypting the entire message twice, only the message digest needs to be encrypted to provide authentication of the sender, reducing the computational requirements. This encrypted message digest is described as a *digital signature*.

(Note: A similar process will be introduced in a later section, in which *symmetric* key encryption will be applied to the message digest. When symmetric key encryption is applied to a message digest, the result is referred to as a *message authentication code* (MAC), rather than a *digital signature*.)

If we reexamine the procedure that we referred to earlier as "double encryption," we see that the computational requirements can be cut nearly in half, since we only encrypt the message once with the receiver's public key (for confidentiality), and encrypt the much shorter digest (typically 128 or 160 bits; 16 or 20 bytes) with the sender's private key. The improved procedure operates as follows:

- The sender calculates the message digest and encrypts the digest using the sender's own private key (insuring authenticity of the sender), thereby creating a *digital signature*.
- The sender encrypts the message (once) using the receiver's public key, insuring confidentiality, since only the receiver possesses the receiver's private key.
- The encrypted message is transmitted along with the encrypted message digest (i.e., digital signature).
- Upon receipt, the receiver decrypts the message using the receiver's private key, which only the receiver possesses.
- The receiver calculates the digest on the decrypted message.
- The receiver decrypts the digital signature using the sender's public key. The decrypted message digest should match the calculated message digest from the decrypted message.
- If the message digest received (from the decrypted digital sign) matches the message digest calculated from the decrypted message, authentication is verified. The receiver then takes whatever action on the message as is appropriate (commonly passing the decrypted message on to the application or process indicated as the destination).
- If the calculated digest and received digest do not match, discard the packet.

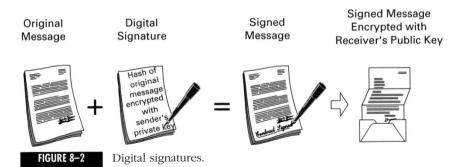

| Original Message | Digital Signature | Signed Message | Signed Message Encrypted with Receiver's Public Key |

FIGURE 8–2   Digital signatures.

There are several indirect benefits of this approach. We have seen that with use of a message digest, the effort to encrypt and decrypt is reduced. The bandwidth required to transmit the message is also reduced, but also the storage requirements of the receiver are reduced, since the digest can be stored along with the message.

Remember that *without* the message digest, authentication was dependant upon the "inner" level of encryption, of the double encryption (i.e., the first encryption done by the sender and the last decryption done by the receiver). If it were necessary to store the "authentication" along with the message, the receiver would have to save a copy of the "inner" encrypted message, before performing the second decryption. Once the second decryption was performed (using the sender's public key), the authentication vanishes with the decryption. The act of decryption provides the authenticity, and once performed there is no storable evidence of the authentication. The only way to "store" the authentication would be to keep a copy of the message before the final decryption is performed, effectively doubling the storage requirements. The two copies refer to the copy that had been decrypted twice, and a second copy that had been decrypted only once using the receiver's private key. With this approach, the second copy would also require an additional decryption each time the message needed to be reauthenticated. Fortunately, use of the digital signature eliminates this duplication.

Although not specifically stated, the private/public key pair used for digital signatures doesn't have to be the same pair that is used for confidentiality. Any user can have multiple sets, as long as they can identify the appropriate set to potential receivers. In fact, it may be advantageous to have separate pairs so that replacing one would not require the other to change, as well.

Although we now have an improved process to provide authentication, in addition to confidentiality, it is based on the assumption that the public keys we use actually belong to the parties that are claimed. Public-key systems are susceptible to forgeries and/or imposters. We need some mechanism to guarantee that the public keys we receive and use truly belong to the parties they claim to be, rather than a clever imposter.

PUBLIC KEY INFRASTRUCTURE (PKI) AND DIGITAL CERTIFICATES

When you meet a stranger for the first time, they may introduce themselves, but may give a false name or claim to be someone else. A more reliable means would be for a trusted friend to introduce them, and vouch for their identity. A similar process might be used to exchange public keys through a trusted intermediary. The trusted intermediary would require that each individual party adequately identify themselves, and once the intermediary is satisfied that each party is who they claim to be, the intermediary can verify their identity.

If the intermediary is trustworthy and their verification process is thorough, it can serve as a reliable source to verify the identity of any party to any other party. Each party could provide "certificates of identity," issued by and signed by the intermediary vouching for the identity of that party.

In public-key encryption, a Certificate Authority (CA) fills this role of trusted intermediary, vouching for the identity of all participating members. Any individual can "enroll" with the CA by providing satisfactory proof of identity, along with the individual's public key. The CA issues a *certificate* that includes the following:

- Identity of the "entity" that is the owner of the public key; name, serial number, IP address, company and/or department name; or other criteria identifying an individual user or network device, such as a host, router, firewall, et al.
- The public key of this entity, which can be an individual user or a network device, such as a host or router
- Digital signature and identity of the CA issuing the certificate
- Dates of validity for this certificate
- Class of certificate — multiple levels; higher-class levels require enrollee provide more substantial proof of identity
- Digital certificate ID# for this certificate

The current standard for certificates is X.509 v3, as defined by the International Telecommunications Union (ITU). Notice that the identity of the issuing CA must be contained in the certificate. Since the CA digitally signs the certificate, the CA's public key must be used to validate the digital signature (which was signed using the CA's private key), and it may be necessary to retrieve the CA's public key before using the entity's public key that the certificate includes and guarantees.

There are a number of companies that develop CA software, including VersiSign®, Entrust® Technologies, Baltimore™ Technologies, and several others. These companies typically will provide the CA as a for-fee service, or will sell the software allowing an organization to manage its own CA. At this time, cross-certification among different CAs is incomplete, although efforts to provide this capability have been proceeding for several years.

The term *Public Key Infrastructure* (PKI) was intended to describe this *ultimate* goal, of complete cross-certification; however, the term is most often used when referring to the partial functionality that is currently available. Current references to PKI should usually be understood to mean that the "infrastructure" is only available within an individual organization that manages their own CA and builds their own "infrastructure," or between organizations that subscribe to a common CA service provider. There is no universality to the infrastructure at this time. Additional information regarding CAs will be included in the IPSec chapter.

Comparing Symmetric versus Asymmetric Methods

As you may have suspected by now, there is a downside to public-key systems. From the above discussion it might appear that asymmetric, public-key systems are superior to symmetric, secret-key systems. If that were that case, there would be no need for symmetric, secret-key systems at all, but things are rarely that simple.

One shortcoming of asymmetric, public-key methods is that they have an entirely different mathematical basis, and require key lengths that are significantly longer that a comparably strong symmetric, secret-key method. Although the ratio varies by key length, asymmetric keys must be roughly 7 to 18 times longer than an equivalent symmetric key to result in the same resistance to brute force attacks. As mentioned earlier in this chapter, Chapter 7 of *Applied Cryptography* by Bruce Schneier (2nd edition, John Wiley & Sons, Inc., 1996) provides several charts comparing key lengths between symmetric and asymmetric encryption methods. In addition to being the author of several books, Mr. Schneier is also the founder of Counterpane™ Labs (formerly Counterpane Systems). The Counterpane Web site contains a wealth of information related to encryption technologies, as well as some excellent downloadable freeware, and can be found at *http://www.counterpane.com/labs.html.*

Due to the increased key lengths required and other factors, asymmetric methods make require as much as 1,000 times more processing power and are, therefore, considered too computationally intensive for general-purpose encryption. Instead, public-key methods are used primarily to distribute or "negotiate" symmetric secret-keys, or other "low-volume" encryption tasks, with symmetric methods used for most bulk, high-volume encryption tasks.

Public-key encryption may be suitable for tasks such as user encryption or decryption of individual email messages, since the time required to encrypt the message can be treated as part of the overall message composition or reading time. Similarly, the CPU utilization is a less significant issue, since the workstation may otherwise be idle while encryption or decryption is performed.

Conversely, public-key encryption would add significantly to the delay and load, if performed by a router or firewall acting as an encryption and decryption gateway for transit traffic.

The Diffie-Hellman Algorithm

The Diffie-Hellman algorithm is the oldest of several variants of public-key algorithms, and is based upon the original work done by Whitfield Diffie and Martin Hellman in the late 1970s. It is used today primarily for what is described as "key exchange," but could more accurately be described as "key creation." It is a special use of asymmetric, public-key techniques to negotiate and generate a symmetric, secret-key for use by a symmetric encryption method, such as DES or 3DES. It cannot be used to encrypt and decrypt messages.

The Diffie-Hellman algorithm provides a mechanism for two parties to dynamically establish a single, shared secret key, known only to them, although they are communicating over an unsecured channel. Neither party creates the key; instead, each makes a contribution to the process, sometimes described as a "half-key." The resulting secret key may be used for DES, 3DES or other symmetric encryption method. The strength of the Diffie-Hellman algorithm lies in the difficulty of computing discrete logarithms in a finite field.

For those readers who are allergic to math, ignore the stuff that looks like math in the section below then continue reading where the text starts again.

For those readers who have an appetite for math, the procedure is described below.

Our old friends, Alice and Bob, want to use the Diffie-Hellman algorithm to derive a secret key known only to them, but need to communicate over an unsecured channel to do so. They begin by agreeing on two numbers: **p** (a very large prime number) and **g** (a number that is less than, and related to, **p**). These two numbers do not have to be kept secret.

Next, each party chooses a random integer value that is less than **p**, which we will call X_A (Alice) and X_B (Bob). Each party keeps this number secret but uses it in an equation:

Alice's Equation: $Y_A = g^{X_A} \bmod p$

Bob's Equation: $Y_B = g^{X_B} \bmod p$

Alice computes Y_A and sends the result to Bob.

Bob computes Y_B and sends the result to Alice.

Alice and Bob use their chosen secret values X_A and X_B in a new equation that includes the values Y_A and Y_B that each received from the other.

Alice: $K = (Y_B{}^{X_A}) \bmod p$

Bob: $K = (Y_A{}^{X_B}) \bmod p$

They now both have the computed value for K, which is the shared secret key. Any other party that may know **p** or **g**, or who intercepts the values Y_A and/or Y_B that are exchanged, will still be unable to determine K, the secret key, due to the difficulty in computing discrete logarithms.

Diffie-Hellman functions because exponentiation does not depend upon on the order that you do the exponentiation. For example: $2^3 \times 2^2 = 32 = 2^2 \times 2^3$

It should be noted that the Diffie-Hellman method does not, by itself, provide authentication of the parties. However, Alice and Bob could use public-key encryption with digital signatures when exchanging the values of Y_A and Y_B, thereby providing authentication.

Perfect Forward Secrecy

The Diffie-Hellman method is particularly useful in generating temporary session keys that are used for the duration of one exchange "session" between two parties, then discarded. A new session requires the negotiation of a new session key. If each new session key is independent of previous session keys, Perfect Forward Secrecy (PFS) can be achieved.

PFS is considered very beneficial since the compromise of any given key will not allow any advantage in determining additional keys. In the absence of PFS, the compromise of one key can provide insight into the values of other keys, making them more vulnerable to attack. This topic will reappear in a later chapter on configuration of IPSec, since Cisco provides a configuration *option* for PFS or no PFS.

RSA Public-Key Encryption

The other significant implementation of public-key encryption is RSA, which derives its name from the developers of the method; Rivest, Shamir, and Adelman. The basis for the strength of this algorithm comes from the fact that it is very easy to multiply two large prime numbers together, but it is almost impossible to determine what those numbers were by factoring the resultant product of their multiplication.

The RSA algorithm was first published in 1978, and since that time has been the most commonly used example of public-key encryption. The description of public-key systems in the earlier part of this chapter are based primarily upon the RSA implementation, and it is by far the most widely deployed of the public-key encryption methods. Over the past 20 years, a number of other public-key methods have been proposed, yet none have received the acceptance enjoyed by RSA.

Message Authentication Codes

A message authentication code (MAC) is another variation on a one-way hash or message digest that has been described previously. It is a procedure is similar to the procedure to create a digital signature, but the purpose is different. With a digital signature, the message digest was encrypted with the sender's private key to provide authentication and integrity check on the message sent. The primary difference is that the hash is encrypted with a secret key to accomplish a similar purpose. MACs will be revisited during the discussion of IPSec, since they are a required element in the configuration of IPSec on Cisco routers and firewalls.

Summary

In this chapter, a broad overview of encryption technologies was presented, focusing upon those elements that are present and/or supported on the Cisco router and firewall product lines. This chapter was intended as a primer for those topics that will be the subject of further discussion in the next two chapters. The goal of this chapter was to provide a foundation for the discussion of IPSec, an adjunct to the IP network layer protocol.

We discussed the secret-key encryption methods, DES and 3DES, that are currently supported by IPSec, and the public-key methods, the Diffie-Hellman and RSA algorithms, that provide the foundation for the key exchange mechanism found in IPSec.

We made no attempt to cover a number of networking and encryption related topics, such as SSL, S/HTTP, S/MIME, PGP, or other application-layer security protocols, since the emphasis of this book is security applied at the Network Layer.

Likewise, this material is not intended to provide as thorough a discussion of encryption-related topics as may be found in the texts referenced earlier in this chapter, *Cryptography and Network Security* by William Stallings, and *Applied Cryptography* by Bruce Schneier. For the reader who is interested in more detail, these two books are excellent sources.

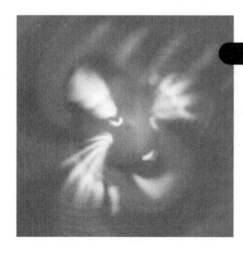

Introduction to IPSec

In This Chapter

*I*n the previous chapter some of the basic concepts and terminology used with encryption were introduced. Encryption was depicted as a fundamental element in the set of tools available to provide security in a public network environment such as the Internet.

The first question that must be decided relates to the characteristics and features that may be provided by encryption technologies that are desirable in such an environment. The features that are on top of that list consist of:

- Confidentiality and privacy of data, messages, and traffic flow
- Authentication of data origin
- Integrity of received data
- Access control for authorization
- Replay protection
- Key distribution and management
- Nonrepudiation

Where to Apply Encryption

The next issue to be decided is how to best apply encryption and related services to provide the desired benefits. In the context of the OSI Reference Model, there are several strategic points where encryption may be applied.

Data Link Layer

When encryption is applied at this level, one benefit is that the encryption can be implemented in hardware devices. The advantage gained from implementation in hardware is the performance and speed improvements that can result from dedicated circuitry, optimized for encryption. When compared to software implementations on general-purpose computers under general-purpose operating systems, a hardware implementation would surely provide better performance.

While this approach can provide superior encryption speed, there is an underlying assumption that the data only needs to cross a single link between two directly connected devices (e.g., two hosts or two routers). If the data path consists of multiple links or hops, decryption and reencryption would need to be performed at each intermediate relaying point, that is, at each router, in order to examine the IP header to make routing decisions.

Since a router inherently strips the incoming data link layer frame and recreates a new frame for outgoing data, the data link layer frame would have to be reencrypted at each "hop." The speed advantage quickly disappears when the data path crosses multiple routers. Additionally, each router would need a different key (and encrypting device) for each other router to which it forwards data, making the logistics unacceptable for a highly meshed network like the Internet.

This approach has historically been used on legacy systems such as ATM machines connected to mainframes over dedicated circuits or even dialup circuits, but would be unsuitable for the multiple hop nature of the Internet.

An alternative approach used by VPN technologies such as PPTP or L2TP is a variation of an encrypted "tunnel." Although slightly oversimplified, this approach can be generally described as follows. A PPP frame can be encrypted then encapsulated inside an IP packet (i.e., the Layer 2 frame becomes the "data" inside a Layer 3, IP packet). The IP packet is then routed as a normal IP packet with the "payload" encrypted. At the other end of the "tunnel" the payload is decrypted and delivered locally as the original PPP frame.

The disadvantage of this method is that the encryption endpoints must be coordinated. If the tunnel endpoints are hosts, scalability is limited, since each pair of hosts should have a separate encryption key, and key distribution and management becomes an issue.

If the tunnel endpoints are routers, the implication is that they share common management and control. If the path is totally within one ISP, this is feasible, but since much of the Internet traffic crosses multiple ISPs, coordination of the tunnel endpoints becomes impractical. As a result, IPSec has generated greater interest as a VPN technology, since it addresses these shortcomings. The approach used by IPSec is considered to provide greater flexibility, and includes a sophisticated key distribution and management system, making it suitable for a wider range of environments.

Network Layer

When encryption is implemented at the Network Layer, several advantages are gained over tradition Data Link layer implementations. If the encryption is applied at the sending station and decryption performed at the receiving station, only a single key is required rather than the multiple keys required for each link in traditional link-by-link encryption previously described. The underlying assumption is that encryption would be applied to the data portion of the IP packet, with the IP header remaining in the clear to provide hop-by-hop routing. Applied at the Network Layer, the encryption would be transparent to upper layer protocols, services, and applications. This allows use of the existing network (and Internet) infrastructure in a manner transparent to the intermediate relaying points (i.e., routers) and only requires that the encryption endpoints be coordinated. The endpoints can be individual hosts or encryption "gateways," such as routers or firewalls. Although this approach seems similar to the methods used for PPTP or L2T, those VPN technologies presume PPP is the data link layer. Applied at the network layer, any LAN or WAN data link types can be supported, such as Ethernet or Frame Relay. In the specific case of IPSec, the key management functionality provides capabilities that are not currently defined for PPTP or L2TP. Although any of the VPN technologies (PPTP, L2TP, or IPSec) might be usable for some situations, IPSec is considered to be a more general-purpose solution, suited for a greater variety of environments.

Transport Layer

When security is provided at the Transport Layer it is assumed that it will be transparent to the upper layers, such as applications. However, that is not the case in practice since applications must request services, reducing transparency. The *Secure Socket Layer* (SSL) is the most widely used protocol of this type, and was originally introduced by Netscape. SSL was designed to be an open protocol and was intended to provide data security layered between applications, such as http, Telnet, ftp, et al., and the Transport Layer (i.e., TCP). As currently employed, SSL provides data encryption, server authentication, and message authentication for TCP-based connections; however, optional client authentication is rarely used. The result is that the server or host is authenticated, but the client is not. The SSL protocol uses TCP port 443.

In a typical scenario, the client connects to a Web server and requests the server to authenticate itself. The server responds by providing its digital certificate. The public key to validate the certificate is included within most browsers for some of the better-known CAs (e.g., VeriSign). Although provision is made for client authentication, since there is no public-key infrastructure, and use of certificates by clients is very limited, most servers do not attempt to authenticate clients. Another limiting factor with SSL is that encryption is only provided to data during transfer. Once the connection is closed, the encryption ends. It is sometimes desirable to provide encryption for data storage or to be stored with the data (e.g., digital signatures).

With Secure Sockets Layer (SSL), public-key cryptography is used to negotiate a symmetric, secret key that is used for actual encryption of data. At this time, SSL is only employed to secure http, although the Internet Engineering Task Force (IETF) is working on a standard referred to as Transport Layer Security (TLS) that is based upon, but significantly different from, SSL version 3.0.

Another Transport Layer protocol is *Socket Security* (SOCKS), although it has not received as wide an acceptance since system calls for each application must be modified, or *SOCKS-ifyed* to operate with SOCKS. A number of applications are available (e.g., Telnet, ftp, finger, whois, etc.), although the necessity to modify applications at the system-call level will probably limit its use.

Application Layer

There are very few Application Layer security protocols since they are inherently application-specific. The notable exception is Secure Hypertext Transfer Protocol (shttp). Due to the popular acceptance of the Internet and near ubiquitous use of http, the critical mass exists, which makes an application-specific protocol viable; however, Shttp has only achieved limited acceptance, with SSL used more frequently.

Shttp is a message-oriented security protocol used to secure messages within an exclusively http environment. It is typically used with public-key systems, but can also be used with symmetric-key systems, with the secret key exchanged out-of-band. Shttp provides the ability to encrypt, authenticate, and/or sign a message, while maintaining the characteristics of http. Shttp clients can interoperate with http, although the security features are not supported.

Goals

The factors detailed above indicated a need for a general-purpose security protocol, and the network layer is considered an appropriate point to implement such security. In that context IPSec was defined and developed to meet a set of broad goals.

- Prevent eavesdropping, alteration, or forgery of traffic between trusted (i.e., authenticated) hosts. Traffic traversing a public (or semipublic) network might pass through any number of unidentified points where it could be susceptible to any of the above hostile actions. The limitation is that encryption and authentication of traffic is host-oriented, and in some cases it is difficult to associate with an individual user, if the host has multiple users.
- Protect the existing base of applications (i.e., email, WWW, ftp, Telnet, et al.), as well as anticipated future applications, while avoiding the necessity to modify or replace existing applications.
- Use the existing unsecured networks, such as the Internet, without requiring significant changes to the existing infrastructure. The security features must be transparent to the existing transport infrastructure (i.e., ISPs and the routing process). It is also necessary to apply security independent of the services currently provided, since it is unreasonable to impose new security requirements upon the service providers, given the existing structure.
- Provide the security features in a fashion that is as transparent to the user as is possible. To the extent possible, apply the security services automatically to traffic on an as-needed basis. Encrypt as much of the packet as possible, while allowing clear-text examination of IP header for routing.
- Provide site-level authentication and encryption. User-level encryption may be desirable and possible under some conditions, although other measures can be employed to provide per-user security. By providing security at the site-level, it will then be possible to create a series of *virtual public networks*, overlaid upon an unsecured public network.
- Provide a mechanism to deal with the logistic and management issues associated with key management. To the extent possible, allow for automatic key generation, and rekeying, along with automatic distribution of the keys in a secure fashion.
- Provide security for the existing IP version 4.0 environments, as well as those anticipated for IP version 6.0.

Overview of IPSec

The suite of protocols collectively known as IPSec meet the goals as defined above. IPSec is a mandatory part of IP version 6.0, and optional extension to IP version 4.0, which makes up the vast majority of existing installations. IPSec offers a standardized method to provide encryption, authentication, and other services between endpoints. These endpoints can be individual hosts or *security gateways* such as routers or firewalls providing services for hosts "behind" the router or firewall.

When used with security gateways, individual hosts are spared the processing overhead inherent in security-related processes such as encryption. In addition, the security function can be applied for all traffic for all hosts in a manner that is totally transparent to the host, applications, and users. No software modification is required for individual hosts or applications. No special procedures or training are required of users.

The result is a standardized set of encryption algorithms and transforms, as well as a standardized, automatic encryption key generation and distribution mechanism to allow for interoperability between IP devices. A basic set of standard algorithms is defined, with provision for other algorithms as desired or required. The IPSec architecture provides a modular structure that is independent of the algorithms used, allowing future extension, or vendor implementation of various different encryption algorithms.

The functionality of IPSec is provided through use of the Authentication Header (AH) and/or the Encapsulating Security Payload (ESP). The AH and ESP consist of additional headers that are inserted between the IP header and the payload of the IP packet as is illustrated in Figure 9-1.

IPSec uses symmetric keys for encryption and keyed Message Authentication Codes (MACs) for authentication. The specification provides for manual configuration of the keys, but also provides for automatic key management through use of the Internet Key Exchange protocol.

The Internet Key Exchange (IKE) protocol provides key management for generation and distribution of keys. IKE is a consolidation of the Internet Security Association Key Management Protocol (ISAKMP) and the Oakley protocol, taking some of its characteristics from each. As a function of key management, each pair of devices forms a Security Association (SA), defining the parameters and functions that are mutually supported on each peer.

A SA is an agreed or negotiated understanding of how various services, such as the encryption algorithm and/or authentication method used, will be handled when exchanging data. Also included are secret key(s) that will be used, a definition of what traffic is to be protected, and the identity (i.e., IP address) of the peer device that will participate in the data exchange. If multiple peers or partners are involved, a separate SA is required for each. The parameters for each SA that a given device has are stored locally in the Security Association Database (SADB), and are identified by a Security Parameters Index (SPI), identifying each individual SA that a given device maintains. There are separate SAs for IKE and for each IPSec option employed. If both

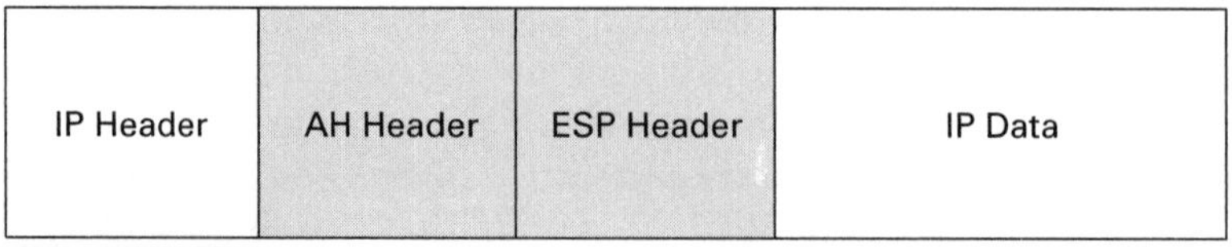

IP Header	AH Header	ESP Header	IP Data

FIGURE 9-1   AH and ESP within the IP packet.

AH and ESP are used, each has their own SA. Since SAs are unidirectional, each peer will have a separate SA for transmitted and received data. If AH and ESP are used along with IKE, each device will have a total of six SAs defined: a pair (one in each direction) for IKE, a pair for AH, and a pair for ESP.

When automatic key management is employed, each SA is established by an IKE negotiation. IKE establishes its own SAs and then also negotiates SAs on behalf of IPSec AH and/or ESP.

The IKE negotiations consist of two phases.

- Phase 1: IKE peers authenticate themselves to one another and establish a secure channel to conduct further communications. This mode is used to establish the IKE SAs. Two different modes are available for this phase: Main Mode and Aggressive Mode. Main Mode is used most commonly, although Aggressive Mode may be used for some situations.
- Phase 2: IKE negotiates IPSec SAs during this phase. A separate negotiation is conducted for each SA required, AH, and/or ESP. In Phase 2 only one mode is defined — Quick Mode.

IPSec SAs terminate when a time limit or traffic volume limit is reached, or can be manually deleted. (Note: An exception exists when manual keying is done and IKE is not used. In these cases, the SAs do not expire and must be manually deleted.) Upon expiration of an SA, the keys are deleted. When new IPSec SAs and keys are needed, IKE automatically performs a new Phase 2 negotiation. Under some circumstances an additional Phase 1 negotiation may also be required (e.g., if the IKE SA has also expired).

The new Phase 2 negotiation results in new SAs and a new key. In most cases, IPSec attempts to anticipate that the existing SA will soon expire, and will direct IKE to begin negotiations so that the new SAs are established before the existing SAs expire. By anticipating the expiration, the new SAs and key can be in place, and communications can continue uninterrupted upon expiration of the first SA and key. The result is that for a very short period there may be two SAs in place covering the same traffic flow, until the first SA expires.

Additional details for IPSec, SAs, and IKE, are included in the sections that follow.

IPSec Details

IPSec can provide protection for data using AH only, ESP only, or both. The services provided consist of:

- Confidentiality (via encryption).
- Authentication; verification of data origin.
- Data Integrity; protection from tampering or modification.
- Antireplay; protection from recording and playback of legitimate traffic.

- Limited traffic flow confidentiality; when tunnel mode is used, identity of devices exchanging data is hidden (details below).
- Access control; when used on a "security gateway," access to protected resources is provided since only properly encrypted traffic can be decrypted at the receiving end, and passed on the protected hosts behind the security gateway.

Since the protection provided is ultimately a function of the algorithms and methods used, IPSec provides a "framework" so that various encryption and authentication methods can be used. It does not require the use of, or limit its use to, any particular algorithms or methods, although a minimal implementation must support 56-bit DES and manually configured keys to insure at least some interoperability between implementations.

Even though DES and manual keying are required, they may not provide the degree of protection required, or scalability for larger installations. It is anticipated that vendors will support additional encryption methods and automatic keying using IKE. (Cisco supports triple DES (3DES) and a full implementation of IKE).

IPSec assumes the use of symmetric keys for encryption and keyed MACs for authentication based upon performances reasons. Public-key methods considered too slow for "bulk" encryption and hence are restricted for use with IKE to provide authentication of peers. As part of the Phase 1 negotiations, IKE provides three options for authentication of peers, two of which use RSA public-key methods (details below).

IPSec operates in one of two modes: transport or tunnel mode. Transport mode is intended for host-to-host exchanges while tunnel mode is for use in gateway-to-gateway exchanges with security gateways such as routers or firewalls. In transport mode, the sending host applies AH and/or ESP, and the receiving host verifies and removes the AH and/or ESP. This requires that the both hosts support IPSec, and have sufficient processing and memory resources to encrypt and decrypt. Each pair of hosts will have a separate SA, and configuration becomes burdensome in one-to-many or many-to-many host environments.

In tunnel mode, the services are applied to traffic transparent to the hosts. Tunnel mode is the preferred mode where a number of hosts are involved since configuration need only be performed on the gateways, rather than each host individually. It is also appropriate where the hosts do not directly support IPSec, as is the case with many current operating systems (e.g., Microsoft supports IPSec under Windows 2000, but not on earlier versions of WinXX). In tunnel mode, the entire original IP packet, including headers, is encrypted and/or authenticated and becomes the "data" for a new IP packet. The source and destination addresses for the new IP packet are the sending and receiving security gateways, respectively. When the new, outer IP packet is received at the destination gateway, the outer header is stripped, the packet deencrypted and/or authenticated and the "inner" IP packet is for-

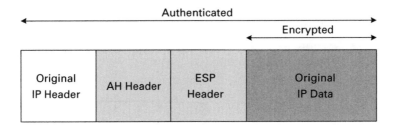

Transport Mode

FIGURE 9-2 IPSec transport mode.

warded on from there, as any other IP packet. This process of carrying the original packet inside of another IP packet is what creates the "tunnel" between the encrypting and decrypting security gateways.

Figures 9-2 and 9-3 illustrate the differences between transport and tunnel mode.

AH — The Authentication Header

AH mode provides authentication for the AH, most of the IP header, as well the upper-layer protocols and data contained within the data portion of an IP datagram. However, some of the fields in the IP header are altered in transit (e.g., time-to-live) and therefore cannot be protected by the AH since their final values are unknown to the sending device. These fields are excluded when calculating the AH. The integrity check provided by the AH consists of a keyed hash using a secret key shared only by the sender and receiver. The authentication extends to cover:

- All IP header fields with the exception of those that are changed in transit
- The AH header, including next header, payload length, reserved field, SPI, sequence number, the authentication data (the keyed hash of the message, which is set to zero for this computation), and padding bytes (if any)
- The upper-layer protocol data, which is assumed to be unchanged in transit

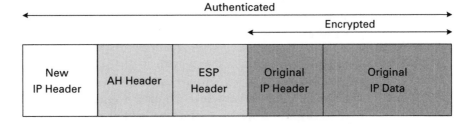

Tunnel Mode

FIGURE 9-3 IPSec tunnel mode.

The following are the unchangeable fields and are included in the AH computation:

- Version
- Internet header length
- Total length
- Identification
- Protocol (this should be the value for AH)
- Source address
- Destination address

The Authentication Header is intended to provide authentication of the originating device and a data integrity verification when used with or without the Encapsulating Security Payload (ESP). However, the ESP provides its own integrated authentication capabilities, rendering the additional authentication provided by the AH unnecessary for most circumstances. As a result, the AH is not typically used with the ESP, but is used when only authentication is required or desired. It can be used in transport or tunnel mode.

ESP — The Encapsulating Security Payload

The Encapsulating Security Payload (ESP) is the portion of the IPSec suite that provides confidentiality of the data via encryption using a symmetric key. As a by-product, the ESP can provide authentication of data origin and data integrity since only the peer device would share the secret key, and could have encrypted the packet. Also included is an antireplay mechanism that is provided through use of a sequence number in the ESP header. This sequence number, which is initially set to zero, can also serve as the "counter" used to determine when the ESP SA is due to expire.

Since the ESP can provide its own data origin authentication, it is rarely used with the AH, since the authentication function provided by the AH is largely redundant. The subtle difference is that the authentication provided by the ESP only covers the payload, and does not include the IP header, as does the AH. For most implementations, the difference is inconsequential.

Because the ESP provides both confidentiality and authentication, it has different algorithms defined as part of its SA. The algorithm used for confidentiality is known as the *cipher* and the algorithm used for authentication is referred to as the *authenticator*.

The current choice of *cipher* is 56-bit DES or 168-bit 3DES. Although IPSec specifies that other encryption algorithms *could* be used, Cisco currently only supports these two. (Note: The IPSec specification provides for use of 128-bit IDEA, triple-DES, and Blowfish. Future support for AES is likely, since that is the new U.S. government standard, intended to replace DES.)

The choice of authenticators is defined as HMAC-MD5 or HMAC-SHA. Both MD-5 and SHA are hashing algorithms that produce a message digest. The MD-5 algorithm produces a 128-bit digest (16 bytes) and SHA-1 produces a 160-bit digest (20 bytes), which is a "fingerprint" of the message. The HMAC refers to a special variation of keyed hash that uses a symmetric key applied to any hashing function, such as MD5 or SHA. Thus HMAC-MD5 is this special form of keyed hash using an MD-5 message digest, and HMAC-SHA is the special form of keyed hash using the Secure Hash Algorithm (SHA). Regardless of which HMAC is used, the result in truncated to 96-bit length (from 128-bit or 160-bit).

Note that this is different from the *digital signature* described in the previous chapter. A digital signature was the result of asymmetric, public-key encryption applied to a message digest such as MD-5, while HMAC-MD5 refers to symmetric, secret key applied to the same MD-5 message digest. *The ESP always uses a symmetric, secret key for both the authenticator and the cipher.*

The ESP SA may have one *cipher* (e.g., DES or 3DES) and one *authenticator* (e.g., HMAC-MD5 or HMAC-SHA). Either of these may be undefined (i.e., NULL) however this is very rarely the case. Since it is possible (although rarely desired) to use the ESP and the AH together, it is possible to have two potentially different *authenticators*, one for the AH and another for the ESP, but there is only one *cipher* allowed.

To clarify the remaining discussion, there are several points that should be emphasized here:

- The IPSec protocol was designed to be a very flexible architecture, usable in a variety of situations. In some cases, there are multiple methods to reach the same end result. In other cases, there are several different options, each producing a different specific result, but where the choice of any of the "options" may produce an equally acceptable solution. This great flexibility, along with the multiple options, will often overwhelm the administrator with too many choices, which may be difficult to differentiate from one another. This has the effect of making IPSec seem very confusing.

- A number of the options and choices are only required for special situations, but are less often used in most "mainstream" environments. In most instances, the default values provided during the configuration stage are suitable for these "mainstream" environments, but other options are available for those that require specific characteristics. The underlying assumption (correct or otherwise) is that the administrator understands the subtle differences and their ramifications, and is able to correctly make informed choices. This is most often the case with Cisco configurations, which will be discussed in the next chapter.

- In practice, these choices sometimes result in an awkward sounding Cisco configuration "rule," such as one that states that there can be (at most) two algorithms defined for authentication, but only one for data encryption. This refers to the rare situation where both the AH and ESP are used as described above.

- In many cases, similar sounding terms have different meanings, while in other cases there may be several terms that describe the same thing. The reader or administrator's first priority should be to understand the "lingo." To the extent possible, we will endeavor to assist in that goal by clarifying our use of the terminology where these situations prevail.
- This material will focus on elements that have the broadest application. Likewise, it is not intended to provide a complete detailed discussion of all aspects of IPSec. Many implementers require only a broad comprehensive understanding, and, hence, the more esoteric details are left to other sources. One excellent source of additional detail is *IPSec* by Naganand Doraswamy and Dan Harkins (Prentice Hall, 1999). A list of the related Internet Request for Comments (RFCs) is included later in this chapter.

In Figures 9-2 and 9-3 we intentionally omitted an additional detail of the ESP. Although the figures illustrate the ESP header, there can also be an ESP trailer. The ESP trailer consists of any padding required by the encryption algorithm, the padding length, and identification of the next header (IPv6). Padding may be added since some algorithms require that the data to be encrypted be a multiple of the key length. The IP packet data plus ESP trailer is considered the encrypted "payload."

If authentication is implemented as part of the ESP (as opposed to separate AH) the ESP trailer is followed by the *authentication data*, i.e., the HMAC-MD5 or the HMAC-SHA. This authenticated data is not covered by the encryption performed on the data payload. The *cipher* is applied to the data payload using the chosen secret key method (e.g., DES or 3DES).

The *authenticated data* consists of the HMAC created by calculating the message digest over the ESP header plus the encrypted payload, and applying the *authenticator* secret key. The HMAC-MD5 or HMAC-SHA is then appended to the end of the encryption of the data "payload" (IP packet data plus ESP trailer). This is important since, upon arrival at the receiving device, authentication will be performed first, followed by decryption. If the authentication fails, there is no need to decrypt the packet, and it will be dropped.

Modes

IPSec operates in one of two modes. The nature of the endpoints determines which of the two modes is appropriate for the circumstances.

TRANSPORT MODE

Since we assume that most Cisco implementations will consist of routers and firewalls providing a security gateway function, we have omitted discussion of AH and/or ESP in Transport Mode, which is used for direct host-to-host IPSec implementations.

TUNNEL MODE

AH • Since the ESP can provide its own authentication without the extra overhead of the AH, we have omitted discussion of the AH.

ESP

There are several advantages to the use of tunnel mode. First, the security protection can be provided transparently to the hosts behind the gateway. No special software or configuration is required on the hosts, and no resources are consumed providing the security protection. For hosts that don't provide native support for IPSec (e.g., Win95, Win98, Win NT, and others), the existing operating systems and applications receive the benefit, and no reconfiguration, additional software, or upgrade is required.

In addition, there is a limited degree of traffic flow confidentiality, since there is no way to determine the identity of hosts communicating through the gateway. All traffic on the public side appears to come from the sending gateway, and destined for the receiving gateway, thereby hiding the identity and traffic patterns of communicating hosts. In VPN situations, IP addresses at remote locations can be numbered as if they were local to the central site, since upon receipt at the receiving gateway, the traffic appears to have been generated locally from the same IP address space. This is true in either direction.

At the sending gateway, the original IP packet is encapsulated or "tunneled" as the data portion of a new IP packet sent from the sending gateway to the receiving gateway (the outer packet). At the receiving gateway, the encapsulation process is reversed and the original IP packet (the inner packet) is delivered in the conventional way. At the sending and receiving end, the encryption and authentication are applied to the "new" IP packet. Since the original IP packet is the "data" for the new packet, the "inner" packet is encrypted IP header and all, providing confidentiality for the packet contents, as well as the original IP header.

The authentication provided in the tunneled packet covers all fields in the "inner" IP packet, rather than only the unchangeable fields listed in the above section on the AH. This is true whether the gateway provides AH, ESP, or both.

In the special case of remote hosts connected via an IPSec VPN to a security gateway, the remote host acts as its own security gateway, by encapsulating its original packet inside another IP packet addressed to the security gateway. It should be noted that the remote host must provide the tunnel mode encryption and authentication functions and, therefore, requires appropriate operating system support for that function. Since in many cases, the remote host is a PC running Win98, WinNT, et al., third-party VPN client software is required, since Microsoft only supports IPSec under Win2000. Further discussion of special requirements for VPN clients will be covered in a later chapter.

SA, SPI, and SPD Defined

As described in the overview above, the Security Association (SA) contains all the relevant parameters to identify a peer (such as IP address), define algorithms and keys to be used, define traffic flows that are to be encrypted, and so forth. There is a SA defined to be applied to outbound traffic, and a separate but complementary SA that is applied to inbound traffic from the same host. A separate pair of SAs (inbound and outbound) must be defined for each peer device. Optionally, there may be more than one pair of SAs per peer device if different traffic types are to receive different treatment, e.g., authenticate only, encrypt with 56-Bit DES, encrypt with 3DES, and so forth. The IP address and a Security Parameter Index (SPI) identify the individual SAs that are defined for each outbound flow and each inbound flow. When transmitting, the sender includes the SPI in the AH and/or ESP header so that the receiver knows which set of procedures, algorithms, and keys to apply to the received data. As such, the SPI must be readily visible in the AH and/or ESP header. Upon receipt of data, the receiver uses the SPI contained in the received header to determine the same procedures, algorithms, and keys to apply to the received data. The catalog of all SPIs is contained in the Security Profile Database (SPD). Security Associations have a "lifetime" determined by a time limit or total byte count, when used with Internet Key Exchange (IKE).

Key Management

The IPSec specification also provides for manual configuration of keys when IKE is not desired or required. In the case of manual keys, SAs do not expire and must be manually deleted. Support for manual keying is required to facilitate (i.e., simplify) interoperability testing; however, automatic keying via IKE is anticipated for most applications in order to provide new keys in a timely fashion, and provide scalability when multiple pairs of peer devices are employed.

Internet Key Exchange

The case for an automatic key exchange is the following: For two network devices (hosts or security gateways) to communicate securely, they must be able to create a secure channel over an initially insecure medium. This requires the use of some type of secure key negotiation and/or exchange method to create the secure channel.

For IPSec, the defined method for secure-key negotiation is through use of the IKE protocol. Although other key negotiation protocols could be used, IKE is mandatory for all IPSec implementations. Although IKE is a mandatory part of IPSec, there is no requirement that it be used. If fully dynamic IKE functionality is not required, a *preshared key* for IKE sessions may be manually configured. Note that this IKE *preshared key* (symmetric key) is used only for IKE exchanges or sessions, and is not the same as the IPSec *manual key* (symmetric key) that may be configured when IKE is not used.

In "fully dynamic" implementations, IKE allows two devices (i.e., hosts or gateways) to dynamically derive the symmetric, secret "session" key for secure IKE communication through the exchange of a series of messages. These exchanges include provision for authentication of peers and/or encryption of some messages, along with protection against flooding, replay, and spoofing attacks. IKE uses a combination of public and private key cryptography, along with keyed-hash functions (i.e., message authentication codes or MACs). IKE also includes provision for the use of *certificates*, in conjunction with a Certificate Authority (CA). The CA can be a private, organization-based system, or may be part of a public system (i.e., public key infrastructure or PKI).

Some have criticized the Internet Key Management protocol as being overly complex, and the corresponding documentation as being vague, confusing, and/or contradictory. Configuration often consists of multiple options, the effects of which are always not clearly understood.

IKE is probably the most complex part of understanding, implementing, and configuring IPSec, but IKE also provides powerful benefits. Once it has been properly configured, IKE is totally automatic, requiring no further administrative attention. When IPSec SAs expire, IKE is automatically activated to renegotiate new SAs and generate new keys. For some environments, this allows the use of "marginally strong" encryption (such as DES), provided that the keys are exchanged frequently enough to make the effort to brute-force the keys disproportionately high, when compared to the advantage gained.

As indicated in the last chapter, if it took 20 hours to break the key, changing the key once per hour implies that only one hour's worth of data would be compromised, and the "cracking" process would always lag by a factor of 20-to-1. As an example, one day's worth of traffic would require 20 days to compromise. If the value of the data diminishes over time, the effort required to "crack" the code would exceed the value of doing so.

While this might not be adequate for archived data, it may be acceptable for some traffic types, where "temporary" protection is sufficient. Although 3DES encryption is considered "mathematically impossible" to break, it requires significantly greater resources (at least triple the effort) to encrypt and decrypt. In situations such as PC-based VPN clients connecting through a security gateway, the PC may simply not have enough processing power to keep up with the data flow.

Since very few organizations have unlimited budgets and resources, each organization must make an independent determination of what constitutes "adequate" protection for their individual circumstances.

Given that IKE can be a very complex protocol, this section will attempt to explain some of the details of IKE and related protocols for those who are totally unfamiliar with the IPSec key negotiation mechanisms. The overall complexity of IKE makes a complete discussion beyond the scope of this book, but we believe some fundamental understanding of the IKE processes is necessary, in order to understand the options that are presented during implementation and configuration.

The challenge is to provide sufficient detail to understand the options and choices, without getting lost in the minutiae. This requires a delicate balance between too much and too little detail. The reader will be left to judge whether or not we have met that goal.

IKE, ISAKMP, OAKLEY, and the DOI

To establish an SA between two devices, they must first agree on the cryptographic algorithms to be used and other details. The peer devices must also have a secure method for exchanging keys or determining keying material, over an insecure channel. IKE provides for session key generation via Diffie-Hellman exchanges, with extensions to provide for authentication of peers, replay protection, and antiflooding protection. It also provides for the negotiation of encryption and/or authentication algorithms or "transforms." Although IPSec is defined as part or the Network Layer, IKE is technically an application-layer protocol, and uses UDP port 500.

One way to learn about IPSec is to read the relevant RFCs, however this quickly becomes a daunting task, given the sheer number and size of the IPSec-related RFCs. (see list at end of this chapter). This is particularly difficult in the case of key negotiation and determination, since coverage is spread over four different documents: IKE, ISAKMP, OAKLEY, and the ISAKMP Domain of Interpretation (DOI). To further increase the confusion, IKE is a hybrid protocol, composed of only *some* elements of several of these other protocols. The major elements of IKE were drawn from:

- Internet Key Exchange (IKE) defines a two-phase process. The first phase consists of authentication of peers and establishment of the secure channel to conduct further IKE negotiations. IKE provides three different methods that can be used to authenticate peers, two of which use public-key technologies. During this phase an IKE SA will be defined. The first phase uses a modified Diffie-Hellman exchange to generate a "root" secret key. This root key will be permutated to generate three additional "session" keys. Phase 2 uses the IKE SA negotiated, and one of the three session keys established in Phase 1 to conduct the negotiations for the IPSec SA.

- Internet Security Association and Key Management Protocol (ISAKMP), which provides the structure for authentication and key exchange. ISAKMP was designed to be independent of any specific key exchange method, and as a result does not define the details of key exchange. Instead, it defines architecture for key exchange, leaving the details to other protocols. ISAKMP describes the message protocol and packet formats, which are created through the use of over a dozen different payloads. Each payload holds a particular type of data used in key negotiation, and may appear in different combinations. By using these various payloads in different combinations, ISAKMP packets can contain all of the data necessary to construct a particular IKE message. Some packet formats and field values are not defined in ISAKMP, but instead in the ISAKMP DOI.
- The Oakley Key Determination Protocol (OAKLEY) describes a series of key exchanges referred to as modes. Some of the Oakley negotiations are used with IKE. Oakley is based upon the Diffie-Hellman algorithm, but with extensions. Oakley provides the details of the individual services provided by different modes, such as authentication, identity protection, and "refreshing" of keys (i.e., using existing keys to generate new keys). Within the context of "rekeying" is the concept of Perfect Forward Secrecy (PFS). PFS requires that a key not be derived from another key, since compromise of the "root" key would jeopardize any keys derived from the root key. PFS requires generation of new keying material, rather than using an existing root key as the basis for new keys. As a consequence, PFS is an IKE configuration option, and is not otherwise assumed.
- Secure Key Exchange Mechanism (SKEME) provides functionality for anonymity of peers, repudiation, and key refreshment or rekeying that is, deriving new keys. IKE's use of public-key cryptography for authentication is inherited from SKEME, while most of the rest of its key management aspects were adapted from OAKLEY.
- The ISAKMP Domain of Interpretation (sometimes known simply as "the DOI") defines an IPSec-specific interpretation of certain parts of ISAKMP headers and payloads. Other DOIs may eventually be defined for non-IPSec or non-IP key negotiation mechanisms.

As is probably apparent, the above items illustrate the difficulty in understanding IKE by reading of the individual component RFCs. It often difficult to determine which elements come from which source, and which elements are actually applicable to IKE. Rather than becoming absorbed in the details, an alternative approach is simply to consider IKE to be a combination of the packet formats of ISAKMP and the exchanges of OAKLEY, but with overtones from another older key management architecture, SKEME.

The sections below provide a more high-level understanding of the operation of IKE.

Basic Key Exchange

To better understand IKE, we will start with the basic Diffie-Hellman (DH) key exchange and add the rest of the procedures in a step-by-step fashion. With Diffie-Hellman (as outlined in Chapter 8), two parties, the initiator (I) and the responder (R), exchange DH "half-keys" (X and Y) to arrive at a mutual session key, k. The advantage of DH is that each party contributes to the result over an unsecured channel, with the mathematical result being a secret key that can be now be used to secure the channel.

The disadvantages of the basic DH exchange are that it has no provision for authentication of parties, and has no capability to prevent replay or flooding attacks. IKE also requires some negotiation mechanism to specify the encryption and/or authentication algorithms that will be used with the generated key.

DH exchanges are susceptible to attacks known as "man in the middle" attacks. To prevent these attacks, both parties must authenticate themselves to one another (i.e., prove their identity). There are several ways this can be accomplished, including the use of public-key technologies, such as digital signatures or certificates.

IKE consists of two phases. Phase 1 creates an IKE SA using a DH exchange, along with one of several forms of authentication. Once an IKE SA is established, all IKE communication between the initiator and responder is protected with secret-key encryption (using the key derived from the Diffie-Hellman exchange), includes an integrity check, and is authenticated. The goal of IKE phase 1 is to establish a secure channel to conduct phase 2 negotiations. IKE phase 2 consists of establishing the appropriate IPSec SAs (i.e., ESP and/or AH).

To establish an IKE SA (sometimes also referred to as an ISAKMP SA), the initiating device (host or security gateway) proposes four items:

- The encryption algorithm used to protect the data
- A hashing algorithm (i.e., message digest) to be applied for digital signatures
- An authentication method for singing the data
- The Diffie-Hellman group number (i.e., set of standard parameters used in DH identified by a group number)

IKE Phase 1

OVERVIEW

When an IPSec session is initially established, the first priority is to establish an IKE SA (also sometimes referred to as an ISAKMP SA). Once the IKE SA is in place, IKE can be use to negotiate multiple IPSec SAs for AH and/or ESP. The IKE SA does not have to be maintained for the IPSec SA to function; however, in practice, IKE SAs have longer lifetimes than IPSec SAs. When an existing IPSec SA expires (or is soon due to expire), the IKE SA is reactivated to negotiate the new IPSec SA. In the event that the IKE SA has also expired, a new IKE SA is automatically established to provide the secure communications channel used to renew the IPSec SA. In either case (e.g., an initial IPSec SA, or renewal of an expiring IPSec SA), an IKE SA is required as a prerequisite to establish the IPSec SA.

In phase 1, IKE uses a Diffie-Hellman exchange to establish *keying material* for encryption and authentication of subsequent IKE exchanges. The keying material will be used to create three symmetric keys: one for IKE authentication, one for IKE encryption, and one used to derive additional (future) keys. Ordinarily, when we discuss Diffie-Hellman we describe the result of the DH as a key. The *keying material* is in fact a key, but rather than use it directly to encrypt or authenticate data, it is used solely to generate additional keys. The additional keys are created by the concatenation (appending) of the *keying material* with other values, then hashing the result to generate a new key. The various different values that are concatenated with the keying material will be described below.

An additional part of the phase 1 negotiation is authentication of each party to the other, using one of three possible authentication methods. Authentication provides protection from man-in-the-middle attacks. In addition, "cookies" (64-bit random numbers) are exchanged to prevent denial-of service attacks against IKE. The Initiator of the exchange contributes C_I, while the Responder contributes C_R. Each peer concatenates his cookie with that of his peer to form a "combined" cookie, $C_I + C_R$. This value is included in all subsequent messages (a complete discussion of the DoS protection provided in this manner is beyond the scope of this material).

Peer authentication is usually performed after the DH exchange so that the *keying material* can be used to encrypt the authentication messages.

PHASE 1 NEGOTIATION

IKE phase 1 can operate in two modes: Main Mode and Aggressive Mode. The result of each mode is the establishment of an IKE SA. Main Mode provides identity protection for the peers, and consists of six messages that are exchanged between the IKE Initiator and Responder. It offers identity protection and considerable flexibility in terms of the parameters and configurations that can be negotiated. Aggressive Mode is an abbreviated variation consisting of three-way handshake, and is therefore faster, but is rarely used.

Figure 9-4 illustrates the six messages that are exchanged in Main Mode.

(*Note:* The contents of some fields in the figure may vary slightly, based upon the specific authentication method employed. The details have been omitted to simplify this discussion. For more complete details, please refer to RFC 2409, the Internet Key Exchange.)

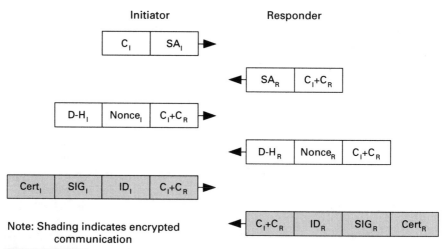

FIGURE 9–4   Main mode message exchange.

In Figure 9-4, the exchange can be described as follows:

- Message 1 — Initiator sends proposals for a SA_I to Responder, along with cookie, C_I.
- Message 2 — Responder replies with SA_R accepted, and concatenates his cookie C_R to the received C_I from Initiator, forming C_I+C_R.
- Message 3 — Initiator sends Diffie-Hellman "half-key" and includes a $Nonce_I$, a random number to be signed by Responder.
- Message 4 — Responder sends his Diffie-Hellman "half-key" along with $Nonce_R$, a random number to be signed by Initiator.
- Message 5 — Initiator sends identification ID_I, SIG_I ($Nonce_R$ signed by Initiator) along with certificate, $Cert_I$ (if applicable).
- Message 6 — Responder sends identification ID_R, SIG_R ($Nonce_I$ signed by Responder), along with certificate, $Cert_R$ (if applicable).

Notice that in the first pair of messages, the IKE SA is determined. The Initiator offers SA_I, which consists of a list of one or more proposals that will be the basis of the IKE SA between the two parties. SA_R is the acceptance by the Responder to the proposal (or one of the proposals if multiple were offered). Each proposal includes list of transforms (i.e., encryption and authentication algorithms) for that proposed SA. The Initiator could offer several proposals, while the Responder must choose only one. If the Responder is unable to find an acceptable match, the IKE SA fails. It is up to the administrator(s) configuring the devices to assure that there is at least one matching set of transforms between any pair of devices. In simple environments, the Administrator may configure only one choice of transforms coordinated across the two peers. However, IKE is capable of operating in much more diverse environments, where multiple choices might exist between any two peer devices. The only choices available are those that have been configured for each device. If there is more than one match, the devices will choose one based upon the priority set by the administrator. (The next chapter discusses this priority setting in greater detail.) Notice that these are the proposed SAs for the *IKE SA, only*. IPSec SAs will be negotiated in phase 2.

In messages 3 and 4, Diffie-Hellman "half-keys" are exchanged, in order to derive the *keying material*. In addition, nonces are exchanged. A nonce is a large random number, from 64 to 2048 bits in length. Since they are randomly chosen, they tend to be unique, contributing to antireplay protection. These values are used in several different ways to provide authentication, using various methods that will be described below.

Messages 5 and 6 are encrypted and authenticated using keys derived from the Diffie-Hellman exchange in messages 2 and 3. The identity of the parties is also included in messages 5 and 6. This identity will be some unique identification of the devices such as IP address, fully qualified domain name, digital certificate, email address, or other. Exchange of digital certificates may or may not occur, depending upon the particular authentication method chosen. These choices are discussed below.

KEY DERIVATION

As indicated in an earlier section, the keying material obtained from the Diffie-Hellman exchange is used as the basis for three additional keys. As defined in RFC 2409, the value *SKEYID* and the key resulting from the DH exchange, DH, are used to derive three additional keys:

$$SKEYID_D = hash(SKEYID, DHK | C_I | C_R | 0)$$
$$SKEYID_A = hash(SKEYID, SKEYID_D | DHK | C_I | C_R | 1)$$
$$SKEYID_E = hash(SKEYID, SKEYID_A | DHK | C_I | C_R | 2)$$

Where: DHK = the key resulting from the Diffie-Hellman exchange
C_I = the cookie created by the Initiator
C_R = the cookie created by the Responder

For those readers who are mere mortals and don't speak the ancient languages of the gods, these expressions can be translated into the following:

To calculate $SKEYID_D$,
Concatenate (append) the binary numbers $DH + C_I + C_R + 00000000$,
Encrypt the resultant number using the secret key, SKEYID (defined below)
Apply the defined hash algorithm to the encrypted result.

The second key, $SKEYID_A$, is calculated similarly, except that the derived key, from the first step, $SKEYID_D$ is added to the beginning of the concatenated string, and the binary value 00000001 is concatenated to the end, before encryption with the key, SKEYID.

The third key, $SKEYID_E$, is similarly calculated by appending the second key, $SKEYID_A$, to the beginning of the string and the value 00000002 to the end.

Each key builds upon the key preceding it, resulting in three different keys. $SKEYID_D$ is the "root" key from which the others are derived. It can be used to derive additional keys that may be required, as long as Perfect Forward Secrecy (PFS) is not required. $SKEYID_A$ will be the secret key used by the IKE SA for authentication, and $SKEYID_E$ will be the secret key used by the IKE SA for encryption.

However, we still have the mysterious value, SKEYID, which was used to derive these three keys. To discover its origin, we need to examine the methods that the peer devices originally used to authenticate themselves in messages 2 and 3 of the Main Mode exchange.

MAIN MODE PEER AUTHENTICATION

IKE supports three basic types of authentication:

1. **Preshared key** — an administrator-defined key manually configured on both devices. This is the simplest method to employ, but (potentially) the least secure and least scaleable. If the key is to be configured on the devices by the same person, key distribution is not an issue, but as the distance between devices increases and the number of peers increase, it becomes difficult to managed. The IKE lifetimes never timeout, but good practice suggests that eventually the keys should be changed.

2. **Digital Signatures** — the IKE specification provides for the use of either RSA signatures or DSS signatures. Cisco supports the RSA signatures, and requires the use of a CA, either public provider (e.g., VeriSign, et al.) or one administered by the individual organization. The $CERT_I$ and $CERT_R$ fields referred to in messages 5 and 6 of the Main Mode exchange reflect the fact that certificates are exchanged, which provide the peer identity and authentication. The initiator and responder exchange digitally signed nonces in messages 5 and 6 using their *private* keys. Each recipient will use the signer's public key to decrypt and verify the message. A secondary benefit with the use of certificates is non-repudiation. (Note: The *Cisco IPSec Design Guide* indicates that DSS signatures are also supported, but that information may be incorrect, and is contradicted by other Cisco documentation.)

3. **Encrypted Nonces** — This option also uses public-key encryption, but does not *require* the use of digital certificates or a CA (i.e., they are optional). The principal difference between this as compared with the other methods is that in addition to the cookies and the DH half-key

sent in message 3, the initiator also includes its identity and nonce, *each encrypted with the public key of the responder.* This requires that the initiator already possesses the responder's public key, and knows its identity since the responder has not transmitted its identity yet. Similarly, in addition to the cookies and the DH half-key in message 4, the responder replies with its identity and nonce, *each encrypted with the public key of the initiator.*

However, another round of public-key encryption is required of both, since digital signatures exchanged in messages 5 and 6 actually perform the actual authentication. The alert reader will note that the encryption in messages 3 and 4 was done using the *public key of the receiver.* By using the receiver's public key, confidentiality is provided for the nonces, but not authentication, since anyone could obtain the sender's receiver's public key.

The slight advantage with this technique is that the nonces are encrypted, making it more difficult to compromise the derived keys without knowledge of the nonces.

The significant disadvantage of this method is that it requires a total of four public-key encryptions, a very resource-intensive process. The second disadvantage is that each peer would typically need to configure the public key of all other peers as part of the IPSec configuration. Since a public key is an inherently larger data block, cut and paste of the public keys is the only reliable (albeit clumsy) method.

The option exists to use digital certificates and a CA, but since multiple public-key encryptions and decryptions are still required, RSA signatures would appear to be preferable.

THE MYSTERIOUS SKEYID

We referred earlier in this section to the mysterious value of SKEYID, and indicated that it was a function of the authentication method used. For each of the three authentication methods, SKEYID is determined in the following manner:

For Preshared Keys	$\text{SKEYID} = \text{hash}(PSK, N_I \mid N_R)$
For RSA Signatures	$\text{SKEYID} = \text{hash}(N_I \mid N_R, C_I \mid C_R)$
For Encrypted Nonces	$\text{SKEYID} = \text{hash}(\text{hash}(PSK, N_I \mid N_R)$

Although we will not delve any further into the specific details, suffice it to say that SKEYID is a "key" derived from a "key," used to make several other "keys." Beyond that, it has no special significance.

IKE Phase 2

Phase 2 of an IKE negotiation is used to negotiate and establish the IPSec SAs that may be required to support AH and/or ESP. It consists solely of one mode referred to as Quick Mode. Phase 2 negotiations occur only after completion of successful phase 1 exchanges, and rely upon the secure channel defined by the IKE SA that is established during phase 1.

QUICK MODE

The purpose of Quick Mode is to generate an SA for an AH or ESP. The message exchanges in phase 2 Quick Mode are far simpler than similar message exchanges for phase 1 Main Mode, and essentially consist of a proposal, an acceptance, and an "acknowledgement" of the acceptance.

Figure 9-5 illustrates the basics elements of a phase 2 Quick Mode exchange used to establish a single IPSec SA.

Several Quick Mode negotiations may be concurrently conducted between two peers, such as SA for AH, SA for ESP, or multiples of either, if multiple traffic streams require different treatment (i.e., algorithms) and, therefore, different SAs. Since each peer will use the same cookie pair established during phase 1, each separate negotiation must have a unique identifier, in order to identify each set of exchanges. The ISAKMP header included in all IKE packets contains a message ID that will serve this purpose.

As indicated in the figure, the Initiator sends a set of one or more proposals for the applicable SA, either AH or ESP, but not both. Also included in the initial message are the cookie pair $C_I | C_R$, a new nonce, $Nonce_I$, and an authenticator, $Hash_1$.

In the second message, the responder transmits the cookies pair, its IPSec SA response, and its nonce, $Nonce_R$. In message 3, the initiator effectively confirms the newly defined IPSec SA. What is now required is a session key to use with the transform defined in the IPSec SA. This new key will be either an encryption key, or an authentication key to be applied to a message digest to produce a HMAC.

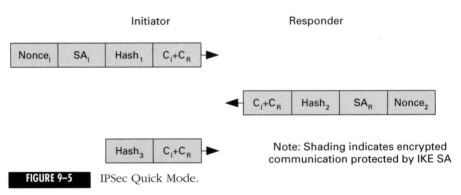

Initiator   Responder

| $Nonce_I$ | SA_I | $Hash_1$ | $C_I + C_R$ | →

← | $C_I + C_R$ | $Hash_2$ | SA_R | $Nonce_2$ |

| $Hash_3$ | $C_I + C_R$ | →

Note: Shading indicates encrypted communication protected by IKE SA

FIGURE 9–5   IPSec Quick Mode.

Since we still have the root key that was used to derive the IKE SA encryption and authentication, we can call it back into service to derive an IPSec session key. Note that the IKE keys are not used for IPSec; however, they may be derived from the same "root " key. The new IPSec key, K_{NEW}, will be derived from the "root" key, and applied to the concatenation of several values. As before we can express the derivation as:

$$K_{NEW} = \text{hash}(SKEYID_D, \text{protocol} \mid SPI \mid Nonce_I \mid Nonce_R$$

Where *protocol* and *SPI* are the protocol and Security Parameter Index, respectively, from the ISAKMP Proposal Payload that contained the negotiated Transform.

Quick Mode can also be used in situations where PFS is required, with a few minor alterations. An IPSec SA is created (using the existing IKE SA) to permit a new Diffie-Hellman exchange. Once the IPSec SA has been established, the IKE SA is deleted and initialized. The new Diffie-Hellman key provides a fresh "root" key, unrelated to any prior keys, and the process begins from scratch. The first and second messages shown in Figure 9-5 are modified to include the Diffie-Hellman half-keys. It should be noted that PFS is not required for all circumstances and environments.

Summary

In this chapter we introduced IPSec, the preferred security protocol suite for IP traffic. The IPSec architecture and operation was outlined, and a relatively comprehensive vocabulary was defined, that should prove useful in the following chapter, which will focus upon the configuration of IPSec on Cisco devices.

Since it is most likely that IPSec will serve primarily as a VPN technology, we focused on those aspects of IPSec that would most likely be employed in such an environment, that is, ESP operating in tunnel mode, using the dynamic key distribution and management capabilities of the Internet Key Exchange.

While all aspects of IPSec are well beyond the limited scope of this book, we have attempted to anticipate the terminology and options that are involved in configuring IPSec. Since IPSec, in conjunction with IKE, provides such a very broad set of sophisticated capabilities, one might anticipate that those features translate into configuration decisions, choices, and options. In the absence of a solid exposure to the fundamentals, configuring IPSec *correctly* is virtually impossible.

While it may have sometimes seemed that we delved too deeply into some of the esoteric details, be aware that there are very few clear-cut choices when implementing and configuring IPSec. Without some basic awareness of the subtle differences and variations, the task of correctly choosing between multiple options becomes little more than a guessing game.

IPSec Documentation

The following is a comprehensive list of RFCs that relate directly or indirectly to the IPSec protocol suite.

RFC 1320   The MD4 Message-Digest Algorithm — (20 pages)
RFC 1321   The MD5 Message-Digest Algorithm — (21 pages)
RFC 1828   IP Authentication using Keyed MD5 — (5 pages)
RFC 1829   The ESP DES-CBC Transform — (10 pages)
RFC 2040   RC5, RC5-CBC, RC5-CBC-Pad, and RC5-CTS Algorithms — (29 pages)
RFC 2085   HMAC-MD5 IP Authentication with Replay Prevention — (6 pages)
RFC 2104   HMAC: Keyed-Hashing for Message Authentication — (11 pages)
RFC 2144   The CAST-128 Encryption Algorithm — (15 pages)
RFC 2202   Test Cases for HMAC-MD5 and HMAC-SHA-1 — (9 pages)
RFC 2268   A Description of the RC2(r) Encryption Algorithm — (11 pages)
RFC 2401   Security Architecture for the Internet Protocol — (66 pages)
RFC 2402   IP Authentication Header — (22 pages)
RFC 2403   The Use of HMAC-MD5-96 within ESP and AH — (7 pages)
RFC 2404   The Use of HMAC-SHA-1-96 within ESP and AH — (7 pages)
RFC 2405   The ESP DES-CBC Cipher Algorithm With Explicit IV — (10 pages)
RFC 2406   IP Encapsulating Security Payload (ESP) — (22 pages)
RFC 2407   Internet IP Security Domain of Interpretation for ISAKMP — (32 pages)
RFC 2408   Internet Security Association and Key Management Protocol (ISAKMP) — (86 pages)
RFC 2409   The Internet Key Exchange (IKE) — (41 pages)
RFC 2410   The NULL Encryption Algorithm and Its Use With IPSec — (6 pages)
RFC 2411   IP Security Document Roadmap — (11 pages)
RFC 2412   The OAKLEY Key Determination Protocol — (55 pages)
RFC 2451   The ESP CBC-Mode Cipher Algorithms — (14 pages)
RFC 2631   Diffie-Hellman Key Agreement Method — (13 pages)
RFC 2857   The Use of HMAC-RIPEMD-160-96 within ESP and AH — (7 pages)
25 documents — 536 pages

Configuring IPSec

In This Chapter

*N*ow that we have a basic understanding of what IPSec is, and what services and options are available, we can set about the task of configuring it on Cisco network devices. This section provides an overview of the steps required to configure IPSec on a Cisco router acting as a security gateway, to form an encryption tunnel for traffic. Although it is possible to configure IPSec for both transport mode and tunnel mode, we will focus specifically on tunnel mode, since this is the mode that will be employed in virtually all cases with Cisco network devices, such as routers and firewalls. Various combinations are permissible, with router-to-router, PIX-to-PIX, and router-to-PIX encompassing the gateway-to-gateway combinations.

Other tunnel mode combinations include client-to-router and client-to-PIX. Although it may not be obvious, the client in these cases will also operate in tunnel mode, and will effectively function as its own security gateway.

To provide a basic understanding of the configuration steps required, and the various configuration options and choices that are available, we will discuss a router-to-router implementation as the foundation. Although the specific details will vary slightly with other combinations, the configuration fundamentals are very similar for other combinations of devices. We will address the subtle variations for PIX Firewalls and client-to-gateway configurations in the next chapter.

As with many other sophisticated feature sets provided with Cisco networking devices, the "configuration" stage assumes that one understands the underlying technology well enough to make "appropriate" choices when presented with various configuration options. A further assumption is that the "configuration" consists of 90% planning and 10% typing of the commands, correctly and completely. The Cisco user interface will not prevent one from making incorrect choices, but only requires that they be syntactically correct.

There is usually a direct relationship between the effort expended in comprehension and planning, and the ultimate success of the implementation. To choose from among multiple choices, a basic understanding of how the elements interact will be necessary. After reviewing the configuration basics in this chapter, it may be useful to reread portions of the previous chapter.

The functional steps for configuring IPSec can be summarized as follows:

- Step 1 — Plan the network design details.
- Step 2 — Configure IKE to provide dynamic key management and distribution (or alternatively, configure manual keys).
- Step 3 — Define the transform sets (algorithms) needed to provide the degree of protection required, as defined by the organization's Network Security Policy.
- Step 4 — Create crypto access lists to define which traffic will be encrypted.
- Step 5 — Create crypto map entries.
- Step 6 — Apply crypto map sets to the appropriate interfaces.
- Step 7 — Test and verify operation.

Each of these steps must be completed for fully functional implementation and will be described in more detail in the sections that follow.

Step 1 — Planning for IPSec

As trite as it may sound, planning for IPSec is one of the most crucial steps. Configuring IPSec can be very complicated, since the actual configuration will provide several different options at various configuration stages. For some environments and under some circumstances the defaults may be totally adequate, while under other circumstances, specific options may be required to achieve the goals of the Network Security Policy. IPSec has been criticized as being too complex, and it has been suggested that such complexity leads to mistakes that can make IPSec less secure. The collection of features and options that have been included in IPSec make this a very general purpose protocol, which can be applied in a variety of ways to achieve different degrees of protection, as well as different degrees of scalability and manage-ability. Each organization will have to evaluate the totality of IPSec against its own goals. In some cases, this may indicate that the configuration can be a relatively simple task, while other cases may be more complex, in order to take fuller advantage of the range of functionality offered.

For some environments it may be tempting to simply encrypt all traffic, using the strongest encryption method, but this is not always practical. Con-sider a scenario with a remote site connected through an encrypted tunnel (i.e., VPN) to a headquarters site. If all traffic from the remote site is destined for the headquarters site, it might be possible to encrypt all traffic, although traffic volumes and performance issues may be a factor. Encryption and decryption is a resource intensive process, and a larger router might be required than would otherwise be necessary, if traffic flow between the two sites was substantial. If triple DES (3DES) is the preferred encryption method, this will be a potentially more significant issue. There are some published sta-tistics describing performance characteristics by platform, and encryption methods, but it is strongly advised that performance issues be addressed as part of the presales support, since each situation will be relatively unique.

If some of the traffic from the remote site is destined for other sites, such as general Internet access, it wouldn't be possible to encrypt all traffic from the remote site. Some process must differentiate which traffic should be encrypted and which needs to remain unencrypted. If different traffic flows have different encryption requirements (e.g., none, DES, 3DES), the definition must also specify which traffic flows fit which category.

Likewise, if the traffic flow has multiple possible destinations, such as traffic from the central site to multiple remote sites, the requirements for each flow to each site must be defined individually. The configuration will require identification of all encrypting peers, definition of the authentication, and encryption methods to be used for each, and other parameters. The SAs described in the last chapter are defined on a per-site basis, but can be even more granular, on a per-host, per-site basis, as well.

The overall complexity (i.e., number of peers) will help determine whether manual keys or dynamic key management via IKE is warranted. In the simplest of cases, with one pair of security gateways, manual keying may be adequate; however, good security practice suggests that the key should be periodically be changed, particularly if DES is used. If manual keys are config-ured, they will also have to be manually reconfigured. Through use of IKE, the encryption and/or authentication key is changed every 60 minutes by default.

Even if IKE is preferred, there are three methods that IKE can use to authenticate peers: preshared keys, RSA signatures, and RSA encrypted nonces. Each has advantages and disadvantages that must be weighed.

Since at least some of the traffic flows are encrypted, any existing access lists or PIX Firewall conduits must be adjusted to permit the encrypted traffic. Since the packet "payload" is encrypted, access lists and conduits will not be able to analyze the packets to the extent that they could analyze unencrypted packets, since only the IP header is readable. The protocol field in the IP header will identify the next header as AH (if used), or ESP (if AH is *not* used), and therefore PIX conduits or router access lists will need to specifically allow this type of traffic.

Although not intended as a comprehensive list, the following summarizes some of the details that must be determined to configure IPSec.

- What is the identity of all peer devices (by host name or IP address)?
- What traffic is to be protected and unprotected?
- What degree of protection is required for each defined traffic flow?
- Which interfaces are involved in the encryption and decryption?
- How often should rekeying be performed?
- What method will be used to perform rekeying?
- Are any adjustments to existing router access lists or PIX Firewall conduits necessary to allow encrypted traffic to flow?

As we continue exploring the additional configuration steps, the answer to these basic questions will be more fully explained.

Step 2 — Configuring Internet Key Exchange (IKE)

Configuring IKE can be either the easiest or hardest part of the configuration. As one might expect, configurations that provide the most powerful features and greatest benefit also tend to be the most complex to configure. IKE configuration is arguably the most difficult part of the task, since there are a multitude of options that must be chosen carefully to achieve the desired result.

Configuring Manual Keys

Before we discuss the specifics of configuring IKE, we should discuss the option of *not* using IKE. It is possible to configure IPSec with a *manual key,* although the benefit of doing so is slight, and is most likely to be offset by the negatives. With manual keys, the SAs do not expire, as they do when IKE is employed; however, the SAs for each peer device must be manually configured, as well. This includes definition of *two* SPIs to identify the *two* SAs, one for inbound traffic and one for outbound traffic. The inbound and outbound SAs are nearly always complementary, mirror images of one another. In common practice they describe the same encryption and authentication algorithms, use the same key to both encrypt and to decrypt, share another key for authentication (keying hashes), and effectively describe the same logical

"IPSec connection" with a shared set of "rules." *Note: The key used for encryption (e.g., DES or 3DES) is not the same key used for authentication (e.g., HMAC-MD5 or HMAC-SHA).* In rare situations, where ESP and AH might be used together, this results in *four* SPIs and *two* SAs, since each SA defines *either* an AH or an ESP, but never both.

Although the SAs are permanent, the key(s) should be changed periodically. Since the key is included as part of the definition of the SA, the existing SAs must be deleted and redefined with the new key, effectively eliminating any advantage to manually defining keys. Support for manual keys is a required part of the IPSec implementation, but was presumably done so to facilitate interoperability testing between different vendors. At this simple, minimal level, the interoperability of basic IPSec functionality could be verified, without the additional complexity of IKE interoperability getting in the way. As will be seen in the remainder of this section, configuring manual keys does not truly result in simplification of the configuration to any significant degree. The default Cisco implementation assumes IKE will be used; therefore, the first step in configuring manual keys is to disable IKE. Although it does not explicitly show in the configuration, the assumed default global configuration statement is **crypto isakmp enable**. (Note that Cisco often refers to IKE by its former name ISAKMP/Oakley. When reference is made to ISAKMP, it is understood to imply IKE.) The specific global configuration statement to disable IKE is:

```
Router(config)# no crypto isakmp enable
```

To manually define the SAs for the peer device, the following additional statements would be required:

For inbound and outbound ESP:

```
Router(config-crypto-map)# set security-association
inbound|outbound esp spi cipher hex-key-string#1 [authenticator
hex-key-string#2]
```

Where:

- *spi* is the Security Parameter Index to identify this SA, and must be coordinated on each peer, that is, the inbound SPI of one peer must match the outbound SPI of the peer, and the outbound SPI must match the inbound SPI of the peer.
- *hex-key-string#1* is the encryption key represented as a hexadecimal string (56-bit for DES and 168-bit for 3DES).
- *hex-key-string#2* is the key to hash the HMAC-MD5 (128-bit) or HMAC-SHA (160-bit) message authentication codes (i.e., keyed hashes). When ESP is used alone (i.e., no AH), this key is required. In rare cases where the AH is also used with ESP, this key is optional since authentication is provided by the AH, and ESP-provided authentication is largely redundant.

The command syntax for AH is included below for completeness. Since ESP has an option to provide its own authentication, AH is not required, but is optional. This syntax is also appropriate if the AH is used alone, with no ESP, however this will rarely be the case. For most environments, the principal benefit of IPSec is encryption, and consequently the AH is rarely used.

For inbound and outbound AH:

```
Router(config-crypto-map)# set security-association
inbound|outbound ah spi hex-key-string#3
```

Where:

- *spi* is Security Parameter Index to identify this SA, and must be coordinated on each peer, that is, the inbound SPI of one peer must match the outbound SPI of the peer, and the outbound SPI must match the inbound SPI of the peer.
- *hex-key-string#3* is the HMAC-key represented as a hexadecimal string (128- bit for HMAC-MD5 and 160-bit HMAC-SHA).

There are additional statements required to complete the configuration that will be described in subsequent sections. A complete sample configuration using manual keys is included at the end of the chapter.

Dynamic Key Management

In most cases, IKE will be used with one of three options. To illustrate the choices, refer to the flowchart in Figure 10-1 below:

As can be seen from Figure 10-1, IKE offers three options to authenticate the peer device: preshared key, RSA signatures, and RSA encrypted nonces. Each has its own strengths and weaknesses, and will be discussed separately.

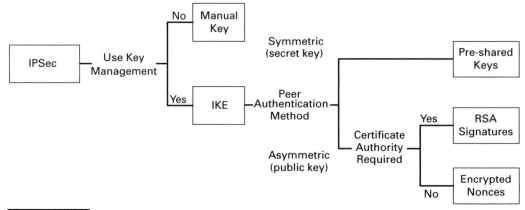

FIGURE 10-1   IKE configuration choices.

PRESHARED KEYS

Of the three choices, preshared keys are potentially the simplest to configure. Notice that this IKE preshared key is not the same as the IPSec manual key. With IPSec manual keys, each peer is configured with the same symmetric secret key for traffic encryption, another key for HMAC message authentication. With IPSec manual keys, SAs must be manually defined, and, as a result, the SAs do not expire. If one party configures both devices, key distribution is not a problem, but rekeying is still a manual process. If different parties configure each device, some secure external, out-of-band mechanism is required to make the key known to both parties.

While it may at first seem counterintuitive to configure IKE for dynamic key management, and then configure a static key, one must remember that it is only the IKE key that is static. The preshared key serves two purposes. The first is authentication of the peer. Like the IPSec manual key, mere possession and use of the IKE shared secret key is considered proof of identity of the peer, since only the peer could possess the shared key. The second purpose is to provide a secure channel to conduct IKE negotiations, the result of which is a dynamically generated IPSec SA, and its corresponding keys (one for encryption and the other to provide message authentication). These IKE-negotiated SAs have a (configurable) lifetime, measured in time or traffic volume. Upon expiration of the IPSec SA, IKE will use the preshared key to authenticate each peer to the other (if the IKE SA has also expired), and then renegotiate new IPSec SAs and corresponding encryption and message authentication keys. The only constant is the IKE preshared key, which is used over and over again.

This approach requires approximately the same level of effort for the initial configuration as IPSec manual keys, but automatically generates new dynamic keys for use by IPSec, making it incrementally better than pure static key assignment done with IPSec manual keys. It does, however, suffer from the same key distribution problem as IPSec manual keys, in that some external, out-of-band channel is still required to make the IKE preshared key known to both parties, if a different person configures each peer.

Although it may not have been made perfectly clear in earlier material, IKE creates its own IKE SA with its IKE peer, in addition to the IPSec SAs. Like the IPSec SAs, the IKE SAs are the rules, parameters, and algorithms by which each IKE entity exchanges information with its IKE peer. As part of the initial IKE phase 1 message exchange, each IKE entity exchanges nonces (large random numbers) with its peer.

In the specific case of preshared keys, these (unencrypted) nonces are concatenated with the preshared key. The result is then hashed to create the "root" key (the mysterious SKEYID from the previous chapter) used by IKE to derive keys for encryption and peer authentication of IKE messages, and a third key that serves as "keying material" for IPSec to derive the IPSec keys (i.e., encryption and message authentication).

We should note that when we refer to authentication, we are sometimes referring to slightly different processes. We have attempted to be specific in describing message authentication, but we should emphasize that message authentication using (HMAC-MD5 or HMAC-SHA) is an IPSec function, and only verifies the *integrity of the message* (i.e., it is unchanged) from the IPSec peer identified in the IPSec SA. When we describe preshared keys as an authentication method, we are referring to the verification of the *identity of the peer*. IPSec assumes the *identity* of the peer is valid (since IKE performed the identity verification) as part of its peer authentication.

Stated differently, IPSec message authentication is always done via a HMAC-MD5 or HMAC-SHA authentication key, while peer identity validation is *inferred* from use of the *IPSec manual* key, or *verified* by IKE using *preshared keys, RSA signatures,* or *RSA encrypted nonces.* In the case of IKE peer authentication, the "authenticator key" is obtained using several different methods, but its primary purpose is to verify the identity of the peer on behalf of IPSec.

The keys used for IPSec encryption and HMAC message authentications are always symmetric, secret keys derived from manipulation of an IKE symmetric, secret "root" key. The IKE "root" key is typically used to generate three keys: one for IKE encryption, one for IKE message authentication, and the third being a "derived" key that will be used as *keying material,* to derive current and future IPSec encryption and message authentication keys.

As we will see with the next two IKE authentication options, public key technologies can also be used for peer authentication. This allows the use of a CA, either managed by the organization for its own use, or managed by third parties as part of a public-key infrastructure (PKI).

RSA SIGNATURES

Another method to authenticate peers is via use of public key technologies, such as digital signatures. As you may recall from Chapters 8 and 9, digital signatures are created when a hash is "signed" by encrypting the authenticating hash with the *sender's private key*. Anyone with the sender's public key can decrypt and verify the hash, but the origin is verified since only the sender could have encrypted the hash. The underlying assumption is that the public key one possesses truly is the correct public key. Public-key technologies are susceptible to man-in-the-middle attacks as illustrated in Figure 10-2.

In Figure 10-2, Alice sends her public key to Bob, but it is intercepted by Manny, who substitutes his own bogus public key in place of Alice's public key. Bob believes the key he receives actually came from Alice.

Similarly, Bob sends his public key to Alice, but it is also intercepted by Manny who again substitutes his own key in its place. Alice believes the public key she received came from Bob.

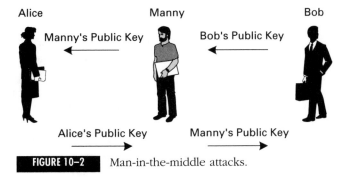

Alice   Manny   Bob

Manny's Public Key   Bob's Public Key

←   ←

Alice's Public Key   Manny's Public Key

→   →

FIGURE 10-2   Man-in-the-middle attacks.

Although this same scenario can have several negative consequences, we will consider the particular case of digital signatures. Alice and Bob enter into an exchange of authenticated messages. Alice digitally signs the message (encrypts the hash) with her private key and sends it to Bob. Manny intercepts the message, strips off Alice's digital signature, alters the message, calculates a new hash for the message, and signs it with his own private key.

When Bob receives the new message supposedly from Alice, he calculates the hash on the (modified) message. To verify that the message truly came from Alice, he uses the public key that he believes belongs to Alice (but really belongs to Manny) to decrypt the received hash. Since the message was altered by Manny, bearing a digital signature created by Manny with Manny's private key, the hashes match, and Bob believes the message is unaltered, and that it originated with Alice.

At any time, Manny could fabricate a message purporting to be either Alice or Bob, and send the message to the other. Each would believe that the message was genuine, and originated with the other.

The fundamental problem is that the authenticities of the public keys themselves are in question. One possible solution is for Alice and Bob to meet in person and exchange keys, assuming that they knew one another, and could verify that neither was an imposter. This is possible, but not often practical for the variety of exchange partners an individual might have. Another alternative is to have a trusted third party vouch for the legitimacy of each public key. This is the function of a CA. The general procedure is to have each party present their respective public keys to the CA (referred to as enrollment) for certification. Once the "enrollees" have established their identity to the satisfaction of the CA, the CA digitally signs the enrollee's public key using the CA's private key, thereby "certifying" the enrollee's public key.

The parties can now distribute their public keys freely, exchange them with other parties, or store them in a publicly accessible place. Any other party who receives the certified public key can verify its authenticity by applying the CA's public key to the signature. If the hash can be successfully decrypted, and matches the hash of the message (i.e., the public key), the recipient of the certificate (i.e., a public key that has been certified) can be assured that the certificate authority has verified the identity of the public key's issuer (but further assumes that the CA itself is trustworthy). The CA serves a role similar to that served by a notary public — a disinterested trusted, third party who can attest to the identities of individual parties.

The application of public-key methods to the IKE process results in a slight modification of the last two messages of the six-message exchange described in Chapter 9. With preshared keys these last messages (messages 5 and 6 of the phase 1 exchange) were encrypted and authenticated using a key derived from an SKEYID that was based upon the preshared key. In the case of RSA signatures, the authentication is performed using a digital signature, (i.e., the private key of the sender). Since the messages also carry the identity of the sender, it is a simple matter of applying the correct public key (i.e., the correct certificate) to authenticate the peer. The certificate can be retrieved from the CA or other publicly accessible source, or, optionally, can be sent along with the message. This option is particularly useful in instances where a party may have multiple public keys. Sending the certificate in the IKE message eliminates the chance of the receiver using the wrong certificate.

The essential point here is that any device can be authenticated through use of certificates, but this choice *requires the availability of a CA*. This option scales well to larger, more complex implementations where any party may have multiple peers. Rather than configuring each device with the public key/certificates or preshared key for all of the possible peers, the sender can include the public key/certificates in the IKE phase 1 message or the receiver can retrieve them from a server on an as-needed basis.

This option also provides nonrepudiation, a by-product of the use of certificates.

RSA ENCRYPTED NONCES

The IPSec specification provides for another form of public-key technology — encrypted nonces using either DSS or RSA public key algorithms. Cisco only supports use of the RSA algorithm. As a result, when reference is made to encrypted nonces, this implies RSA encrypted nonces in Cisco environments. This form of public-key technology does not require the use of CAs, but can support use with a CA if available.

In the more general case (without a CA), the configuration requires that the public key of all peers be installed on the device as part of the configuration. This option is more cumbersome than preshared keys, but is more secure and might be considered more scalable, as will be explained in the following discussion.

In previous description of IKE phase 1 exchanges, we described messages 3 and 4, which typically carried the cookies and Diffie-Hellman "half keys." These are used in various combinations with the "root key," SKEYID, to derive other keys. In addition to the cookies and Diffie-Hellman half-keys, with this third option (i.e., encrypted nonces) the initiator also includes its identity and a nonce *encrypted with the public key of the responder.* This requires that the sender already have the public key of the responder, since the responder has not yet transmitted its identity. In addition to the cookie and DH half keys, the responder replies with its identity and nonce *encrypted with the public key of the initiator.*

Since the responder can learn the identity of the initiator by decrypting the identity field of the previous message, the responder does not necessarily need to have the public key of the initiator, beforehand. The responder could retrieve the key on an as-needed basis, although this is not typically the case in practice.

Note that this requires a public-key encryption and decryption by each party, but authentications of the parties are not yet accomplished. Since each encryption was done using the *public* key of the other party, confidentiality has been achieved, but authentication will take place in messages 5 and 6. The authentication in messages 5 and 6 consists of hashing the concatenation of the cookies (from messages 1 and 2; cleartext) with the nonces (messages 4 and 5). The test of authenticity is simple. Since messages 3 and 4 were encrypted using the other party's *public* key, only the legitimate device could learn the value of the encrypted nonces by decrypting those messages with their own *private* keys. If messages 5 and 6 contain the correct values for the encrypted nonces, each party assumes that the values could only be correct if decryption of the previous messages (3 and 4) were successfully accomplished. Notice that the authentication (messages 5 and 6) requires an additional public-key encryption and decryption for the authentication hashes, resulting in two public-key encryptions and decryptions for each device. Recall from previous discussions that public-key encryption is orders of magnitude slower and more CPU-intensive than equivalent secret-key encryption and decryption.

At the beginning of this section we referred to this option as more secure. The reasoning is as follows. To learn the values of the nonces, the encryption performed in messages 3 and 4 would need to be "broken." Since the nonces are used to derive the root key SKEYID, knowledge of the nonces could be used to "break" any key based upon the nonces.

By encrypting the nonces, this option simply adds an additional hurdle that must be overcome to attack SKEYID and other keys derived from it.

We also referred to this option as possibly more scalable than preshared keys. This method of encrypted nonces can optionally be used with a CA, although the RSA signature method is considerably easier to configure, since encrypted nonces require that the initiator must possess the responder's public key before IKE phase 1 can begin. This typically indicates that the peer's public key must be manually configured. Unless the additional protection afforded by encryption of the nonces is desired, and the additional public-key encryption and decryption is acceptable, one of the other methods is likely to be a better choice.

CONCLUSION

Preshared keys are considered the simplest to configure for smaller environments, however scalability becomes an issue in more complex environments.

RSA signatures are more scalable, but require a CA. This is the Cisco
configuration default.

RSA encrypted nonces are theoretically more secure, but at the expense
of an additional public-key encryption and decryption. In addition, the public
key for each peer must be included as part of the router configuration. (Based
upon *IPSec User Guide for the Cisco Secure PIX Firewall Version 5.3*, this
option is not available for IKE implementations on the PIX Firewall.)

PFS and SA Lifetimes

IKE SAs generally have a lifetime greater than IPSec SAs. By default, IKE lifetimes are approximately one day, while IPSec SAs have default lifetimes of
one hour (PIX default is eight hours). *Lifetime values for IKE SAs and IPSec
SAs are configurable options.* Both values are configuration options. As a
result, an IKE SA will usually be in place when any given IPSec SA expires.
The effect is that IKE will only need to conduct a new phase 2, Quick mode
message exchange to renegotiate the new IPSec SAs. The IKE phase 1 Main
mode (or Aggressive mode) is only necessary to establish a new IKE SA.

This Quick mode exchange will include an exchange of nonces
between the two peers. A hashing function is applied to the concatenation of
the following values:

- The protocol field in the IKE header
- The new SPI number in the IKE message header
- The two new nonces contributed by each peer
- The "keying material" generated in the original phase 1 exchange

You *may* recall that the "keying material" (SKEYIDD), was derived from
the "root key" (the mysterious SKEYID) by applying a hash function to the
concatenation of the IKE phase 1 "root key" hashed with the cookies from the
original phase 1 exchange.

It is not crucial to remember the specific details of its origin, but only
that "this key was derived from some other key." This violates the principal of
PFS, since this key was based upon a manipulation of a former key. If the
former key was compromised, the information can be used to compromise
the new key. PFS assumes that there is no relationship to any prior keys.

To achieve PFS, the IKE phase 2, Quick mode includes an option for a
new Diffie-Hellman exchange to provide a new "root" key. With PFS activated, each time that IPSec SAs expire and require a new key, IKE Quick
mode performs a new DH exchange and a new "root" key is generated that
has no relationship to prior keys. The IKE configuration on Cisco devices
includes an option for PFS.

Other IKE Configuration Options

So far we have discussed several of the options available when configuring IKE. There are two others we have not directly discussed. We have described in some detail how the IKE peers authenticate each other via preshared keys, RSA signatures, or RSA encrypted nonces. We have also seen in some (painful) detail how IKE derives encryption and message authentication keys to protect phase 1 (Main or Aggressive mode) and phase 2 (Quick mode) message exchanges. What we have not yet discussed is what encryption and HMAC algorithms IKE uses with these keys. Fortunately, the remaining choices are simple. For encryption of IKE messages (some phase 1 and all phase 2), 56-bit DES is the only choice. For message authentication (some phase 1 and all phase 2) the choice is HMAC-MD5 (128-bit) or HMAC-SHA (160-bit). HMAC-SHA is a mathematically, more secure algorithm, but the differences are not significant. The default on Cisco routers and PIX Firewall is HMAC-SHA.

The only remaining option is the Diffie-Hellman group. The Diffie-Hellman algorithm defines a large prime number, p, and an integer, g. The IPSec specification defines five acceptable sets of numbers and refers to them as Group 1, Group 2, Group 3, Group 4, and Group 5. *Cisco supports only Group 1 (768-bit modulus) and Group 2 (1024-bit modulus).* These groups use traditional exponentiation over a prime modulus. Groups 3 and 4 are used with elliptic curves. Group 5 is similar to Groups 1 and 2 except with a 1680-bit modulus. A more complete discussion of the mathematics is beyond the scope of this material, but may be found in *Applied Cryptography, 2nd Edition,* by Bruce Schneier (John Wiley & Sons, 1996). Additional information may be found in RFC 2631 — Diffie-Hellman Key Agreement Method.

Command Syntax for IKE

As indicated at the beginning of this topic, use of IKE is the assumed default with the Cisco router IOS. An additional assumed default is that the identity of the device will be the IP address of the interface used to communicate with the peer (an option exists to specify hostname). The command syntax that is assumed, but not explicitly shown in the configuration is:

```
Router(config)# crypto isakmp enable
Router(config)# crypto isakmp identity address
```

To define a specific policy to be used with IKE, an additional global configuration statement is required.

```
Router(config)# crypto isakmp policy priority
```

where *priority* is a number value, indicating the priority for a particular IKE "policy." If any device has multiple peers, it is quite conceivable that a different set of options may be chosen for different peers, for example, preshared keys for one, RSA signatures for another.

If more than one policy is defined, IKE will attempt to negotiate the policies in order of priority, where lowest number is highest priority. If only one policy is defined, the number is inconsequential but must be included for proper syntax. IKE will begin with the highest priority policy, and attempt to match a policy with any given peer. If there is not a match of policy between any two peers, IKE fails, and, correspondingly, IPSec fails.

Once a match is found and agreeable to both peers, the IKE SA is established using the definition contained in the policy. It should be obvious that policies must be coordinated on each peer. While each peer device may have multiple policy definitions, it is up to the administrators to guarantee that each pair of peer devices shares at least one policy.

If the above command is entered, an IKE-specific configuration mode is entered. In this IKE-specific configuration mode, options may be chosen other than the default values. The command sytax to set specific options is:

```
Router(config-isakmp)#authentication [RSA signatures|pre-
share|rsa-encr
Router(config-isakmp)#hash sha|des
Router(config-isakmp)#encryption [des]
Router(config-isakmp)#group [1|2]
Router(config-isakmp)#lifetime seconds
```

If the defaults are to be used, simply type the global statement, and exit the IKE-specific mode with **exit** or **^z**. For example:

```
Router(config)#crypto isakmp policy 100
Router(config-isakmp) ctl-z
Router#
```

By creating a policy numbered 100, and specifying no options, the defaults will be used. The defaults are:

```
Router(config-isakmp)#authentication RSA signatures
Router(config-isakmp)#hash sha
Router(config-isakmp)#encryption des
Router(config-isakmp)#group 1(768-bit D-H group)
Router(config-isakmp)#lifetime 86400(1 day)
```

With the possible exception of authentication method (i.e., RSA signatures require a CA), the defaults will probably be adequate for a most circumstances.

Step 3 — Defining Transform Sets

The transform sets are simply the algorithms that will be used to provide IPSec encryption and authentication that are the basis for the IPSec SAs. They do not have to be the same algorithms specified for IKE encryption and message authentication, and used for IKE SAs, but in many cases they are.

A transform set is named and describes the collection of algorithms that will be used for the AH, ESP, or both, that will define the SAs between peers. The transform set also indicates whether the transforms are to be used in transport or tunnel mode.

Multiple sets can be defined for different traffic flows and/or different peers. As before, the crucial element is that each peer must have a matching set of transforms for the establishment of an SA to succeed. The command syntax allows for multiple transform sets to be offered by the initiator, with one of the offered proposals accepted by the peer. When multiple named sets are offered, they will be offered in the order indicated in the configuration. In many cases, only one transform set will be defined for all traffic, but IPSec and IKE allow for great flexibility to accommodate special or complex situations, and consequently multiple transform sets may be offered for different peers and/or different traffic flows to any given peer.

The choices are fairly simple:

- The transforms can be used in transport or tunnel mode, but not both within the same transform set definition (i.e., the same SA). If some traffic is transport and some is tunnel, two transform sets must be defined.
- If AH is to be used, HMAC-MD5 or HMAC-SHA are the only choices.
- If ESP is to be used, 56-bit DES or 168-bit 3DES are the encryption choices.
- If ESP is used, but not AH, ESP can provide its own message authentication using either HMAC-MD5 or HMAC-SHA. If AH is also used, it is still possible to define an ESP authentication method, but it is largely redundant.
- If AH and ESP are both used, the authentication included in ESP is unnecessary, and the authentication transform may be defined as NULL (i.e., none).

The last item on the list is sometimes expressed in an odd-sounding rule that states that a transform set may specify at most one encryption transform and two authentication transforms. The reference to two authentication transforms is to the transform specified for AH and to the optional ESP authentication transform that may be specified.

Under most circumstances the configuration choices will be even simpler. Security gateways, such as routers and PIX Firewalls operate in tunnel mode. Transport mode is intended for direct host-to-host communications.

Since most uses of IPSec will be specifically to provide encryption, ESP will be used in virtually every case. Since ESP can optionally include its own authentication, AH will rarely be used. In cases where these generalities are true, the choice narrows down to DES or 3DES for encryption and HMAC-MD5 or HMAC-SHA for authentication. The differences between HMAC-SHA and HMAC-MD5 are not of major significance, but HMAC-SHA is the more secure choice.

The primary decision will be whether to use 3DES or DES. This decision may be more challenging. Since 3DES is achieved by three encryptions with a 56-bit key, it is easily 300 percent more resource intensive. Depending upon platform and traffic flow, 3DES may be ruled out for performance reasons. Each organization must make this judgment based upon their requirements, circumstances, and budget. As indicated earlier in the material, it is an appropriate topic during presales support, since it is difficult to make meaningful generalizations.

Configuring Transform Sets

The global configuration command statement to define and name a transform set is:

```
Router(config)#crypto ipsec transform-set setname transform1
transform2 transform3
```

where *setname* is the name assigned to this transform set, and *transform1*, *transform2*, *transform3* are the keywords that describe the transforms.

The allowable transform keywords are:

- ah-md5-hmac
- ah-sha-hmac
- ah-rfc1828
- esp-des
- esp-3des
- esp-md5-hmac
- esp-sha-hmac
- esp-null
- esp-rfc1829

The references to RFC 1828 and 1829 are for backward compatibility with earlier implementations of IPSec, and are not normally used.

The command syntax to define the mode as transport or tunnel is a "transform-set specific" statement. An example illustrates the configuration statements required to create a transform set named "CPUeater," and define 3DES for encryption and HMAC-SHA for ESP authentication.

```
Router(config)#crypto ipsec transform-set CPUeater esp-3des esp-
sha-hmac
Router(cfg-crypto-trans)#mode tunnel
Router(cfg-crypto-trans)#^z
Router#
```

Step 4 — Create Crypto Access Lists

Crypto access lists are used to define the IP traffic that will be protected by IPSec (AH and/or ESP) and which IP traffic will be unprotected (e.g., cleartext and/or unauthenticated). They are simply another way to use the syntax of access lists to describe the "profile" of traffic that will be treated in a certain fashion. (For the purpose of simplifying this discussion, we will assume encryption is performed using the ESP, but the AH is not used. However, the same rules would normally apply to traffic protected by the AH, as well.)

Crypto access lists do not block traffic, per se. They are used to differentiate the traffic we want to protect (permit=encrypt) from the traffic that should not be unprotected (deny= don't encrypt, cleartext). They are used to describe the profile of traffic that is covered by a given SA, either an ESP or AH.

In IPSec terminology they are described as the *selectors* and are defined in the Security Policy Database (SPD) associated with a specific SA. The criteria that may be included as a *selector* in the definition of an SA includes source address, destination address, protocol (next-header field in the IP header), and/or upper layer port number. Since this also corresponds to the criteria that can be defined in an extended access list, the ACL server as a perfect tool to define the criteria. The *selectors* stored as part of the SA in the SPD, describe what services (e.g., encryption using DES with a specific key) should be applied to outgoing traffic, for outbound SAs, and what services (e.g., decryption using DES and a specific key) are to be applied to incoming traffic as defined in the inbound SAs.

The crypto access lists *must* be mirror images of one another. If, for example, the outbound SA of one peer indicates Telnet traffic from IP address 10.0.0.1 to IP address 20.0.0.1 should be encrypted using a specific 56-bit DES key, the corresponding inbound SA of the peer must indicate that Telnet traffic from IP address 10.0.0.1 to IP address 20.0.0.1 should be decrypted with the same 56-bit DES key.

The less obvious consequence is that if one end would encrypt traffic with a certain profile, it also assumes that it should decrypt the equivalent traffic received from the other end. Consider this example of a statement on Router A:

```
access-list 100 permit tcp host 10.0.0.1 host 20.0.0.1 eq telnet.
```

This statement will be used to populate two SAs on router A. The first is relatively obvious. The outbound SA will effectively state:

For *outbound* packets with a source address of 10.0.0.1 and destination address of 20.0.0.1 and destination port 23 (telnet), *encryption* is required.

What is less obvious is that this statement creates a corresponding entry in the inbound SA that effectively states:

For *inbound* packets with a source address of 20.0.0.1 and source port 23 (telnet) and destination address of 10.0.0.1, *decryption* is required.

The interesting consequence is that the peer, Router B must have a corresponding statement that does encrypt the outbound traffic. The "mirror image" of the access list statement on Router B must be:

```
access-list 100 permit tcp host 20.0.0.1 eq telnet host 10.0.0.1
```

If Router B is not configured correctly, and does *not* encrypt the traffic, Router A will receive packets that it believes need to be decrypted. Since the decryption process will fail, the packet will be dropped. As a result, the configurations of each peer must be carefully coordinated to ensure that they are complementary. Cisco strongly recommends that the extended ACL statements be as specific as possible, and discourages the use of "any" as part of the definition, since there are many ways this may be misinterpreted by the SA.

For example, consider a scenario where all traffic between two sites is to be encrypted. Cisco documentation indicates that traffic generated *by* each router (routing updates, Telnet sessions originating from one of the routers, etc.) will not be encrypted. Assume the statement that creates the outgoing SA at one peer, Router A, reads:

```
access-list 100 permit ip any any
```

When Router A defines the incoming SA it will assume that all *incoming* traffic should also be encrypted, and will drop any packets that are not encrypted, such as routing updates, CDP packets, or any other packets that are originated by the other router.

Since we are unable to describe all the combinations that might not work correctly, we will merely end this discussion with a note of caution. It is important to remember that the same extended access list is used to evaluate both *inbound* and *outbound* traffic, since the same ACL statement defines the SA *selectors* in each direction.

Although crypto access lists may appear to be identical to extended access lists, they are not applied to the interface in the same manner as extended access lists. Instead, they are used as a traffic profile included in a "crypto map," which will be discussed in the next section.

Step 5 — Creating Crypto Maps

Crypto maps are the mechanisms to pull all of the pieces together as a composite rule set that will then be applied to the appropriate interface. The elements that make up a crypto map include:

- Which traffic should IPSec protect? (as defined in the crypto access lists)
- What is the granularity of the traffic to be protected by a given set of IPSec SAs? (also defined in the crypto access lists)
- What is the local address (or name) that will be used to identify this device to the peer device in IKE negotiations and when the peer defines IPSec SAs? (defined in the **crypto isakmp identity** statement)
- What type of protection should be applied to incoming and outgoing traffic? (defined in the **crypto ipsec transform-set** statement)
- What mode of IPSec should be used? (also defined in the **crypto ipsec transform-set** statements)
- How are SAs established — manually or via IKE? (defined by the **crypto isakmp enable** or **no crypto isakmp enable** statements)
- If IPSec manual keys are used, what are the keys? (defined in the **set security-association** statements)
- If IPSec manual keys are used, what are the SPIs used to identify individual IPSec SAs? (defined in the **set security-association** statements)

As can be seen from the above list, we have defined all of these parameters elsewhere in the configuration. A crypto map pulls all the pieces together into a single comprehensive set of rules. Likewise, we may have defined different transforms and different traffic flows for different interfaces. The crypto map specifies which transforms and which flows should be applied to which interface. Even on the same interface, to the same peer, there may be different types of traffic that receive different types of protection, each identified by a different SA.

The global configuration command that creates a crypto map is:

```
Router(config)# crypto map name seq# method
```

Where:

- *name* is the name assigned to label this crypto map set.
- *seq#* is a number that determines the order that crypto map sets should be proposed when attempting to establish matching policies with a peer (i.e., same transforms, peer authentication method, et al.). If multiple are defined, lower sequence numbers are proposed before higher sequence numbers.
- *method* is the key management method; manual keys, IKE-negotiated, or Cisco Encryption Technologies (CET), a preIPSec Cisco proprietary method.

Once the crypto map has been created and named, the next step is to define the elements that make up this set. When the **crypto map** statement is entered, it opens a crypto map-specific configuration mode where the additional commands may be entered. The command sequence and individual commands would resemble the following:

```
Router(config-crypto-map)#match address [acl# | acl-name]
Router(config-crypto-map)#peer [hostname|ipaddr]
Router(config-crypto-map)#transform-set setname
```

Where:

- *Acl#* or *acl-name* is number or name of the extended access list that defines the traffic to be protected.
- *Hostname* or *ipaddr* is the host name or IP address of the peer device. Host name can be a fully qualified domain name if **ip domain** has been defined in the configuration and DNS server has been identified.
- *Setname* is the name of the transform set that is applicable. If multiple *setnames* are listed, they will be proposed in the order listed, when initiating IKE phase 2 Quick mode negotiations. When the peer initiates IKE, this is the list of acceptable proposals, and the initiating peer indicates the order of preference.

For the special case of IPSec with manual keys, the format of the commands is slightly different, and there are additional commands that are required to define the SAs and SPI numbers to use for the SAs.

```
Router(config-crypto-map)#set match address [acl#|acl-name]
Router(config-crypto-map)#set peer [hostname|ipaddr]
Router(config-crypto-map)#set transform-set setname
Router(config-crypto-map)#set security-association inbound
|outbound esp spi cipher hex-key-string1 [authenticator hex-key-string2]
Router(config-crypto-map)#set security-association inbound
|outbound ah spi hex-key-string3
```

Where:

Spi is the SPI number used for this SA, and must be coordinated with peer so that inbound SPI of one peer matches outbound SPI of the other, and vice versa.

hex-key-string1, *hex-key-string2* and *hex-key-string3* are the keys for ESP encryption, ESP-HMAC authentication, and AH-HMAC authentication, respectively.

Note that the syntax of the other commands changes slightly with IPSec manual key. Also note that only one transform set is allowed, and only one permit statement is allowed in access list definition. Due to these limitations, as well as the fact that keys need to be manually reconfigured, use of IKE is the preferred approach, even if preshared keys are used.

Step 6 — Applying Crypto Maps to an Interface

This is often the easiest part of the configuration, since the choice of interfaces may be obvious. The syntax to apply a crypto map to interface S0 would be as follows:

```
Router(config)#interface s0
Router(config-if)# crypto map name_of_cryptomap
```

Step 7 — Test and Verify

There are numerous commands to display the status of individual SAs, definitions of transform sets, crypto maps, and other information that may be used to verify or debug an IPSec configuration. The following represents a list of some of the more useful ones:

```
Router#show crypto ipsec transform-set
```

Displays a listing and configured parameters of all currently defined transform sets.

```
Router#show crypto ipsec security-association lifetime
```

Displays the configured lifetimes of all SAs.

```
Router#show crypto ipsec sa
```

Displays the settings of all current SAs. This command has several optional parameters that allow display to be tailored to a specific crypto map. With the optional keyword **address**, displays all existing SAs sorted by destination address, then by AH or ESP.

```
Router#show crypto map interface int_type_number
```

Displays the crypto map applied to the specified interface.

```
Router#show crypto map tag map_name
```

Displays the crypto map identified as *map_name*.

```
Router#show crypto isakmp policy
```

Displays all of the current IKE policies

```
Router#show crypto isakmp sa
```

Displays all of the current IKE SAs and their status.

In addition to the status displays available with the various **show** commands, there are several **debug** commands that allow the administrator to monitor the progress of IKE phase 1 and phase 2 negotiations, and the contents of the individual messages exchanged. Two of the more informative commands are:

Router#**debug crypto isakmp**

and

Router#**debug crypto key-exchange**

To observe and monitor the IKE phase 1 and phase 2 IKE negotiations, clear the current IKE SA then clear the corresponding IPSec SA. Generate traffic across the IPSec connection. The sequence is as follows:

- When IPSec has traffic to protect, it looks to see if there is an existing IPSec SA. Since the IPSec SA has been cleared, it will look to see if there is an existing IKE SA to negotiate a new IPSec SA.

- Since the IKE SA has been cleared, IPSec will trigger a new IKE SA to be formed. The first stage is the phase 1 IKE (Main mode) exchanges to establish the IKE SA, followed immediately by a phase 2 (Quick mode) exchange in which the IPSec SAs are established.

To clear the IPSec SA held in the SPD:

Router#**clear crypto sa**

To clear the IKE SA:

Router#**clear crypto isakmp** [*connection_id*]

When used without the optional *connection-id*, all current IKE SAs will be deleted. They will automatically be reestablished once IPSec needs to renegotiate new IPSec SAs (but not necessarily before they are needed).

There are a number of error messages that may appear during the process, although a proper configuration should not produce error messages. We will not attempt to describe them here; however, they are reasonably understandable by "mere mortals," given some knowledge of the message exchange for each phase.

These error messages (if they appear), will provide the best indication of why the process fails, and should be among the first tools used to define the problem (assuming that the configuration has already been visually verified).

Sample Configurations

Included are some very simple, sample configurations. Their purpose is simply to allow the reader to become familiar with the location and contents of the elements created in the step-by-step procedure presented. The first task after configuring the step-by-step tasks is to review the configuration for completeness. Each step outlined in this chapter will result in a set of related statements grouped together. Although the steps are not all grouped together in the configuration, with very little effort one should be able to identify the IKE configuration, the crypto access lists, the crypto maps, and other elements described for each step. A step-by-step visual verification of the configuration is clearly a good habit to develop. For completeness, we included some of the traditional router configuration information (e.g., passwords, routing protocols, et al.) although they do not directly relate to the IPSec configuration. The purpose is to familiarize the reader with the location of IPSec information within the body of a relatively complete configuration.

Sample Configuration #1 — IPSec Manual Keys

```
no service password-encryption
service udp-small-servers
service tcp-small-servers
!
hostname RouterA
!
enable secret 5 k3wf5odpf3rwef
!
! IPSec Manual key configuration
no crypto isakmp enable
! Transform set defined DES with HMAC-SHA
crypto ipsec transform-set sample1 esp-des esp-sha-hmac
! Cryto map named MANUAL
crypto map MANUAL 10 ipsec-manual
 set peer 10.20.30.41
 set session-key inbound esp 500 cipher abcdefabcdefabcd
authenticator 1234567890abcdef
set session-key outbound esp 501 cipher abcdefabcdefabcd
authenticator 1234567890abcdef
set transform-set sample1
match address 100
!
interface Ethernet0
ip address 172.16.1.1 255.255.255.0
!
! Apply crypto map to interface
interface Serial0
 ip address 10.20.30.40 255.255.255.0
 crypto map MANUAL
```

```
!
router eigrp 200
 network 172.16.0.0
!
no ip classless
! Define crypto access list
access-list 100 permit tcp 172.16.0.0 0.0.255.255 192.168.10.0
0.0.0.255
!
line con 0
 login
 password cisco
 exec-timeout 0 0
line vty 0 4
 login
 password cisco
```

Sample Configuration #2 — IKE with PreShared Key

The sample configuration #2 is illustrated in Figure 10-3. In this sample we have eliminated the traditional configuration information that the router would normally contain, such as passwords, routing protocol, et al., to focus on the elements that are required.

```
crypto isakmp policy 100
 hash md5
 authentication pre-share
 lifetime 43200
crypto isakmp key SaMpLeKeY address 192.168.2.1
!
crypto ipsec transform-set WestSet esp-3des esp-sha-hmac
!
!
 crypto map WestMap 10 ipsec-isakmp
 set peer 192.168.2.1
 set transform-set WestSet
 match address 100
!
interface Serial0
 ip address 192.168.1.1 255.255.255.0
 crypto map WestMap
!
access-list 100 permit ip 172.16.1.0 0.0.0.255 172.16.2.0
0.0.0.255
```

FIGURE 10-3

Router B

```
crypto isakmp policy 200
 hash md5
 authentication pre-share
crypto isakmp key SaMpLeKeY address 192.168.1.1
!
crypto ipsec transform-set EastSet esp-3des esp-sha-hmac
!
!
 crypto map EastMap 10 ipsec-isakmp
 set peer 192.168.1.1
 set transform-set EastSet
 match address 120
!
interface Serial0
 ip address 192.168.2.1 255.255.255.0
crypto map EastMap
!
access-list 120 permit ip 172.16.2.0 0.0.0.255 172.16.1.0
0.0.0.255
```

The configuration as shown is fairly straightforward; however, there is a surprise for those readers who are very observant.

There is a discrepancy between the configured lifetime of 43200 seconds (12 hours) on RouterWest and the default IKE SA lifetime of 86400 (24 hours) on RouterEast. While at first it would appear that there is a mismatch in IKE policy between the two peers, this is a discrepancy that has a resolution. Rather than declare a mismatch, RouterWest will defer to the lower IKE SA lifetime of RouterEast. In the special case of SA lifetimes, the peers will compromise at the lower value.

Summary

In this chapter we introduced a step-by-step procedure to configure basic IPSec, along with most of the common options on a Cisco router, acting as a security gateway. We will review configuration of IPSec for other device combinations in the next chapter.

We discussed the sophistication and corresponding complexity of IKE, and described the various IKE options — no IKE (i.e., manual IPSec keys), or IKE used with pre-shared keys, RSA Signatures, or RSA encrypted nonces. In the discussion of each we highlighted the pros and cons of each approach.

The concept of transform sets was introduced, and we discussed how they are used to describe the encryption and message authentication algorithm that are to be used by IPSec.

Crypto maps were defined as a mechanism to pull all the pieces together into a single composite definition, including IKE parameter, transform sets, peer identification, and traffic profiling using crypto access lists.

Hopefully, this will provide a solid foundation for most IPSec implementations; however, we will provide additional detail in the next chapter for the more advanced implementations (e.g., those that require a CA) or other special circumstances, such as client-to-gateway configurations, that many associate with the term VPN.

Virtual Private Networks — VPNs

In This Chapter

- ◆ Motivation for VPNs
- ◆ Why VPNs
- ◆ VPN Technologies
- ◆ Authentication Limitations
- ◆ Summary

*C*ommunication has become the lifeblood of nearly any modern organization. In addition to the telephone, fax, and various forms of mass communication, the Internet has now become another essential vehicle for business-to-business communications, as well as business-to-consumer communication. While its promise as the preeminent business-to-consumer vehicle has yet to reach its promised potential, the Internet's role in business-to-business communications is becoming firmly established, from simple email to elaborate corporate Web sites that provide technical support, product information, customer service inquiries, and other information. Even government agencies and political and religious organizations have discovered the magic of information dissemination via a well-constructed Web site. Newspapers, magazines, publishers, radio and television stations, and other mass media types have their own Web sites, complementing (or in some cases, duplicating) their mainstream media formats. Everyone wants to have a foothold, and all fear being left behind or left out.

Unknown, unproven, unprofitable companies have made initial public offerings (IPOs) and raised hundreds of billions of dollars on the speculation that they will be the "hot" item on the Internet.

Along with its exploding popularity comes an entirely new vocabulary of dot-com companies, e-commerce, B2B (business-to business), B2C (business-to-consumer), PKI (public key infrastructure), digital signatures, Certificate Authorities, VPNs (virtual private networks), et al.

The purpose of this chapter is to define or refine the common meaning or some of these terms that are often misunderstood in casual use. The first term we will explore is *virtual private networks* or VPNs. This term is so vague that it has been used to describe any number of network implementations and variations. It has even been used to describe telecommunication networks built from dedicated leased lines, or frame relay technologies, but in most usage the definition is intended to mean something much more narrow in scope.

So the question becomes, "What is a Virtual Private Network (VPN)?"

When we say that a VPN is a *network*, we mean that multiple "entities" can exchange information. It also usually implies that the number of entities is arbitrary, relatively unlimited, and is not limited to two entities. It further implies that any entity can communicate directly with any other entity.

When it is referred to as private, we refer to the fact that entities are members of a *private*, closed community. The architecture and structure are that of a *private* network. By definition, a private network creates a closed community of users, allowing them to access various network-related services and resources. It further implies that there is traffic isolation, that is, traffic on the private network does not affect, nor is it affected by, other traffic. This is not necessarily the case in all circumstances hence the confusion begins.

The third characteristic of a VPN is that it is *virtual*. According to *Webster's New Universal Unabridged Dictionary* the word *virtual* means "being such in power, force, or effect, though not actually or expressly such;" in other words, illusionary.

The telephone network is clearly a public *network* in that it is publicly accessible. However, once a call is placed to a particular number, it effectively results in a *private* communication channel between the two parties, if we ignore wiretaps and other forms of eavesdropping. A *virtual* circuit is put in place between the two parties (i.e., a switched virtual circuit or SVC).

By this broad interpretation, the public switched telephone network (PSTN) could also be called a *virtual private network*, too!

The accepted (albeit broad) definition of a VPN can be stated as follows:

"A VPN is a private communications environment created by segmentation of a shared communications infrastructure, in order to imitate the characteristics of a physically separate network."

Access to the communication environment is limited to interconnections within a defined community, although the underlying shared communications infrastructure provides services on a nonexclusive basis. Although this is still an overly broad description, we will refine the definition in the following sections.

Motivation for VPNs

To better understand why VPNs might be desirable, we should take a look at how we arrived at the current state-of-the art in data communications.

Over the course of the last 30 to 35 years, data communications has evolved along a path that paralleled voice communications. Through most of the 1960s, data communications in the U.S. was offered by virtually one company — AT&T. The circuits available were relatively low speed (i.e., 2400 bps), and the modems were always included as part of the monthly charge. As the modem monopoly held by AT&T was lifted by the 1969 Carterphone decision, other vendors entered the market. The advancements in technology progressed over the course of roughly the next 10 years, with 9600 bps being considered state-of-the-art by the early 1980s. High-speed data communications required a dedicated analog "data-grade" voice circuit, (commonly referred to as a 3002 circuit), and these lines often had to be specially "conditioned" to permit data communications at these speeds.

These "dedicated lines" were not switched through the public switched telephone network (PSTN) since the PSTN was subject to "noise" introduced by the call switching process, which was harmful to data communications. The data communications circuit was "hardwired" between two points (although *multi-drop* circuits could daisy-chain more sites). Since this circuit was dedicated to a specific customer and the capacity unavailable for others to use, the customer leasing this dedicated circuit paid for 24/7 use, regardless of the actual usage. The advantage to the customer was that they had a dedicated, private circuit that was available for their exclusive use, not subject to other users.

The disadvantage was that the customer paid for the circuit even if it wasn't being used, and the monthly charge was related to the length of the circuit. Longer circuits passed through more switches, and capacity had to be reserved in each switch that the circuit passed through. There were almost no meaningful guarantees on the quality of the line, but the user was permitted to operate any speed modems that would operate successfully over the line. Whether a customer had 2400 bps, 4800 bps, or 9600 bps, the line cost was the same. An organization could upgrade to a higher speed modem but the line cost remained the same.

AT&T® offered an alternative to these analog lines in the form of DATA-PHONE® Digital Service (DDS), an all-digital end-to-end circuit. Initially offered at specific speeds of 2400 bps, 4800 bps, and 9600 bps, this service was later expanded to 56 Kbps. The significance of 56 Kbps was that this was actually a 64 Kbps circuit that the carrier retained 8 Kbps to insure line quality. DDS came with service guarantees that limited the number of line errors and, instead of a modem, used a Data Service Unit (DSU).

At the time, voice circuits were commonly digitized at 64 Kbps using Pulse Coded Modulation (PCM) at the point where a call entered the telco network. As a comparison, a DDS circuit required the same bandwidth as a common voice call or analog modem attached to a data-grade circuit, but was "value-priced" at a much higher level.

Within the switching environment inside the telco, these various 64 Kbps circuits (DDS, voice, or modem over a data-grade voice circuit) were grouped together in bundles of 24. The individual 64 Kbps bit encoding was described as a DS-0. When 24 of these were grouped together, the result was DS-1 encoding, commonly referred to as a T1 circuit. In the hierarchy of T-carrier bundles there were different increments — T1, T1C, T2, T3, and so on.

After the breakup up of AT&T in the early 1980s, it became much more economical for large organizations to "buy in bulk" using T1 circuits, with the organization providing their own digitization for voice calls at the PBX level, and sending them to the carrier in a group over a single T1 circuit, rather that paying for 24 individual voice circuits.

The economics were so attractive that many organizations discovered that they could use T1 circuits for their voice requirements, and any bandwidth left over could be used for data (in increments is 64/56 Kbps). By using any additional bandwidth for data, with the cost paid for by savings on voice circuits, the data communications would essentially "ride for free."

In addition, the premium pricing of 56 Kbps circuits resulted in some strange economics. It was common for the cost of a T1 circuit to be about the same as three 56 Kbps DDS circuits. For organizations that had three or more 56 Kbps DDS circuits, a single T1 circuit could replace these, with approximately ten times the capacity. Since the individual organizations were providing their own digitization, and they could group the individual 64 Kbps channels in any increments they needed.

As an example, a single T1 could be carved up into the following increments:

- 512 Kbps to one site (8x64 Kbps)
- 384 Kbps to another site (6x64 Kbps)
- 6 voice circuits (6x 64 Kbps)
- 4 circuits of 56 Kbps each to four other sites (4x64 Kbps; DDS still requires the additional 8 Kbps per circuit for service quality guarantees.)

As long as the organization has the appropriate equipment to multiplex or "channelize" the data and digitize the voice, the above could be leased for approximately the same monthly cost as three individual 56 Kbps circuits. When coordinated with the telco, the voice calls could be fed into the public switched telephone network (PSTN) or be dedicated voice circuits between sites (often referred to as "tie lines"), with the data circuit routed to one or more remote locations. If the volume of intrasite calls was sufficient, this alternative was often less expensive than dialed long-distance calls between the same sites.

As time passed, competition and technology improvements led to additional changes in the offerings and economics. Additional increments between 56 Kbps and T1 were offered (i.e., fractional T1) in increments of 64 Kbps. The overall quality of lines improved as the carriers deployed more fiber-optic cable in their networks. Errors caused by line noise diminished, and the benefit of the 8 Kbps (i.e., 64 Kbps channel less 56 Kbps DDS) required by DDS diminished. The carriers began to offer "clear-channel" 64 Kbps (DS-0) without the 8 Kbps overhead, as an alternative to 56 kbps DDS service.

The price of 56 Kbps DDS-equivalent (trademark of AT&T) or clear-channel 64 Kbps fell below the price of the older, more limited 3002 data-grade analog circuits that still required expensive modems, and are limited to 19,200 Kbps or possibly 38,400 on most circuits. The price structure of analog compared to digital has effectively eliminated analog circuits as economically viable choices today, resulting in a nearly all-digital world (except for voice). Larger volume bundles became available in the form of T3, and later fractional T3. A T3 circuit is nominally rated at 45 Mbps, but it is the result of bundling 28-T1s or 672 – DS0s. (Note the international equivalents of these are E1-based and have a higher capacity of 2.048 Mbps.)

Why VPNs

Even with these improvements, there is still a requirement that the circuits be dedicated between any two sites to achieve these capacities. Traditional private networks provide connectivity among various network entities through a set of dedicated circuits (T1, E1 T3, etc.). In the U.S., these are leased from interexchange carriers (IEX), such as AT&T, MCI WorldCom, Sprint, et al., or local-exchange carriers (LECs), such as the Regional Bell Operating Companies (RBOCs) or other local carriers.

The capacity of these links is fixed, and the only traffic on these private networks is that of the organization deploying the network. This allows the traffic to be managed by an organization in such a way as to provide the desired quality of service (QoS) that the organization desires, since the traffic is totally under their control.

However, this level of control has a price. Since these are dedicated circuits, they must be configured and installed (i.e., provisioned) by the carrier. The time to provision a link varies from weeks to months, depending upon the carrier, location, and circumstances. International circuits have additional complicating factors. Since these are dedicated circuits, they are relatively expensive, and more so if international locations are involved.

The planning stage of these networks involves detailed estimates of the applications, traffic patterns, desired response times, and anticipated future growth rates. Planning and provisioning are lengthy processes that can adversely affect a company's ability to react quickly to changes. New sites cannot be added, nor old sites rearranged quickly. The pressure today is to be able to quickly react to changes and, therefore, a flexible information technology infrastructure is crucial.

An additional consideration is the mobility of today's workforce. Many organizations have "extended" networks that include employees traveling or working from an office in their home, using desktop computers, as well as laptops and palm-based devices. To support the requirements of these mobile users, organizations must have a method to extend their "Intranet" to numerous remote locations so that employees can access company information from remote locations. In the past, this was done via large modem pools for remote dial-in. The cost and complexity of installing, managing maintaining, and securing these modem pools can be substantial, and are limited to speeds available from dialup modems or Integrated Services Digital Network (ISDN) access. Except for special circumstances, there is no provision for use of DSL (digital subscriber lines) or cable modem technologies.

An additional cost with mobile or small office remote users is the long-distance charges or toll-free numbers paid for by the company, which typically range from five to seven cents per minute (in the U.S.). If we consider full-time access at five days x eight hours per week, the monthly cost for dialup is approximately $500 to $700 per month, and limited to pseudo-56 Kbps (i.e., 56 Kbps in one direction, only. If both ends are 56 Kbps modems, real bandwidth is 33.6 Kbps). Even if access is only two hours per day, the monthly cost would still be approximately $125 to $175. If we consider international calling, the costs can be considerably higher. ISDN can provide greater speeds, but in most U.S. locations, the cost will be disproportionately higher than analog dialup using modems.

Also note that this monthly cost is a variable, and does not include the cost associated with the organization's modem pool. The cost will also vary based upon the number of remote users and their usage patterns, another variable.

Also note that the server-centric nature of common PC-LAN technologies, such as Microsoft Windows environments, indicates that performance over low-speed connections is abominable, without the use of remote access software, which is not applicable in all circumstances.

The use of higher speed access media like cable modems and DSL via an Internet connection can reduce or eliminate the access speed limitations, but firewall technologies and security policies limit access from "outside" the organization's perimeter. It is sometimes possible to define a conduit for remote access, if the IP addresses are fixed. Authentication and authorization can also be performed, but the issue of data confidentiality and privacy remains. It is considered extremely bad practice to extend the organization's internal network or *Intranet* over the Internet without encryption.

In addition to remote access by employees, e-commerce applications can provide considerable advantages over traditional paper-based, business-to-business exchanges. These applications may include purchasing, invoicing, inventory management, and various forms of electronic data interchange (EDI). In most cases, support for these applications requires access to some database within the organization's Intranet. Order entry and invoicing are two vivid examples. The economic advantage of EDI for these types of applications has been clearly established, provided that access can be tightly controlled.

In traditional private networks, this kind of access is easy to control, but expensive, and sometimes impractical since it requires dedicated links between each participant. For an organization with many business partners, the complexity and cost can be serious concerns. In addition, there is little or no flexibility, since change of any partner requires provision of another dedicated circuit. If reliability is a serious issue, provision must be made for redundant circuits or dial backup, further adding to the cost and complexity. It may sometimes be necessary to quickly add or change business partners, but the inflexibility of dedicated circuits limits the organization's ability to adapt quickly.

A properly applied VPN can be a preferred solution to many of these situations described above and can provide a very flexible IT infrastructure. Global VPNs using the Internet can provide access to most international locations at a fraction of the cost of dedicated links. VPN services can also provide high-speed remote access to the organization's Intranet at a significantly lower cost and higher speeds than dialup or ISDN. In addition, the VPN architecture can support various authentication and authorization methods, such as PAP, CHAP, RADIUS, and TACACS+ to provide controlled access to the organization's Intranet via the Internet from virtually any location, and using any combination of analog modems, ISDN, cable modems, DSL dedicated circuits, or wireless.

VPN Applications

There are three primary types of environments where VPN technologies may be employed:

- LAN-to-LAN for extended Intranet service
- Dialup-to-Intranet service
- Extranet services business-to-business e-commerce

LAN-TO-LAN VPN

LAN-to-LAN VPNs allow an organization to extend their Intranet to local area networks located at multiple geographic areas using a shared network infrastructure. Various industry-oriented shared infrastructures exist, such as the Automotive Network Exchange (ANX) for the automotive industry. This shared network infrastructure could take many forms, but the Internet is the single best general example, and will be the basis for our discussion.

A LAN-to-LAN VPN is often used to connect multiple geographic locations of a single organization, such as smaller offices connected with their regional and main offices. This type of VPN service can provide a cost-effective alternative to dedicated, leased lines or frame relay links.

A simple example of a LAN-to-LAN VPN is shown in Figure 11-1.

As shown in the example, one advantage of a VPN is the ability to increase the capacity of an individual site, as circumstances may warrant. As applications change over time, the flexible VPN architecture can be adapted to meet the needs. Further, additional geographic sites can be added to the VPN with little effort.

Under most circumstances, there is a cost savings, as well. Dedicated leased lines are usually based upon the distance between sites. Although frame relay pricing is usage-base (i.e., committed information rate or CIR), there is often an incremental charge for each permanent virtual circuit (PVC) defined, and the carrier must provision the additional PVCs. With a shared infrastructure such as the Internet, distance between sites is not a price factor and additional PVCs do not have to be defined to reach any site. Effectively, the cost of the Internet "backbone" is included with Internet access, although this "backbone" is itself virtual, and actually comprised or one or more ISP backbones.

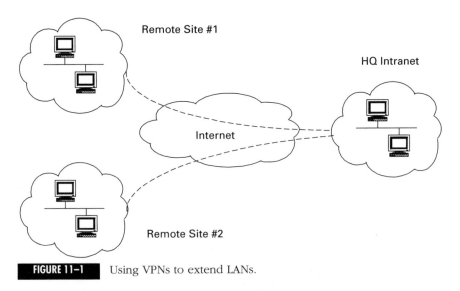

FIGURE 11-1   Using VPNs to extend LANs.

An additional benefit is the ease of adding another site or moving or removing an existing site. As long as the site has Internet access, it is merely a matter of defining or redefining the VPN, with physical changes not usually required. Also note that although the underlying network infrastructure is shared, VPN technologies allow traffic to be isolated and/or secured to varying degrees, depending upon the VPN technology employed.

DIALUP VPN SERVICES

A dialup VPN service allows mobile and telecommuting employees to access the organization's Intranet from remote locations. A typical dialup VPN is shown in Figure 11-2. The remote employee/user dials into the nearest ISP point-of-presence (PoP) and connects to a Network Access Server (NAS). The NAS typically supports combinations of analog modem access or ISDN. The user typically authenticates to the NAS using username, password (and possibly other information, depending upon the VPN technology employed).

In one type of dialup VPN model, using the Layer 2 Tunneling Protocol (L2TP), the NAS creates a "tunnel," that is, the NAS establishes a connection to a complementary NAS server located within the organization's Intranet. Upon completion of successful authentication, the connection enables the user to transparently connect to the Intranet. Since the data is tunneled to the Intranet (i.e., carried inside an IP packet addressed from NAS to the Intranet server at the other end of the tunnel), an IP address can be assigned from the organization's address space rather than being assigned to by the ISP. The L2TP model is a form of static VPN and is usually aimed at home offices and telecommuters who dial-in to a specific NAS since the VPN is defined and configured by the ISP. Using this type of tunnel/VPN requires participation from the ISP, and limits user access to the organization's Intranet. (Additional details will be provided on L2TP in a later section.)

Another VPN technology uses the Point-to-Point Tunneling Protocol (PPTP), and is more suitable for mobile users, since the user may dial-in to any local ISP. After initial authentication of the user by the ISP, the user initiates the connection to the specific VPN servers located inside the company's

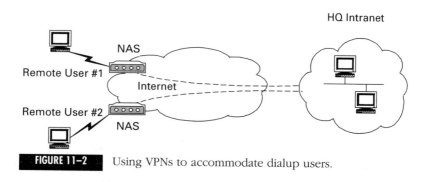

FIGURE 11–2   Using VPNs to accommodate dialup users.

Intranet. A second authentication mechanism validates the user and establishes user's network access privileges on the organization's Intranet.

As compared to the L2TP model, the local NAS at the ISP point-of-presence (POP) does not establish the VPN connection; rather, the clients, establish the VPN. The benefit is that no participation of the ISP is required; however, since PPTP is a Microsoft-specific protocol, it is usually only applicable with Windows clients to a Windows NT or Windows 2000 Server. Since the client is only receiving basic Internet access from the ISP, it can also be used with higher access speed services, such as DSL and cable modems.

A dialup based VPN can result in significant, immediate, and tangible cost reduction. If any significant number of the remote sites require a long-distance call, the savings can be dramatic, since for a flat monthly charge of about $20, nearly anyone can get unlimited local Internet access. When compared to the previous estimates for dialup access, a dialup VPN can be employed for a fraction of the cost of straight dialup service. The savings are immediate and ongoing. In addition, the dialup VPN avoids the capital and ongoing costs to install and manage a modem pool.

In addition, the same VPN technologies that are used for dialup access are also applicable to higher-speed access services, such as DSL and cable modems, although calling this dialup access is a bit of a misnomer. DSL or cable modem can overcome some of the speed limitations of dialup, but assumes access is always from a fixed location.

EXTRANET VPN SERVICES

An extranet VPN, as shown in Figure 11-3, is primarily for business-to-business (B2B) e-commerce, and to a smaller degree, business-to-consumer (B2C). In many ways, it may include the elements of dial-in or LAN-to-LAN VPN types, with the primary difference being that it connects "outsiders" to the organization's resources. As a consequence, it may not terminate on the organization's internal network or intranet, but rather in a controlled access area such as a DMZ behind the firewall. The presumption that "outsiders" are not as trustworthy as "insiders" is a debatable point; however, extranets usually require much more limited access than is required for intranets. While a remote or traveling employee might need access to a range of different network resources or services, an extranet VPN is intended to allow access to a much more narrowly defined set of resources, possibly a single server. This type of extranet allows controlled access for vendors, suppliers, and/or customers, to a specific resource or resources to place orders, check status, monitor inventory, or stock levels. An example might be an insurance company represented by independent agents. To perform price quotes for clients, the agents typically need access to the insurance company's policy pricing systems. If the resource that the independent agents need to access is on the organization's internal network, additional risk is introduced. Instead, the resource might be located in an isolated DMZ, created specifically for that

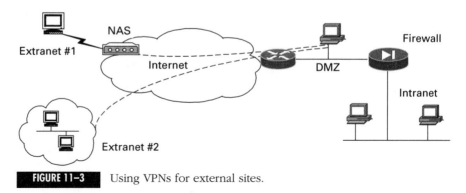

FIGURE 11-3   Using VPNs for external sites.

purpose. This approach leads to a better balance between access and exposure to risk.

As stated earlier, an extranet VPN may be a mixture of dialup and LAN-to-LAN VPN types, with the primary difference being to whom the access is granted, and where the accessible resource is situated.

The flexibility provided by an extranet VPN helps allow the addition or deletion of new external suppliers, customers, or other type of users with a minimum of time and effort. There are no new circuits required, provided that the new addition already has Internet access. In addition, access speed or capacity can be upgraded at either end or both ends of the VPN with considerably less effort than would be required with the use of dedicated lines or frame relay PVCs. There is also no necessity to share the line costs, or related equipment, since each party pays for their own Internet access.

The ability to have direct online access to information between business partners is valuable in a number of e-commerce applications, where timeliness of the information is crucial to the application. The ability to provide this type of exchange promotes cost savings, as well as better management of resources, as typified by applications, such as just-in-time inventory and production systems.

VPN Technologies

While the definition of VPN can be construed to mean nearly anything one wants it to mean, we will limit our discussion to a fairly narrow set of protocols that are most commonly indicated when discussing VPNs. Some would argue that frame relay is a VPN technology, because it possesses many of the characteristics that we described, but we believe that including them in our discussion would only serve to confuse the issues. If we want to stretch the definition to its limits, we could describe the voice telephone network as a virtual private network, since once a call is set up there is a virtual, private, isolated circuit between the two parties.

Of all the things that could be loosely described as VPNs, there are three current protocols designed with the primary purpose of providing VPN functionality. These and others typically operate at the Data Link or Network layers of the OSI reference model. While other protocols such as SSL or SHTTP could also be considered as having VPN qualities, they are not general purpose enough to suit our purposes, and, therefore, we will discuss only those that operate at the Data Link and Network layers in this material. The three protocols that were specifically intended to provide VPN functionality are:

- PPTP — the Point-to-Point Tunneling Protocol
- L2TP — Layer 2 Tunneling Protocol
- IPSec — as discussed in a previous chapter, IP-related network layer

The first two protocols on our short list are related, and a brief history of their relationship is probably appropriate. Two protocols were proposed as "the standard," PPTP and Layer 2 Forwarding protocol (L2F). Microsoft and Ascend® (now part of Lucent® Technologies) proposed PPTP. The PPPT protocol was a creation of the PPTP Forum, a group formed by Microsoft, Ascend, 3COM®, US Robotics® (now part of 3COM) and ECI Telematics®. The L2F Protocol was proposed by Cisco, and is effectively proprietary since no other vendors have chosen to support it. The compromise was a combination of the two proposals, and a combination of the two names — the Layer 2 Tunneling Protocol. While L2TP is officially the standard, many vendors have not yet implemented it. On the other hand, while Microsoft has indicated that L2TP is their direction, there is a significant installed base that runs PPTP and does not yet support L2TP. As a result, the de facto standard is effectively PPTP, and it most likely has the largest installed base of the three, although that will almost certainly change over time. For that reason, it seems appropriate to briefly discuss PPTP for purely practical reasons.

PPTP

PPTP originated with Microsoft, and is the oldest of the three. Intended to facilitate a VPN between Windows clients and Windows NT server, PPTP was later expanded to provide LAN-to-LAN VPNs, as well. The premise behind PPTP was to allow use of the Internet to create private tunnels between remote clients and an organization's server. Remote users could simply dialup a local ISP and securely connect to their corporate network.

PPTP is built around use of PPP, the most common Data Link layer, serial line, dialup protocol used for Internet access. PPTP encapsulates PPP packets inside of IP packets, using a variation of the Generic Route Encapsulation (GRE) protocol. GRE is also used by Cisco as the basis for tunneling IPX and AppleTalk inside an IP packet to transport these protocols over an all-IP network. As a result, PPTP can be used to carry protocols other than IP.

Since PPTP uses PPP, it also inherits the other aspects of PPP, such as the use of Password Authentication Protocol (PAP) and Challenge Handshake

Authentication Protocol (CHAP). As you may recall from earlier chapters, PAP passes username and password as cleartext, while CHAP sends an encrypted hash of the username and password concatenated with other information. This requires the receiving device to have a copy of the password in cleartext to hash for comparison to the hash received from the authenticating party. Since Windows NT does not store passwords in cleartext, Microsoft created a special variation referred to as MS-CHAP, which is supported as an alternative to standard CHAP.

PPTP also includes data encryption using Microsoft Point-to-Point Encryption (MPPE). MPPE is based upon the RC4 from RSA Security, and uses a 40-bit symmetrical key. A software upgrade option exists for U.S. and Canadian users for use of a 128-bit session key.

Microsoft includes support for PPTP in Windows NT Server and provides free client software for most Windows clients. Since these are either bundled or available for download, PPTP has achieved wide acceptance in Microsoft Windows-based environments. Third-party support exists for several other client platforms, as well, although PPTP remains a primarily a Microsoft-specific VPN.

PPP

Since PPTP assumes PPP as the underlying protocol, it seems appropriate to briefly describe the basic operation of PPP in a dialup environment. PPP is composed of two primary elements and a number of optional components. The two primary elements are the Link Control Protocol (LCP) and the Network Control Protocol (NCP). The LCP is primarily responsible for establishing the physical connection — call setup and tear down. NCP is responsible for negotiating optional parameters for upper-layer protocols, and separate NCPs exist for IP, IPX, AppleTalk, DECnet, and others.

Once the LCP has established the connection, that is, placed the call and recognized that the call was answered, the specification calls for an optional authentication phase using PAP or CHAP. If the authentication phase is implemented, a successful authentication is required before the LCP will complete the connection. If the authentication fails, the call is abandoned. While PPP considers this authentication phase to be optional, it will virtually always be implemented by ISPs, since this is the primary mechanism to control access through their network to the Internet.

Although PAP sends passwords in cleartext, and there is no protection against eavesdropping or playback attacks, it is still used by many ISPs. CHAP uses a "three-way handshake." The handshake consists of a CHAP *initiator* that indicates a desire to establish a connection, and indicates CHAP is to be used. The CHAP *responder* issues a *challenge* consisting of a time stamp and random number. The CHAP *initiator* concatenates this challenge with the password, hashes the result, and forwards it to the CHAP *responder*. The *responder* uses the username provided to look up the password stored in cleartext on the *responder*, concatenates the copy of the password with the challenge, and performs the same hash on the result. If the hash computed by the *responder* matches the hash sent by the *initiator*, the *responder* concludes that the *initiator* must have used the correct password and authenticates the *initiator*. (Note: CHAP provides the option for mutual authentication, while PAP does not. PAP is a purely master-slave relationship. In addition, CHAP provides the option to issue additional challenges at any time during the connection.)

Notice that an initiator never sends the password at any time during the exchange, but only a hash of the password. The mathematical property of hashes is that the hash inputs cannot be deduced from the hash result. However, hashes are susceptible to "dictionary attacks" in which a dictionary is used as input, with every word hashed in an attempt to match a given hash. The challenge is included both for antireplay protection (i.e., the challenge is constantly changing) and to help thwart dictionary attacks.

In addition to PAP and CHAP, the PPP specification has been extended to include the Extensible Authentication Protocol (EAP) that is described in RFC 2284. EAP provides for multiple authentication mechanisms, and does not perform authentication during the LCP, as does PAP and CHAP. Rather, it postpones the authentication to a latter stage, allowing the *responder* to request more information from the *initiator*. This is particularly useful when using a separate authentication server with RADIUS or TACACS+ protocols, as well as token servers that were described in an earlier chapter.

PPTP TUNNELS

Once the user has been authenticated and the PPP connection established, PPTP takes on the role for creating the packets that constitute the "tunnel." PPTP creates a TCP connection between the client and server for status and control information, and creates the IP packets that will be exchanged between the client and server carrying the PPP packets using GRE. A simplified illustration of these tunnel packets is shown in Figure 11-4.

The Ethernet (or other header) is the LAN or WAN protocol that the ISP uses to reach the "next hop." The IP header includes the source and destination IP addresses of each end of the tunnel: the client and server. The grayed area with the PPP header and data payload is the data that are sent through the tunnel.

Ethernet (or other)	IP Header	GRE Header	PPP Header	PPP Data Payload

FIGURE 11-4   PPP encapsulation using GRE.

PPTP allows the tunnel to be created by the remote client, or created by the ISP on behalf of the client. If the remote client creates the tunnel, this fact is transparent to the ISP, and the packet is treated like any other routable packet. This requires that the client supports PPTP, and can connect to the server on the organization's Intranet without involvement of the ISP. This is useful in cases where the ISP is not able to support PPTP, or the organization does not require the value-add of ISP VPN support and corresponding cost.

This results in the separation of tunnels into two categories: voluntary and compulsory. A *voluntary* tunnel is created by the client for himself, in order to reach a specific server. The client also has the option of general Internet access, not using the tunnel. This allows the client the greatest flexibility if the client needs both general Internet access in addition to the VPN to the organization's Intranet, but requires that the PPTP software support be loaded and configured on the client. The caveat is that the ISP must assign the IP address dynamically from the ISP's address space. When connecting to the organization's Intranet, the IP address will not be predictable, and will vary from connection to connection. Depending upon your organization's security policy this may or may not be desirable.

A *compulsory* tunnel is created by the ISP on behalf of the client, without the awareness or consent of the client. The client is essentially "hardwired" into the VPN and is unable to have general Internet access through the dialup connection, and can only access the organization's Intranet. Since all packets are "piped" to the organization's Intranet, IP addresses may be assigned to the client from the organization's Intranet address space, making the client appear to be a local device inside the Intranet. Again, depending upon your organization's security policy this may or may not be preferred.

A compulsory tunnel requires nothing on the part of the client, but does presume that the VPN is able to offer the service at any remote location that the organization may require. This is rarely the case.

In the case of compulsory tunnels, they may be *static* or *realm-based*. Static compulsory tunnels require the use of dedicated equipment or manual configuration. The user may be required to dial a certain number to be connected to these automatic, "hardwired" tunnels. With realm-based or manual compulsory tunnels, the Network Access Server (NAS) examines a portion of the user's name to determine which tunnel (of possibly numerous tunnels) to use to send that user's data (e.g., jim@mycorp where @mycorp identifies a specific VPN to My Corp).

L2TP

The Internet standard for Layer 2 VPNs is L2TP. As indicated earlier, it is a hybrid of Microsoft's PPTP and Cisco's L2F protocol. It has only achieved limited acceptance in the marketplace as compared to PPTP or IPSec. This is due in part to the "newness" of L2TP when compared to PPTP. When compared to

IPSec, it lacks many of the essential features many expect from VPNs, specifically encryption. The L2TP specification does not include provision for encryption, but recommends that it be used with IPSec to use the encryption capabilities of IPSec. The problem with that logic is that if one uses IPSec, there is little value in also using L2TP since IP sec is a far more flexible, feature-rich protocol suite.

The primary distinguishing characteristic that sets L2TP apart is its support for IPSec-based encryption. However, there is some question whether it is better to simply use IPSec instead of L2TP.

Since many of the characteristics of L2TP come from PPTP, it would be a little redundant to elaborate on them here. Although the terminology varies slightly, there are very strong similarities. Due to L2TP's limited current acceptance in the marketplace, and the far greater acceptance of IPSec, we will forgo a more complete discussion of L2TP.

IPSec

Since IPSec has been covered at some length in previous chapters, it would be redundant to repeat that material here. It is probably safe to say that IPSec is far more feature-rich and sophisticated than either PPTP or L2TP. At risk of over-generalizing, it appears that the marketplace believes IPSec is the preferred method to build.

One plausible reason is that encryption is a primary requirement for securing VPNs. When we place the three side by side, with encryption as a primary consideration, IPSec clearly wins.

Authentication Limitations

When PAP or CHAP is used as the authentication mechanism, authentication is usually associated with a specific workstation or device. If you have ever used dialup networking on a Windows machine, you probably noticed the check box option for Windows to remember your password. This little convenience saves the user the tedium of typing in the password each time they connect to the network. What you may not have considered is that anyone else using that machine benefits from this preprogrammed password, as well. Like other choices that are available, this may or may not be desirable, and each circumstance may be different.

One alternative is to not save the password, instead typing it in each time. Another alternative is to use a more sophisticated authentication mechanism such as one-time passwords or token cards. To use these more sophisticated, authentication mechanisms, the NAS must provide support for those methods. One common way is through use of a dedicated authentication server, using RADUIS or TACACS+ protocols. This will be discussed further in the next chapter.

Summary

No book on network security would be complete without a discussion of VPNs. However, most books that cover VPNs focus on PPTP, L2TP, or other technologies, with little or no mention of IPSec. Although PPTP and L2TP can both create VPNs without the aid and assistance of an ISP, their architecture favors ISP-based VPNs — L2TP more so than PPTP.

The current situation with ISP-based VPNs is something of the classic chicken-or-egg situation. The ISPs are reluctant to do a full-scale rollout until there is sufficient demand. The customers are reluctant to commit to ISP-based VPNs since service is often not available in all locations required by a given organization. In the interim, organizations have discovered that they can implement IPSec VPNs without the involvement of ISPs, and are swiftly moving along that path. Whether ISP-based VPNs will flourish in the future, only time will tell.

This chapter attempted to illustrate the basic advantages and value of VPNs for various circumstances and environments. We provided a brief discussion of PPTP and L2TP VPNs, but made no attempt to be as thorough as the coverage of IPSec in previous chapters, since it appears that IPSec is the near term VPN technology of choice. It is also consistent with the degree of emphasis that Cisco places on IPSec as compared to PPTP and L2TP, which we used as a guideline.

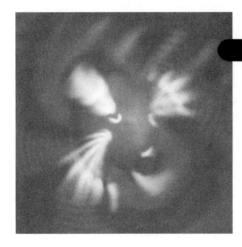

Cisco's Other Security Products

In This Chapter

◆ Access Control

◆ Vulnerability Assessment

◆ Intrusion Detection

◆ Summary

*T*he previous chapters focused on the primary Cisco security products; however, best current practices recommend a "layered" approach to security, as opposed to relying upon a single individual product. In this chapter we will review several other Cisco security-oriented products that are often used in conjunction with firewalls, access lists, and other traditional security products. Although the scope of this book does not permit a thorough treatment of these other products, we believe it useful to include and position them relative to the products and technologies previously discussed.

Access Control

In previous chapters we made reference to RADIUS and TACACS+. These two protocols are commonly used with access control products. These protocols are used to provide authentication, authorization, and accounting in conjunction with access control devices, such as access servers, modem pools, and other dialup access products. However, they can also be used in other circumstances in which authentication and authorization are required. The purpose these protocols serve is to allow authentication, authorization, and accounting to be centralized, rather than configured individually on each network access device. Figure 12-1 illustrates this point.

In Figure 12-1, a network access server (NAS) is located at each of several remote locations providing access to a common network, which could be the Internet, an organization's Intranet, or other controlled-access network. The authentication and authorization verification information (e.g., username and password) would be configured on each NAS individually as part of the NAS configuration. For a small number of users that are always seeking access from fixed locations, this may be an acceptable alternative. However, if users are mobile and/or don't always access the network through the same NAS, this approach does not scale well, since username and password would have to be configured on each and every NAS that the remote user could use. For a large number of NAS locations and/or large numbers of remote access users, the configuration of each NAS becomes unmanageable, particularly as users are added and deleted, since the information would have to be duplicated in many locations.

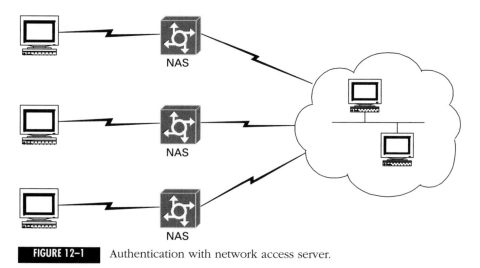

FIGURE 12-1   Authentication with network access server.

The better solution in these cases is to centralize the verification of user authentication and authorization using a common database on a central server. As users attempt to access the network from any location, the local NAS would relay the authentication information (e.g., username and password) to the central server for verification of username and password. Upon successful authentication, the central server would reply with the appropriate authorization for that user, and other parameters that might be applicable to the user. Note that this authorization and other parameters can be specific to a given user. For example, some users might require different protocol support than other users to reach certain servers or services. Some might require support for Apple's Remote Access Protocol (ARAP) while others might use IP and PPP. This and other user-specific parameters could be defined and included as part of the authorization.

The mechanism for the NAS to relay the authentication information to the central server, and receive authorization from the central server, can be either Remote Authentication Dial In User Service (RADIUS) or Terminal Access Controller Access Control System (TACACS).

TACACS is described in RFC 1492; however, this RFC is informational only and does not define a standard. Cisco has made several extensions to the simple, original TACACS, known as extended TACACS (XTACACS) and TACACS+. While Cisco still supports the older variants of TACACS, they recommend (and this discussion assumes) the latest variation, TACACS+, which is not compatible with the older two versions. Although this protocol is not Cisco proprietary, Cisco is one of a relatively smaller number of vendors that actively supports TACACS+ (as compared to RADIUS), and it is Cisco's preferred choice.

RADIUS was originally developed by Livingston® Enterprises (now part of Lucent® Technologies), and has since been defined as an Internet standard. The current specification for RADIUS is described in RFC 2138 and 2139. Nearly all vendors of remote access products support RADIUS.

At the most basic level, although both protocols serve a similar purpose (i.e., authenticating users), they do not share all the same capabilities. TACACS+ has a higher degree of granularity and is able to support functionality that RADIUS cannot; hence, TACACS is the "better" choice for Cisco environments.

The operation using TACACS+ or RADIUS is illustrated in Figure 12-2.

The reference in Figure 12-2 to the AAA server is the generic name sometimes used to describe an access control server (ACS), and the two terms are often both used to describe the function. The specific Cisco product that fills the role of AAA server is the Cisco Secure Access Control Server (ACS), and is available for both Windows NT/2000 and some Unix platforms. Cisco Secure ACS is network security software that helps authenticate users by controlling dial-in access to a network access server (NAS) device, and can also be used to authenticate access for PIX Firewall or routers.

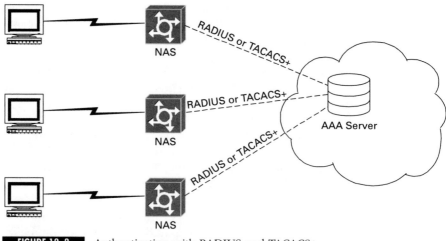

FIGURE 12–2   Authentication with RADIUS and TACACS+.

In the diagram, the remote user would typically use PPP for dialup and, therefore, most often use either PAP or CHAP authentication to the NAS. The NAS would take the username and password provided by the remote user in a PAP or CHAP message and relay it to the AAA server for authentication and authorization of privileges, using RADIUS or TACACS+. The Cisco Secure ACS replies with a success or failure response to the NAS, which permits or denies user access. Once the user has been authenticated, Cisco Secure ACS may also send any special authorization attributes to the NAS, and the accounting functions (if any) are initiated.

In this context, there are two client-server relationships. One is the remote user (client) to the NAS (server), but the second is the NAS (client) to the AAA server (server). This second client server relationship between the NAS and AAA server is transparent to the remote user.

AAA or ACS servers are used to define which users can access the network and what services are authorized for those users. A profile containing the username and password for each user is stored on the server to authenticate each user. The user profile on the AAA server also includes authorization information for each user. While the authentication information validates the identity of each user, the authorization information defines the nature and limits to access allowed each user. The Cisco Secure ACS can send user-specific profiles to the NAS that define the network services the user can access or the level of service to which the user is subscribed. Different users and groups may have different levels of service. Authorization may be differentiated according to levels of security, access times allowed (i.e., time-of-day or day-of-week), services permitted, or number of maximum concurrent sessions.

When AAA servers are employed, they allow the authentication and authorization information to be centralized on the AAA server, rather than configured on each NAS. Each NAS must support either RADIUS or TACAC+ and be configured to relay authentication information to the AAA server.

In addition to its use with NAS, the AAA server can also be used in other situations where access must be controlled and users authenticated. Other examples include access to Cisco routers and access through a PIX firewall.

In Chapter 3 we described the option of using user-specific passwords for router administrative access. In the example we describe the mechanism to configure username and password, as an alternative to the more common practice common of assigning a "port-level" password for basic users and inbound Telnet. We will repeat the command syntax here for convenience.

```
Router(config)#username yourname password somepassword
Router(config)#line vty 0 4
Router(config-line)#login local
```

While there are additional commands required to configure the router for AAA, the specific changes to this command are very simple. The configuration statement defining the username as *yourname,* and the password as *somepassword* would be eliminated since this information would be stored on the AAA server. In place of the reference to **login local** we change this to **login tacacs+**.

In Chapter 6 we discussed controlling inbound and outbound access through the PIX Firewall. We stated that for inbound access a conduit would be required, but that we could overlay this conduit with an additional authentication step. For outbound access, we referred to the default condition, which placed no limits on outbound connections initiated by internal users. However, we could require that outbound connections be authenticated as a precondition. In both cases, we could use the AAA server to verify the authentication and provide the authorization parameters. These authorizations could include user-specific or group-specific access lists, and a wide range of other authorization privileges that could be provided. These are a few of the uses for the Cisco Secure Access Control Server, but there are others, as well.

Although Figure 12-2 alludes to the Cisco Secure ACS as the database for usernames, passwords, and authorization privileges, the ACS could also be a front-end proxy to other authentication and authorization servers, including other RADIUS and TACACS+ servers, Windows domains and Active Directory, Novell NDS, token card servers, and several others.

The proxy feature enables the Cisco Secure ACS to automatically forward an authentication request from a NAS to another AAA server. Once the user is authenticated, the authorization privileges that have been configured for that user on the remote AAA server are passed back to the originating Cisco Secure ACS. The Cisco Secure ACS response to the NAS includes the user's profile information that is to be applied for that session on the NAS.

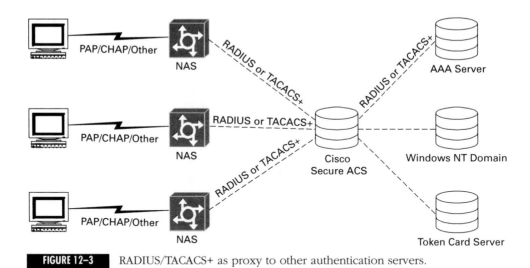

FIGURE 12-3   RADIUS/TACACS+ as proxy to other authentication servers.

With the Cisco Secure ACS, network security administrators can use a variety of different authentication methods, including PAP, CHAP, token card, and other one-time-passwords (OTPs). Figure 12-3 illustrates the AAA server operating as a proxy to other authentication servers.

In Figure 12-3, the Cisco Secure ACS is shown forwarding RADIUS or TACACS+ information "upstream" to another RADIUS or TACACS+ server. These can be arranged in a hierarchical or distributed fashion to provide scalability and reliability. Although not shown, the NAS could be configured to relay information to an alternative Cisco Secure ACS server, for redundancy. Both TACACS+ and RADIUS are flexible in this regard.

For example, the Cisco Secure ACS can be configured with a specific order in which to try alternative remote AAA servers if there is no response from the primary AAA server. If an authentication response is not received, the next server in the list is selected, until an authentication response is received from some AAA server. If Cisco Secure ACS does not receive a response from any server listed, the authentication fails.

The Cisco Secure ACS is also shown relaying authentication information to the Windows NT domain, but recent versions of the Cisco Secure ACS also support Windows 2000 Active Directory, as well as Novell NDS. The tight integration of Cisco Secure ACS with the Windows NT and Windows 2000 environments allows an organization to utilize the user and group information already configured on Windows NT and Windows 2000 servers, eliminating the time and effort to duplicate and maintain additional authentication information on the Cisco Secure ACS. This also permits a single login (single-sign-on), since the same authentication used for server access is also used to grant dial-in access.

In the case of Windows environments, the Cisco Secure ACS imitates the request made directly by a client. The Windows domain or Active Directory assumes that the request is being made directly by a client, rather than some proxy server. This is a value-added feature of the Cisco Secure ACS and is not a RADIUS or TACACS+ function.

Likewise, the proxy for token card servers works in a similar manner, and does not use RADIUS or TACACS+ for the exchange between Cisco Secure ACS and the token card server. Instead, the Cisco Secure value-added feature imitates the request made by a token card client. For this reason, Cisco does not support all token card servers. The Cisco Secure ACS can serve as a proxy for the following authentication mechanisms:

- Windows NT
- Windows 2000 Active Directory
- Novell® NetWare Directory Services (NDS), version 4.6 or greater
- Cisco Secure ACS or other RADIUS/TACACS+ server
- AXENT token-card servers
- CRYPTOCard (server included in Cisco Secure ACS0
- SafeWord® token-card servers
- RSA Security (Formerly Security Dynamics, Inc.)
- Generic Lightweight Directory Access Protocol (LDAP)
- Microsoft Commercial Internet System (MCIS)
- Relational databases fully compliant with Microsoft Open DataBase Connectivity (ODBC)

In addition to the authentication and authorization functions, the Cisco Secure ACS can also serve as a central repository for accounting information. Each user session authorized by the Cisco Secure ACS can be recorded including start/stop times for the session stored in a file on the Cisco Secure ACS. This accounting information can be exported to a comma-separated-variable (CSV) file for use in applications for billing, capacity planning, and/ or security audits.

For further information, refer to the *Cisco Secure Access Control Server for Windows NT/2000 Servers User Guide* available on the Cisco Web site.

Vulnerability Assessment

The Cisco Secure Scanner (formerly known as Net Sonar) is an easy to use network vulnerability testing tool. By running vulnerability tests against their own network, an organization is able to gauge their current security position, manage security risks, and eliminate vulnerabilities in most cases. The intent of this type of tool is to discover and repair network security weaknesses of any IP-based network before an intruder has a chance to exploit those weaknesses. The Cisco Secure Scanner permits an organization to automatically build a database of network devices (i.e., clients, servers, et al.). Once the devices are identified, each is subject to a battery of preprogrammed tests, to identify any vulnerability that these devices may have. This list of discovered vulnerabilities is presented in various formats for reporting to different levels of the organization. The vulnerabilities are categorized by host type, by severity, by IP address, by frequency of occurrence, etc. The canned reports are reasonably easy to understand, and customized reporting capabilities are supported.

Since scanning tools such as the Cisco Secure Scanner may be misused, the software includes a unique electronic fingerprint that is embedded in each licensed copy of the scanner software.

Although the Cisco Secure Scanner can provide a one-time assessment of an organization's network, it is best used on a recurring basis as part of scheduled and random security audits. Since networks are in a constant state of change, new vulnerabilities will invariably be introduced over time. The built-in scheduling function allows network scans to be established on a regular or random basis. Once the scan is initiated, it needs no user interaction, and can easily be preprogrammed to run unattended.

Although the Scanner can test the network, the task still remains for someone to evaluate the output and take appropriate steps to remedy any vulnerabilities discovered. For that reason, it is appropriate to designate some-one to that task, with sufficient responsibility and corresponding authority to see that remedies are put in place.

There are ongoing stories in the trade press about network security incidents that occur all the time. In all too many cases, the vulnerability that was exploited had a solution (i.e., security or version patch) but the solution was either unknown, or known and not implemented. It is only a matter or time before some organization is held accountable for not having taken appropriate precautionary action, or "due diligence."

With regard to scheduling, the Scanner uses several methods to "discover" devices; however, these methods are imperfect. They do not always discover all the devices on the network, especially if the device was unavailable or heavily loaded at the time of the test. For that reason, it is best to run the scans when the network is least active, and when all devices are available, although that might be a contradiction. For these reasons, the scans should probably be scheduled for different hours to maximize the likelihood that all devices will be discovered.

Recurring scans should be run periodically, each time there is a significant change to the network, or, ideally, each time new devices are added to the network, to limit exposure to new vulnerabilities that may be introduced.

Cisco describes the operation of the Cisco Secure Scanner as a six-phase process:

- Phase One — Network Mapping
- Phase Two — Data Collection
- Phase Three — Data Analysis
- Phase Four — Vulnerability Confirmation
- Phase Five — Data Presentation and Navigation
- Phase Six — Reporting

Phase One — Network Mapping

During this phase, the Scanner attempts to discover all active devices on the network, by scanning all IP addresses and all ports in the range selected by the party running the scan. The allowable choices are a single host, all hosts, or a selected list of hosts on different segments. The "probe" for active devices consists of an ICMP Echo Request (i.e., Ping) to the specified address or addresses. The Scanner builds a database of all the hosts that respond to the Ping. Since Ping is used, the scan may cover several segments separated by switches or routers, although care should be taken that access lists permit the free exchange of ICMP Echo Requests and Echo Replies.

Phase Two — Data Collection

Each of the hosts discovered in Phase One are then subject to a scan of all ports (or only those that are specified) to determine what services are running on those devices.

Phase Three — Data Analysis

The Cisco Secure Scanner uses a patented vulnerability analysis engine (i.e., process) to identify the following characteristics.

- All IP addressable devices, including routers, switches, firewalls, network servers, desktop computers, workstations, and printers
- Operating system and version number
- Services Provided — for example, netBIOS, http, Telnet, dns, ftp, smtp, snmp, et al.
- Potential vulnerabilities, including known security "holes" in Windows NT or Unix, routers, or firewalls that are misconfigured, unsecured services (e.g., rlogin, rsh, anonymous ftp), known deficiencies of various versions of Sendmail, general system misconfigurations, et al.

The scan uses an internal rules database, which recognizes various combinations of elements. It is important to note that during this phase the tests are not invasive. They do not attempt to exploit the vulnerability detected, but only to identify them.

Phase Four — Vulnerability Confirmation

Once the scan has identified a potential vulnerability, the Scanner issues the appropriate commands to the target device to verify the vulnerability. While these tests are "invasive," the Cisco Secure Scanner does not perform any destructive tests that would be harmful to the host, such as DoS attacks.

Phase Five — Data Presentation and Navigation

The results of the scans are made available in several standardized formats.

Grid Browser — This format is the basic "list" that can be oriented in several ways. To provide more or less detail of each individual host, vulnerability, frequency of vulnerability, severity of vulnerability, etc.

Network Security Database (NSDB) — This is a catalog of more detailed information on each potential vulnerability, including basic description, degree of severity, potential consequence of the vulnerability, link to additional sources of information regarding this vulnerability (including patches, etc.), the systems and/or services that are affected by this vulnerability, and a user-defined "comments" section to add notations.

Charts — the data can be presented in nearly all manner of charts and graphs including 2D and 3D formats.

Phase Six — Reporting

The Cisco Secure Scanner includes a report wizard to define the type of report that best fits the intended audience. The predefined categories include:

- Executive — summary only; no technical details
- Brief Technical Report — "short-form" technical summary
- Full Technical Report — full report including all technical details (Note: This report can be *very* large if printed, often hundreds of pages.)
- Custom Report Templates — allows for modest degree of customization

While the Cisco Secure Scanner can identify most "known" vulnerabilities, like any test procedure it is not foolproof. Likewise, it merely identifies potential problems. It does not *fix* any problem. Further, not all potential problems are *actual* problems. Someone with a thorough understanding of the IP protocol and/or operating system behavior will need to evaluate the potential problems. Like the rest of the network security environment, this is not a "magic silver bullet," but only a powerful tool in the hands of someone who can properly interpret the output.

The Cisco Secure Scanner is available for both Window NT and Solaris™ platforms. Further information is available in the *Cisco Secure Scanner User Guide* that can be found on the Cisco Web site.

Intrusion Detection

While a network vulnerability scanner such as the Cisco Secure Scanner can identify certain specific vulnerabilities, it has no ability to monitor traffic for activity to which all systems may be vulnerable, such as DoS, Distributed Denial-of Service (DDos), port scanning, and other malicious activity. To monitor traffic in real-time, a monitoring system is required that can recognize malicious traffic and either report it or block it. This is where intrusion detection systems (IDSs) enter the picture.

IDSs are relatively recent developments in the network security product spectrum. They were developed to cover problems that are not addressed by firewalls, access lists, vulnerability scanners, and other network security devices. While these other systems and devices play an important role, they are also subject to certain limitations that may allow intruders to slip past them.

As defined by Cisco, intrusion detection is the ability to analyze data in real-time in order to detect, record, and/or stop malicious activity as it occurs. The topic of intrusion detection has been the topic of several books, and we make no pretense that this section will be more than simple introduction.

IDSs are commonly host-based or network-based and include a library of "signatures" of potentially malicious activity or traffic. In the case of network-based IDS, these "signatures" are designed to recognize the profile of a single packet or series of packets that are representative of the hundreds of known network attacks or intrusions.

The Cisco Secure Intrusion Detection System (CSIDS), formerly known at Net Ranger, is representative of the network-based approach. Other vendors may offer host-based products or combinations. While each approach has its pros and cons, the general consensus is that some combination of host-based and network-based IDSs can offer the greatest protection.

In the case of the CSIDS, the network-based approach consists of two primary elements — a Director and one or more Sensors.

The IDS Sensors are dedicated network appliances that monitor and analyze all traffic on a given network segment. They operate similar to a protocol analyzer or "packet grabber," by operating in Ethernet promiscuous mode copying every packet on the network. Unlike a protocol analyzer (which often doesn't do much "analysis"), the IDS Sensor compares the packet or packets to a known database of packet types or packet sequences that are representative of network intrusions. These "suspicious" packets are identified and details are forwarded to the IDS Director, which is the primary display and reporting station for further analysis and action from the analyst monitoring the IDS Director.

Recently, Cisco has supplemented these stand-alone Sensor appliances with other sensor-like devices. The Catalyst 6000 Intrusion Detection System Module is now available as an add-on "sensor" inside the Catalyst 6000, and the Cisco Secure Integrated Software (router-based firewall) can detect and report on a subset of the approximately 400 total signatures maintained in the Network Security Database (NSDB).

The Director operates under (and requires) HP OpenView, and acts as the primary monitoring console. The "alerts" generated by individual Sensors and sensor-equivalents are displayed on the IDS Director console as icons, color-coded according to severity level:

- Green — Normal state — level 1 (information only)
- Yellow — Marginal state — level 2–3
- Red — Critical state — level 4–5

The icons can be "drilled down" to get more detailed information, such as IP source and destinations address, brief description of the type of alert, and NSDB reference for more complete description of the type of "suspicious" packet(s). The IDS Director includes a high-level network map that allows the analyst to determine the location of the IDS Sensor that generated the alert. This is essential in the case of multiple sensors.

Although placement of the IDS Sensors is discretionary on the part of the organization deploying the IDS, there are several logical vantage points, as indicated in Figure 12-4.

In Figure 12-4, the IDS sensors are shown in several possible locations. Some would argue that a sensor should be placed in "front" of the firewall, but there is at least one good reason why that is not a particularly good choice. Since the sensor would record any number of intrusion attempts that were thwarted by the firewall, some would reason that it is good practice to know what attempts have been made, even if unsuccessful. On the other hand, there could potentially be an enormous number of alerts that are not of any particular consequence. On one network we observed, there was a total of approximately 3,000,000 alerts generated by three sensors over a 30-day period. Most were inconsequential "false positives," but their sheer volume easily overshadowed the few that were truly of interest.

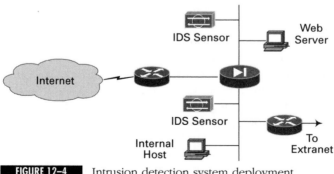

FIGURE 12–4   Intrusion detection system deployment.

The more meaningful point to monitor activity is at the Web server in the DMZ. Even though this segment is "protected" by the firewall, it is still a semipublic area, much like the lobby of a building, and it is very useful to be alerted to malicious activity there. Figure 12-4 also illustrates a sensor on the internal network. Since the firewall does not protect internal resources from insiders, this is a very common position to monitor, given the high incidence of abuse or misuse from insiders. Similarly, the internal sensor could be positioned at the endpoint of an extranet to business partners.

The security of your internal network could be compromised if the business partner failed to prevent unauthorized access originating from their end of the link. As President Reagan once said. "Trust, but verify." That is sound advice for extranets, as well.

The one difficulty in deploying sensors inside an organization is that the sensor can't "see" the entire intranet if Ethernet switching is employed. A sensor would have to be connected to the *span* port of each switch, in order to see all the traffic through the individual switch. That is a contributing factor to Cisco's introduction to the Sensor module for the Catalyst 6000 series switches.

The choice of these or other locations will vary from organization to organization. This is a very relevant topic to be discussed in presales support.

Reacting to Alerts

Although the IDS Sensors can be configured to drop connections and/or download access lists to a given Cisco router in response to certain types of alerts, this is not the most common practice. Since there are often a significant number of "false positives" (i.e., false alarms), many organizations are reluctant to take fullest advantage of the automatic, dynamic ability of the CSIDS to "shunt" traffic.

The common complaint with all IDS offerings is the great number of these false positives. The simple underlying reason is that the IDS will report many suspicious, but harmless packet patterns. This puts the burden on the analyst (i.e., human operator) to make a judgment, based upon (sometimes) limited information. After the initial installation, there is likely to be an adjustment period, in which many of the nuisance alerts can be identified and accommodated.

The other significant limitation is that the packets must match a "known" pattern, and the IDS will be unable to recognize patterns that are not currently known. Although different techniques are being evaluated for second-generation IDS that can overcome that limitation, they are not yet available from any vendor.

Nonetheless, the current IDS technology employed by the CSIDS is a good complement to other security technologies, and definitely warrants consideration in most medium-to-larger organizations. The technology is also applicable to smaller organizations; however, the deployment cost may be prohibitive. In cases such as that, there are a growing number of third-party services that offer 24/7 monitoring and intrusion detection services at a price within the reach of most organizations.

Summary

The aim of this chapter was to introduce some of the other relevant network security products that are available. Since several of these could be the topic for an entire book, we did not attempt to cover them thoroughly. In the case of intrusion detection, in particular, there are several good texts available, including *Network Intrusion Detection—An Analyst's Handbook* (1999, New Riders Publishing), by Stephen Northcutt, and *Intrusion Detection—An Introduction to Internet Surveillance, Correlation, Trace Back, Traps, and Response* (1999, Intrusion.net Books), by Edward Amoroso. In addition, the SANS Institute Web site (*http://www.sans.org*) has a wealth of information related to intrusion detection.

Index

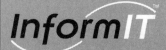

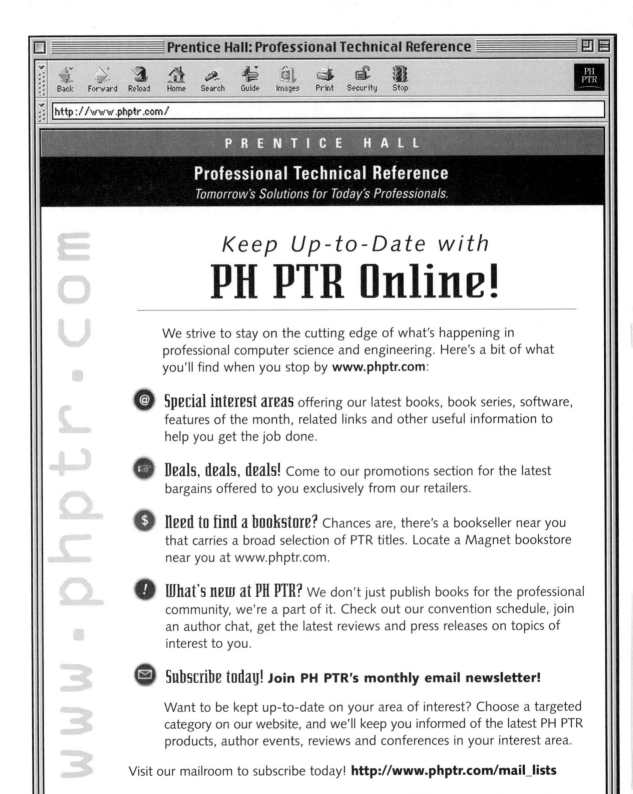